Foundations for New Economic Thinking

Foundations for New Economic Thinking

A Collection of Essays

Sheila C. Dow
Emeritus Professor of Economics, University of Stirling

First published 2012 by
PALGRAVE MACMILLAN

Palgrave Macmillan in the UK is an imprint of Macmillan Publishers Limited, registered in England, company number 785998, of Houndmills, Basingstoke, Hampshire RG21 6XS.

Palgrave Macmillan in the US is a division of St Martin's Press LLC, 175 Fifth Avenue, New York, NY 10010.

Palgrave Macmillan is the global academic imprint of the above companies and has companies and representatives throughout the world.

Palgrave® and Macmillan® are registered trademarks in the United States, the United Kingdom, Europe and other countries.

ISBN: 978–0–230–36910–8

This book is printed on paper suitable for recycling and made from fully managed and sustained forest sources. Logging, pulping and manufacturing processes are expected to conform to the environmental regulations of the country of origin.

A catalogue record for this book is available from the British Library.

A catalog record for this book is available from the Library of Congress.

10 9 8 7 6 5 4 3 2 1
21 20 19 18 17 16 15 14 13 12

Printed and bound in Great Britain by
CPI Antony Rowe, Chippenham and Eastbourne

To Alistair

Contents

List of Illustrations   viii

Preface and Acknowledgements   ix

1   What Kind of New Theory in Light of the Crisis?
A Focus on Theoretical Approach   1

2   Schools of Thought in Macroeconomics:
The Method Is the Message   15

3   Animal Spirits and Rationality (jointly authored with
Alexander Dow)   33

4   Beyond Dualism   52

5   Uncertainty about Uncertainty   72

6   The Appeal of Mainstream Economics   83

7   Mainstream Economic Methodology   105

8   Methodological Pluralism and Pluralism of Method   129

9   The Non-neutrality of Formalism (jointly authored with
Victoria Chick)   140

10   Structured Pluralism   162

11   The Meaning of Open Systems (jointly authored with
Victoria Chick)   178

12   The Issue of Uncertainty in Economics   197

13   Variety of Methodological Approach in Economics   210

14   Afterword   231

Bibliography   236

Index   257

Illustrations

Tables

5.1	A taxonomy of uncertainty	77
8.1	Pluralism in economics	132
11.1	Conditions for open systems	182
11.2	Conditions for closed theoretical systems	183

Figures

11.1	Mainstream economics	193
11.2	Critical realism	193
11.3	Our position	194

Preface and Acknowledgements

Addressing the crisis in the economy and in economics requires a heightened awareness among economists of how we approach our subject and the capacity to form judgements about it. Only then can we seriously address where we have gone wrong and how we might make improvements. Such awareness would provide the foundation for constructive new developments in economics.

The motivation for putting together this volume was an appreciation of how difficult it is for economists to be aware of what we do at the level of methodological approach. It is even more difficult to be aware of the way we frame reality and apply a particular mode of thought. This is not surprising. To engage in theory development and policy advice in settled times we need to start from somewhere. But the current climate calls for new economic thinking, and this requires that everything be up for discussion. Indeed, even in settled times it is important to be aware enough of the underpinnings of our economics to be able to engage with economists who build on different underpinnings and to be ready to engage and adapt.

Single papers are not enough to get this across. This volume is designed, therefore, to gather material on different aspects of methodological approach and mode of thought in an attempt to get across what is involved in developing this kind of awareness, addressing some of the issues it raises. These essays are illustrative of a much wider literature available to those who want to pursue enquiry at this level. It is an attempt to explore some foundations for new economic thinking.

Since the papers were written over a long span of time, they have benefited from input from a very wide range of colleagues. I would particularly like to single out the early influence of my colleagues at the University of Stirling, Brian Loasby and Peter Earl, and of Victoria Chick. I am grateful to Victoria for agreeing to the inclusion of two of our joint papers, but even more for the encouragement, support and guidance she has given me over the years. But the greatest debt is owed to my husband Alistair (Alexander), who first sparked my interest in methodology, with whom I have had countless discussions about economics and its methodology over the years and who has provided particular support and guidance on this volume (including agreement to the inclusion of one of our joint papers). Finally, I am grateful to Taiba

Batool of Palgrave Macmillan for the encouragement to put together a volume like this and to Ellie Shillito of Palgrave Macmillan for nursing the project along.

I am grateful to the following for permission to draw on previously published materials, as follows (by chapter number):

Australian Economic Papers

2. 'Schools of Thought in Macroeconomics: The Method Is the Message', 22 (2), 30–47 (1983).

Taylor and Francis

3. with A. C. Dow, 'Animal Spirits and Rationality', in T. Lawson and H. Pesaran (eds), *Keynes' Economics: Methodological Issues* (London: Croom Helm), pp. 46–65 (1985), reprinted in 2009 by Routledge.

Cambridge Journal of Economics

4. 'Beyond Dualism', 14 (2), 143–58 (1990).
6. 'The Appeal of Neo-classical Economics: Some Insights from Keynes's Epistemology', 19 (6), 715–34 (1995), under the new title 'The Appeal of Mainstream Economics'.
7. 'Mainstream Economic Methodology', 21 (1), 73–93 (1997).
9. with V. Chick, 'Formalism, Logic and Reality', *Cambridge Journal of Economics*, 25 (6), 705–22 (2001), under the new title: 'The Non-neutrality of Formalism'.

Edward Elgar

5. 'Uncertainty about Uncertainty', in S. C. Dow and J. Hillard (eds), *Keynes, Knowledge and Uncertainty*, pp. 117–27 (1995).
8. 'Methodological Pluralism and Pluralism of Method', in A. Salanti and E. Screpanti (eds), *Pluralism in Economics: Theory, History and Methodology*, pp. 89–99 (1997).
12. 'The Issue of Uncertainty in Economics', in P. Mooslechner, H. Schuberth and M. Schuerz (eds), *Economic Policy-making under Uncertainty: The Role of Truth and Accountability in Policy Advice*, pp. 191–203 (2005).

Journal of Economic Methodology

10. 'Structured Pluralism', 11 (3), 275–90 (2004).
11. with V. Chick, 'The Meaning of Open Systems', 12 (3), 363–81 (2005).

Journal of Economic Surveys

13. 'Variety of Methodological Approach in Economics', 21 (3), 447–19 (2007).

1
What Kind of New Theory in Light of the Crisis? A Focus on Theoretical Approach

Introduction

There is an appetite among economists, as well as among policymakers and concerned citizens, for new economic thinking. What was previously regarded as standard economic theory seems to many to have failed us, not only in addressing the series of crises which began in 2007, but also in being implicated in the causes of the crises.

This book is addressed to those who want to consider how much is up for discussion – what features should continue in any new economic thinking and how much is open to challenge? Should we consider aiming for a new standard theoretical approach to replace the old or should we contemplate fostering a range of theoretical approaches? (Should economists be intimidated by jokes about our inability to agree?) There is much discussion currently at the level of theory and policy, but the emphasis here is at the level of methodology, which is sometimes discussed explicitly, and mode of thought, which normally remains implicit and even unconscious.

Considering methodology is regarded by some as an optional extra at best, particularly when policy issues are pressing. But this volume is built on the premise that it is foundational. We all use some methodology – and some philosophy of science – or another, whether we are

This chapter draws on a paper entitled 'What kind of new theory to guide reform and restructuring?', presented to the first Annual Conference of the Institute for New Economic Thinking, Cambridge, April 2010. It has benefited from comments from Victoria Chick and Alexander Dow.

aware of it or not. New economic thinking could well involve changing methodology and/or philosophy of science, with implications for theory and for policy. But we need first to bring to the surface the methodology and philosophy of science on which we and others implicitly base our theory and policy if we are to contemplate considering possible changes. Even more, we need to bring to the surface the mode of thought we employ: how we conceptualise the world, communicate about it and form arguments about it. This is not easy; we normally function by taking these things for granted. Nor can we necessarily expect to alter our mode of thought. But awareness of the source of differences is a great aid to better understanding different approaches. It is awareness at this level which provides foundations for new economic thinking.

Such awareness can have direct policy implications. A central issue which has arisen in the response of economics to the crisis has been the issue of meaning of concepts. It is a recurring theme in this volume that the economy is conceptualised differently, and concepts have different meanings, within different methodological approaches. Thus, for example, the concept of 'rationality' plays a special role and has a particular meaning in mainstream economics which does not correspond to the role and meaning of rationality in other approaches. Yet policy is being designed to address what has been identified as irrationality in financial markets often without recognition of the range of ways it can be understood and applied.

As a contribution to this process of consciousness-raising, this volume is a collection of essays on economic methodology which explore the meaning and significance of different methodologies and philosophies of science applied to economics in different circumstances. The essays have been selected as being those most relevant to the current search for new economic thinking. Other than the first and last chapters, they represent a development of ideas about economic thought over a period of 30 years, published in a range of outlets and presented chronologically (with varying amounts of revision from the original versions).

It is hoped that, representing a gradual build-up of ideas, the essays will be helpful to those setting out to engage with the methodological aspects of their habitual thinking and the possibilities for new economic thinking. The thread of argument which runs through the essays is that economics would benefit from a wider acceptance of the legitimacy of a broader range of approaches than the mainstream, from learning about the content of different paradigms, and from engaging in debate across paradigms.

Some of the essays were written during earlier periods when economics was thought by many to be in crisis. It is instructive to get some perspective on the current situation; a perception of crisis is not new, although perhaps it is more widespread than it has been for many decades. So we can learn from previous examinations of the discipline. While some essays include reviews of the state of economics in a series of decades (Chapter 2 on the 1980s, Chapter 7 on the 1990s and Chapter 13 on the 2000s), all include references to the history of economic thought and the history of thought in the methodology of economics. It is only by looking back that we can really understand where we are now, and therefore where we may go in the future.

Considering economics at the level of methodological approach in itself helps us to understand better earlier theoretical contributions which have come to general attention again because of the crisis. There is renewed interest in great thinkers of the past such as Smith, Marx, Hayek and Keynes. But there is a limit to how far their ideas can be incorporated in the quite different modern mainstream approach, since they adopted different methodological approaches on the basis of different modes of thought. Much of the discussion throughout the volume focuses on issues surrounding any difference in approach to economics. While we will refer quite frequently to Keynes's approach, there is discussion also of other approaches. The purpose is not to argue for one approach rather than another, but to draw attention to what is involved in a difference of approach and the potential benefits of much wider awareness of the approaches we adopt, what they enable, but also what they constrain.

In this introductory chapter, we proceed to consider the financial crisis, and how it has been analysed and explained from different perspectives, in order to illustrate the practical importance of the way we think in economics. Different policy prescriptions follow, depending on which approach is taken. Different approaches in turn are not just a matter of one theory rather than another, but also different ways of perceiving the reality of economic processes and different criteria for deciding on a good theory. New economic thinking may well require a new way of understanding the reality of the economy and how to approach building up analysis of it. But the first step is to recognise what we currently take for granted in economics and that other approaches are possible.

In the process of considering further below the search for new thinking in light of the crisis, it will be explained how each of the subsequent chapters elaborates on particular arguments on which we draw in this analysis. In addition, each chapter will be introduced with an explanatory paragraph connecting the subject matter with our current concerns with new economic thinking.

Economics and the financial crisis

The current economic environment poses unusual policy challenges. All sorts of policy developments have occurred over the last few years which had previously been outside the normal range of theoretical analysis and policy discussion, such as activist fiscal policy, quantitative easing and partial socialisation of banking. These initiatives were introduced even while active discussion was ongoing as to how best to frame the theoretical analysis of the crisis. Some new thinking seemed to be required because of the lack identified in mainstream economic theory. The crisis had not been predicted by most economists, and it was taking some time for theoretical explanations to be forthcoming. But unbeknownst to most economists explanations (and general predictions) already existed in approaches to economics outside the mainstream. The significance of a difference of approach, much of it rooted in the subconscious level, is that it limits understanding across methodological divides.

For many economists, the basic issues surrounding the build-up to the crisis seemed to rest on inappropriate pricing of risk at market level. It generally had been presumed that, through the price mechanism, competitive markets would ensure an equilibrium outcome which maximised social welfare. This was particularly the case for financial markets, which were known for their competitiveness, which had been enhanced by the deregulation of the 1980s, as well as the technical skills of market players.

Therefore, leading explanations for the crisis, taking this view of markets as the starting point, rested on some impediment or other to the free operation of market forces. Of these, the main impediments were identified as asymmetric information and a regulatory structure which encouraged moral hazard. A range of policy prescriptions followed from these explanations: in particular, measures to improve the valuation of assets (especially with respect to risk) and to reduce the incentives and/or opportunities for moral hazard. Other explanations have been sought beyond the normal theoretical framework. They refer to what are taken to be irrational motives for behaviour, 'greed and fear', 'hubris', and so on. The policy solution is to discourage irrational behaviour.

The existing mainstream theoretical framework has thus now provided a basis for reform and restructuring which follows from the palpable distance which had emerged between theory and reality. In what sense is this new thinking? The proposals address new developments in financial markets, including the role of the authorities. But they are designed essentially to make markets more like the way they had been depicted by existing theory. What is assumed but rarely made explicit is that this would produce the best outcome for society, according to a particular set of (utilitarian) values, including the judgement that rationality (according to its theoretical definition) should be promoted. To support these proposals is to make the (contestable) value judgement that the theoretical outcome would indeed be best for society. Further, to design these proposals may require a theory of the process of institutional and behavioural change which requires a different sort of analysis.

Assumptions are deeply embedded in our thinking, whatever our approach, and they often go unacknowledged. There is the question just noted of what is best for society. But there is also the understanding of how economies work. For example, the mainstream theoretical approach is built on a view of economic systems as being essentially stable, which is why crises are so shocking. But there are other understandings which underpin different approaches to theory. Thus, for example, neo-Austrians view the economy as in a constant state of flux, though not unstable in a macroeconomic sense, except due to interference by the state. Post-Keynesians view the economy as inherently unstable (and thus crisis-prone), requiring intervention by the state. Minsky's (1986) theory of financial instability along these lines has attracted significant attention as offering an explanation for the crisis. But only that part of Minsky's theory which points to the systemic risk resulting from interconnectedness of portfolios has been picked up and is now being addressed by new work on network theory. Here we see an example of the importance of methodological approach. The foundations and wider implications of Minsky's analysis have not been widely recognised, chiefly because *they do not make sense* within a rational optimisation framework (Dow, 2010).

The first step in teasing out the nature and significance of different approaches to economics is to make the case for understanding different theoretical and policy positions in terms of the underlying methodology and ultimately the mode of thought. Groupings tend to coalesce around a shared mode of thought and approach to methodology, within which there may be differences of opinion about theory and policy. Chapter 2, entitled 'Schools of Thought in Macroeconomics: The Method is the Message' takes a case-study approach to spelling out what this means, considering three approaches in the 1980s: the general equilibrium approach, the Post-Keynesian approach and the neo-Austrian approach. In each case, differences are considered at the conceptual, theoretical and policy levels in order to demonstrate the practical significance of difference of approach and the usefulness of a methodological basis for classification.

Mainstream economics has of course moved on from the general equilibrium approach of the 1980s. But as we proceed with our analysis of approaches to economics through the chapters up to the present day we find that, at the level of methodological approach, the core principles remain in what we will term 'mainstream' economics. According to Lakatos's (1970) framework of scientific research programmes, any approach is defined by various propositions about the hard core (HC), and also by positive and negative heuristics (PH and NH) which guide theory development. The following is a Lakatosian representation of neo-Walrasian general equilibrium theory based on Weintraub (1985a) and Backhouse (1991):

HC1   There exist economic agents

HC2   Agents have preferences over outcomes

HC3   Agents independently optimise, subject to constraints

HC4   Choices are made in interrelated markets

PH1   Go forth and construct theories in which agents optimise

PH2   Specify the model-specific meanings of equilibrium and disequilibrium and analyse the model in terms of these

PH3   Construct theories in which agents have a well-defined set of information about relevant phenomena

PH4   Construct fully-specified, consistent models, simplifying where necessary in order to be able to do this, and draw only those conclusions which can be proved to be implied by the models

PH5   Specify the rules governing the interaction of agents (in terms of game theory, make the game explicit)

NH1   Do not construct theories in which irrational behaviour plays any role

NH2   Do not construct theories in which equilibrium has no meaning

NH3   Do not test hard core propositions

We will proceed to use the term 'mainstream economics' to refer to theory which is built on this core, encompassing terms such as 'general equilibrium theory', 'neo-classical economics' and 'orthodox economics'. As will be explained in Chapter 2, we use commonality of methodological approach to define a school of thought, even though there may be a range of different theories within the approach. Any such categorisation is of course a simplification, but this is the point of categories (as discussed in Chapter 10).

Perhaps the most important development in mainstream economics in response to the crisis has been to challenge NH1, considering the possible relevance of irrational behaviour, and NH3 on the basis of experimental evidence. Rationality is in fact one of the central concepts in debate over financial instability, with much of the mainstream understanding of the crisis revolving around different views as to possible irrational behaviours which have interfered with normal market processes. But the centrality of the hard core has coloured the way in which this development has occurred, such that there is pressure to absorb experimental evidence and analysis of irrationality into the hard core (Dow, forthcoming, a).

The meaning of the term 'rational' here is very specific, referring to well-informed optimising choice in pursuit of specified goals. The third chapter, jointly authored with Alexander Dow, 'Animal Spirits and Rationality', considers a different possible understanding of rationality as 'reasonableness' in the face of uncertain knowledge. This alternative analysis builds on a mode of thought which does not separate rationality and irrationality in a dualistic way, but rather sees sentiment, or emotion as an integral part of decision making (Dow, 2011). Thus, reason requires a foundation in conventional belief (just as the Bourbaki project found that deductive mathematics cannot be constructed as a self-sufficient system) and must be combined with the exercise of the imagination, along with emotion, to motivate behaviour. For Keynes (as for Hume and Smith), far from being something to be discouraged *per se*, sentiment (or emotion) is necessary for decision making.

Making sharp distinctions, for example between rationality and irrationality, is a pervasive feature of much of Western thought – 'dualism'. But again, while this is in particular a central feature of the mainstream mode of thought there are other possibilities, and the issues to be considered are explored in the fourth chapter, 'Beyond Dualism'. This habit of thought is well engrained. We see it having concrete consequences in the treatment of rationality, and theory design more generally. But it is only a habit, which needs to be brought to the surface and discussed.

One alternative non-dualistic approach, for example, would foster a range of partial analyses which together add weight to argument, rather than one complete formal model as the whole argument. Thus, for example, there would be no need to try to squeeze the contributions from psychology into a standard deductive, axiomatic argument in an equilibrium framework. (Indeed this approach provides arguments against such a procedure.) Yet this seems to be a widespread aim in behavioural economics (see Kahneman, 2003; and DellaVigna, 2009, for example), illustrating the continuing importance of the core mainstream principles set out above.

The meaning of rationality is closely related to whether or not allowance is made for uncertainty, referring to the availability or not of full knowledge. But the term 'uncertainty', like 'rationality', takes on different meanings according to the underlying mode of thought. These different meanings are explored in the chapter entitled 'Uncertainty about Uncertainty'. An important feature of different understandings of uncertainty is the degree to which it is in fact acknowledged by decision makers, which ultimately depends on psychological make-up and social environment. Here we see that different meanings of uncertainty will have more relevance to some circumstances than to others.

Keynes (1937) argued that we cope with uncertainty by relying on conventional judgements (Davis, 1994). But conventions may be challenged by events – they too evolve. Confidence in the conventional low assessment of risk increased as markets followed a relatively stable path up to 2007. This psychological state had real consequences in employment, production and expenditure. Conventional judgements in the form of market sentiment were part of the reality, in turn affecting the reality, while reinforcing themselves reflexively as asset prices continued to rise (Soros, 2008). Market players framed the reality in terms of mainstream theory, which suggested that rational market behaviour was expected to produce the pricing of assets in line with true risk and the best outcome for society (or at least this framing was used rhetorically). But conventional risk assessment was thrown into disarray with the crisis, and it took some time for new, more wary, conventions to become established. In such situations, market players can find it difficult to price assets; indeed, this is the normal pattern when markets undergo structural change. To contemplate an objective risk measure, which markets are to identify, is to presume that the future is knowable, at least stochastically, as in mainstream theory. (New Keynesian theory challenges the 'full knowledge' assumption in terms only of limited access to full information.) Unpredicted structural change challenges such a presumption. The more general case for economists to contemplate is some degree of fundamental uncertainty or unquantifiable risk. It becomes more compelling to take fundamental uncertainty seriously when current conventions of risk assessment are challenged by events.

If the crisis is understood, as Greenspan (2009) suggests, by irrational greed and fear taking over market sentiment, then the policy solution is to reduce the incentives and opportunities for irrationality. But the approach we have just considered as an alternative possibility is to take market sentiment seriously – not as something to be ignored or eliminated as irrationality, but rather as the normal mechanism for market judgement in the face of uncertainty. Theory used to understand developments in financial markets would therefore include analysis of decision-making under uncertainty, including any changes in the institutional environment which might alter the process of arriving at, and perpetuating, judgements. This would suggest input from 'old' institutionalist theory (Rutherford, 1994; Hodgson, 1999) and 'old' behavioural theory (Earl, ed., 1989; Sent, 2004) which (unlike the 'new' versions of this theory) are not constrained to analyse behaviour in terms of rational optimisation by atomistic individuals. These other approaches would aid understanding of market sentiment and what causes it to change, but also point to different types of policy intervention in order to stabilise markets (see Dow, forthcoming, c and d). Conventions may depart from what the authorities regard as reasonable (rather than narrowly rational) judgement, and psychological theory can inform the analysis (see Tuckett and Tafler, 2008; and Tuckett, 2011, for example). This implies, first, the development of mechanisms for monitoring market sentiment, and second, addressing monetary policy (especially communication of monetary policy) to moderating market sentiment when it is judged to be lacking a grounding in reality.

Economists too face varying degrees of uncertainty about their analysis in the face of new circumstances and rely on a range of conventions as to how to proceed. The methodological conventions of the mainstream approach have attracted support over a long period of time and the possible reasons for this are explored in the sixth chapter, 'The Appeal of Mainstream Economics'. But the current crisis has increased uncertainty about which is the most appropriate way for an economist to proceed in formulating policy advice. For any economist, deciding on one approach or another is necessary for knowledge to be developed, to inform policy. The adoption of one conventional approach rather than another involves putting higher value on what that approach allows relative to what it precludes. This chapter suggests that there is a trade-off between the internal certainties of deductivist analysis and the uncertainty of its application, when, as is normally the case, the theory's assumptions are not satisfied. Theories are inevitably abstract, but for theory to be applied there needs to be a reasoned process of moving from abstraction to reality.

The philosophy of logical positivism implies that economists can choose theories with confidence on the basis of empirical testing. But philosophers of science long ago declared logical positivism unsatisfactory. The economic methodology literature which followed (led by Caldwell, 1982) concluded that, while reasoned justifications can be made, there is no absolute basis for choosing one approach over another. Choice for economists, as for economic agents, requires the exercise of judgement.[1] The seventh chapter, 'Mainstream Economic Methodology', serves as a brief account of how thinking in the field of economic methodology has evolved over the last century. The aim here too is to uncover the different modes of thought implicit in different positions on methodology.

One topic in economic methodology which has attracted particular interest and support in recent years has been pluralism. But this is yet another term which has a range of meanings; lack of clarity as to what is meant has led to some confusion. It is particularly important for this concept to be clear for the current volume, since the exercise of considering a range of approaches to economics can be understood as an exercise in pluralism. The eighth chapter, 'Methodological Pluralism and Pluralism of Method' attempts to distinguish between some of the different uses of the term, referring to the level at which pluralism is being discussed. The two most commonly confused are pluralism at the level of approach (methodological pluralism) and pluralism as a *particular* methodological approach (pluralism of method). The first means acknowledging a range of legitimate approaches to economic knowledge, while the second means using a range of methods.

The dominant method of mainstream economics is deductive mathematical logic. The ninth chapter, jointly authored with Victoria Chick, 'The Non-neutrality of Formalism', explores the implications of this being the dominant method required of economics. Mathematics is often discussed as being like a language – a particularly clear and precise language. But the possibility is explored in this chapter that

---

[1] Of course, such choices are not entirely 'free'; any discipline involves its own institutions and educational frameworks which encourage particular approaches to the discipline.

mathematics is not neutral because it delineates the subject matter of economics and thus alters theories. For example, the chapter addresses the issue raised above about moving from abstraction to reality. Most (though not all) approaches to economics would agree that mathematical models can play a useful part, as a way of expressing partial arguments in a clear way. But if an approach focuses on uncertainty, conventions and emotions, as well as the non-deterministic evolution of institutions which cannot be modelled in the conventional deductivist way, then any argument based on a formal, closed model is inevitably partial and requires putting together with other lines of argument and different forms of evidence in order to increase its weight (Lawson, 2009). It is worthwhile to consider that, while Keynes referred to the usefulness of formal models, he nevertheless warned about the importance of keeping in mind the closures which models require but which need to be relaxed for application of the model's conclusions, as well as the meanings underlying mathematical terms (Keynes, 1936, pp. 297–8).

Not everyone supports methodological pluralism. It has been criticised by some as being incoherent – 'anything goes'. Such an approach would indeed by insupportable. But economics, with all its different schools of thought, is not incoherent. Like any other subject, it functions within loose communities, each identified (as we will see illustrated in Chapter 2) by shared methodological approach. A workable form of pluralism is explored in the tenth chapter, 'Structured Pluralism', where different approaches are structured around schools of thought. Rather than warring factions (as many have depicted the different parties to debates in the 1970s), the category of schools of thought is simply a shorthand method by which to identify the work of particular groupings of economists, with some understanding of their methodological approaches.

Schools of thought evolve, of course, and new synthetic schools of thought emerge. Within the system of economic thought, schools of thought are thus delineated by boundaries which are themselves evolving and which are permeable, allowing some communication between them. Such issues are even more important for how we analyse the economic system itself. The most important methodological distinction, arguably, is between the economy as an open system and the economy as a closed system, since important implications follow as to the best way to analyse it. But because these terms too are used differently by different economists, Chapter 11, jointly authored with Victoria Chick, is devoted to exploring 'The Meaning of Open Systems'.

The nature of the subject matter and how it is understood does in fact seem like the best place to start when considering new economic thinking to address the current series of crises and to formulate policy advice. The reality of an increase in uncertainty and the awareness of uncertainty have often been noted. One current of thought (neo-Austrian economics) has argued that policymakers should refrain from action because of their own uncertainty, while for others the onset of crisis evidently required some sort of action. But our current institutional structures mean that, even on a routine basis, action is required. For example, central bankers are required to make regular monetary policy pronouncements, no matter how much uncertainty they and the economy face. The problems posed by uncertainty are explored in the twelfth chapter, 'The Issue of Uncertainty in Economics', taking monetary policy as a case study.

Where then does modern economics stand as we contemplate new developments? The aim here is simply to attempt to open up the field for new economic thinking by drawing attention to what is being taken as given in economics and to the different possibilities which currently exist and on which we might build. But some have argued that economics is already pluralistic. We examine this claim in the thirteenth chapter, 'Variety of Methodological Approach in Economics'. Certainly, mainstream economics has evolved a wide range of different theories and employs a wider range of methods than in the past. But what is lacking is what this volume is intended to address: a discussion and justification of methodological approach. Even where new methods are employed, the aim is still given as being to build the results into a more refined deductivist theoretical structure which is amenable to mathematical expression. By presuming economics *in its totality* to be defined by this methodological approach, consideration of alternative possibilities is ruled out. This chapter then reviews the main themes that have been covered in more detail in earlier chapters. Some thoughts on the way forward are set out in the Afterword.

Conclusion

The aim here has been to make a start at setting out what is involved in different possible approaches to economics which can inform policy (not just different theories within one approach). This is the first step towards developing new economic thinking as the reality evolves. Each approach starts from its own view of the nature of the economy, categorises it accordingly and establishes criteria for good argument (including what are acceptable methods). It has been suggested that a deductivist approach continues to dominate mainstream economics and mainstream economic policy (in spite of challenges from evidence). But this should not be regarded as the only option. For all its attractions, this approach limits coverage of important issues which have become particularly noticeable with the crisis. Any approach must be selective about the types of issues which can be addressed. As new issues arise, there needs to be awareness of the selections currently made and whether others might be more fruitful. Considering the mainstream approach, the starting point of rational optimising individual behaviour limits the scope for understanding market sentiment (indeed any sentiment, with respect to fairness for example) and how it may change. It also limits the scope for analysing trust and considering how it may be restored. Even for those who conclude that the deductivist approach on balance is still preferable, the challenging nature of the current and real policy problems we face requires that such a judgement be justified in relation to alternative approaches.

While I, like any practising economist, have my own understanding of reality and a preferred way of approaching economics, the purpose here is not to argue for one approach over another. Rather the argument is for an open attitude to the possibility of alternative approaches and a willingness to make the case for one approach over another, that is, methodological pluralism. This is the first step to seeing one's own approach, with all its tacit assumptions, afresh. This is not at all to go to the other extreme of advocating that 'anything goes', but rather that reasoned judgement be applied to considering which is most useful among the range of possibilities. (These approaches each represent a set of conventions among groups of economists as to how to build knowledge.) We have illustrated the significance of a difference of approach briefly in terms of policy to address the current crisis.

Whatever approach we take will require the exercise of judgement at various stages of theorising, testing and application to policy. The best place to start in exercising judgement is an account of the reality to be analysed. The crisis has drawn attention to the real uncertainty faced by agents and by economists. Keynes argued that society addresses uncertainty by developing conventions, such that uncertainty is generally less evident than now (though always present in some degree). In contrast, mainstream economics ascribes stability in 'normal' times to the successful working of competitive markets, with uncertainty only arising in 'abnormal' times as a symptom rather than a cause. The dominance of mainstream economics, which tends to be taken for granted rather than explicitly justified, can itself be seen as a convention to assist economists in analysing a complex reality. As available reason and evidence change, then we would expect conventions too to change. But Keynes argued that non-conventional action in spite of uncertainty also requires animal spirits. It is to be hoped that the extreme circumstances of the crisis may fire up the animal spirits of economists to be aware of, reconsider and challenge their own conventions in a constructive way.

2
Schools of Thought in Macroeconomics: The Method Is the Message

It is tempting, when looking for constructive new theoretical developments, to look for a consensus stance on theory (and policy). Yet debates persist now, as they have done in the past, about which are the best new theories. These debates would be clarified if there were a better understanding of the different methodological underpinnings of each theory. Mainstream economics, neo-Austrian economics and Post-Keynesian economics of the 1970s and early 1980s are taken as case studies to illustrate the argument that different bodies of theory can usefully be classified in terms of their underlying methodological approaches. It is shown how each employs a quite different way of conceptualising the economy and economics. Further, by considering a historical period, we can recognise the principles guiding each of the three schools of thought independently of current theoretical discussion. Yet on reflection we may see these principles continuing to guide modern developments in each of the three traditions.

Introduction

'We are all monetarists now' (Laidler, 1981, p. 31)

This is an abridged version of an article published in *Australian Economic Papers*, 22(2), 1983, 30–47, which had benefited from the helpful comments and suggestions of Peter Earl, Paul Hare, Jan Kregel, David Laidler, Brian Loasby and an anonymous referee.

In presenting the case that this proposition is true in some, if not all, senses, Laidler was acting in the long-standing tradition of distilling a synthesis from apparently different schools of thought. He was echoing an earlier statement attributed to Milton Friedman that 'We are all Keynesians now'. Certainly, if agreement is possible, then efforts to promote it must be welcomed. At the same time, if disagreement persists, then it is instructive to explore the sources of that disagreement.

The search for synthesis reflects a desire to ensure the progress of economics as a science.[1] The natural sciences may be expected to 'progress' in that they deal with subject matter which has not changed fundamentally during the history of modern science (though even that is controversial). But the social sciences deal with behaviour, preferences and institutions which inevitably do change, changing the framework within which choice is framed and expressed. As a result, the social sciences may be expected to change both their emphasis and their mode of analysis to suit their times (in the sense of both economic conditions and prevailing understandings and ideologies). As such, it is likely that there will be, at any one time, strong differences of opinion as to which approach does best 'suit the times'.

The approach employed here to explore these differences of opinion as they apply to macroeconomics is that of Kuhn's (1962) theory of scientific revolutions. According to this theory, prevailing paradigms progress by means of 'normal science' and they are defended against attack until some incontestable fact demonstrates the inability of the paradigm to deal with what are perceived as current problems, and a new paradigm becomes orthodox.[2] Progression then consists of adopting new paradigms which are more relevant to these problems, rather than a continuous process of improving on existing theory.

The relative merits of Kuhn's theory in general, and as it is applied to economics in particular, have been debated elsewhere.[3] It is not the purpose here to go over that ground again (but see further Chapters 4 and 10). Rather, we start with the simple hypothesis that Kuhn's approach allows insights into the demarcation between schools of thought and

---

[1] Even the return to the Quantity Theory of Money advocated by Friedman in 1956 was interpreted as an element in the march forward of economics by Johnson (1971). He argued that both Keynes and Friedman exaggerated their break with the orthodoxies which prevailed in 1936 and 1956, respectively, for sociological and psychological reasons.

[2] A financial crisis can be understood in these terms as challenging the view that markets are efficient and are equilibrating.

[3] See for example Lakatos and Musgrave, eds (1970), and Latsis, ed. (1976).

the degree to which synthesis between them is possible. We proceed to attempt to demonstrate the validity of this hypothesis in the context of macroeconomic theory and policy.

Clarifying the paradigm concept in response to his critics, Kuhn (1974) argued that each paradigm is expressed in terms of its own 'disciplinary matrix'. This matrix represents the methodology of the school of thought, where the concept of methodology is broad enough to encompass not only the range of methods used but also the underlying world-view which determines the choice of questions raised and the way in which phenomena are perceived. While paradigms may have some features in common, then, the exclusiveness of each overall methodology to its paradigm precludes neutral synthesis between paradigms.[4] But theories expressed in terms of the same methodology, and thus the same paradigm, are conducive to synthesis by the process of normal science.

This approach, then, allows a categorisation of economic theory by methodology which necessarily cuts across other classifications. In so doing, we can conclude which differences between schools of thought are irreconcilable, reflecting differences of paradigm, and those which are not. To examine differences of approach in this way is not to attempt to promote discord. Rather, once differences of theory and policy prescription are seen to emerge necessarily from particular world-views combined with their particular methodological frameworks, the debate between paradigms may concentrate on the appropriateness of each for answering particular economic questions. No economic theory can perfectly model reality; policymakers still have to make a choice between the different representations of reality which are available.

The methodological criterion suggests theory groupings from which we take three as case studies from the 1980s: mainstream general equilibrium theory[5], neo-Austrian theory and Post-Keynesian theory. That these three groupings were of disproportionate size in terms of numbers of economists they represent is to be expected in a Kuhnian context, as a range of forms of mainstream theory constituted the ruling paradigm. Where economists recognise elements of their own methodologies as belonging to more than one grouping, they have adopted an additional paradigm

---

[4] See Dow (1980) for a demonstration of this point in the context of the capital controversies.

[5] While mainstream economics is no longer so widely classified explicitly as general equilibrium theory, most of the core elements are still present, as discussed in Chapter 1. In the 1980s, the mainstream general equilibrium grouping included a variety of theories, such as the monetarism and 'hydraulic' Keynesianism, which normally were treated separately.

which can be distinguished from those discussed here, and they can thus be expected to have difficulty in reconciling their economics with any one of these paradigms. The three groupings are not intended to be all encompassing, but to be of sufficient importance to demonstrate the usefulness of the methodology demarcation criterion.

Three key elements in the framework of macroeconomic theories are singled out for special attention as reflecting their different methodological approaches: the treatment of microfoundations, the use of the concept of equilibrium and the modelling of expectations.

Microfoundations

The advantage the social scientist has over the natural scientist is in understanding, by introspection, the motivation of the subject matter – *verstehen*, as a source of scientific evidence (see Ziman, 1978). The possibility of *a priori* reasoning on this (albeit subjective) basis has been seen as compensating to some extent for the relative difficulty of testing results. Aggregative macroeconomics, as it developed from the Keynesian revolution (although diverging from Keynes, as we will see below), forewent that advantage by driving a wedge between economics at the micro level and at the macro level. Indeed, this was regarded as a virtue by logical positivists who put the major emphasis on empirical testing of theoretical results.[6] The most extreme position was taken by Friedman (1953) when he argued that empirical verification was sufficient to support theory: verification of assumptions, particularly those with respect to individual behaviour, was unnecessary, and indeed undesirable.[7] But, uncomfortable with a lack of scope for *verstehen* in macroeconomics, and motivated to build a complete deductivist structure for economics, a range of economists attempted to rebuild the microfoundations of macroeconomics.

Mainstream theory

The general equilibrium theorists' search for microfoundations[8] started from the position that the neoclassical macroeconomic model, as

---

[6] Logical positivists reject value judgements as unscientific and advocate the uniqueness and universality of the scientific method (see Katouzian, 1980, ch. 3 and Caldwell, 1982).

[7] In Popperian terms, the scientific method requires an absence of falsification rather than verification, although in practice the principle is rarely maintained (see for example Blaug, 1980, ch. 15 and Coddington, 1976).

[8] The first major contribution was the Frydman and Phelps (1970) volume. See Weintraub (1979) for a survey.

expressed by the logical positivists, was inconsistent with neoclassical microeconomic theory. First, the emphasis on aggregate demand precluded considerations of scarcity. Second, Patinkin's (1965) exploration of the process of adjustment to money supply changes raised the question of the behaviour of markets in disequilibrium. Then the observed positive relationship between the rate of change in nominal wages and employment, captured by the short-run Philips curve, seemed to flout the representation of the labour market as clearing at full employment unless wages are held artificially high.

Within mainstream theory, such an inconsistency was profound and disturbing. The only logical distinction within this theory between the microeconomic level and the macroeconomic level was the degree of aggregation of markets in equilibrium. Implicitly, each component market of an aggregated market was also in equilibrium. If the economy is in disequilibrium at the macroeconomic level, then no presumption is admissible as to the equilibrium of any component market, however small. Following Leijonhufvud (1976), Weintraub (1979) distinguished between macroeconomics as dealing with 'coordination failure' and microeconomics as dealing with 'coordination success'. But it was difficult for such a distinction to make sense in a general equilibrium framework in which coordination failure in any market means coordination failure in at least one other market.

In fact, particularly in applied mainstream economics, reductionism was not taken as far as has been suggested above as being logically required by much general equilibrium theorising. While presented as representing individual behaviour, much of mainstream microeconomics in fact adopted the Marshallian concept of the representative individual, who acts like an 'average' individual.[9] This form of microeconomics thus referred to aggregative behaviour, allowing for stochastic deviations from the average on the part of individuals. No scope was given for individual behaviour which was inconsistent with macroeconomic outcomes. Coordination success depicted at the micro level was in fact equivalent to coordination success at the macro level. The possibility of any systematic variance from the average among different groups of individuals was subsumed in the aggregate outcome.

Coordination failure at the macroeconomic (and thus, also, microeconomic) level was incorporated into the analysis as a disequilibrium

---

[9] Machlup (1987) defended neoclassical microeconomics against charges of lack of realism on the grounds that the depicted behaviour is more representative than actual behaviour. Expressions of the 'pure' Arrow-Debreu model do, however, refer to 'individual' behaviour (see Hahn, 1981).

state, the product of imperfect information. The economy moves up or down short-run Phillips curves, for example, only when expectations differ among different agents and from the actual outcome. Once all expectations are formed on full information, a Walrasian process brings the economy back to the long-run equilibrium position. Thus, individual behaviour still could be modelled as utility or profit maximising, but constrained by the availability of information.

General equilibrium theory developed markedly during the 1970s to deal with disequilibrium, pursuing concepts such as temporary equilibrium and 'neo-Walrasian' adjustment mechanisms. Since the underlying methodology did not change, however, we continue to use the term 'general equilibrium' on the understanding that we are thereby encompassing the developments of the 1970s. By the same token, as explained in Chapter 1, we will use the term 'mainstream' to encompass developments beyond the 1970s.

Neo-Austrian theory

Problems of information are central to neo-Austrian theory, and indeed form the basis of their critique of mainstream theory. Both approaches share a worldview whereby the operation of free markets is, on balance, beneficent.[10] In the neo-Austrian theory, this beneficence stems from the ability of individual economic agents to coordinate information in a manner superior to a central agency such as government.

Economies are characterised as being perpetually in a state of imperfect information, and thus perpetually prone to change as new information emerges. Since decisions must always be made with respect to the future, on which there is only disparate, differential and uncertain information, it is virtually impossible that information should ever be uniform, and uniformly correct. If attainment of general equilibrium is virtually impossible in practice, then it is regarded as more relevant to actual economic conditions to focus on the process of change. The neo-Austrian method, then, eschews macroeconomic analysis as a discipline distinct from microeconomic analysis. If market information is the most relevant information for propelling the economy in the 'correct' direction, then any adjustment to that information arising from government policy simply impedes that process (see Hayek, 1931). Indeed, since aggregate behaviour is simply the aggregation of the behaviour of

---

[10] Unlike neo-Austrian theory, mainstream theory does point to particular Pareto-optimal forms of intervention (ranging from the taxation of activity causing external diseconomies to central planning.)

all individuals searching as well as they can for the best information, it is argued that no additional useful information can be gleaned at the aggregate level. If the macroeconomy is best served then, by market signals emitted by and to actual individual agents, macroeconomics simply consists of aggregating microeconomics, which may not be a feasible operation and in any case serves no useful purpose.[11]

Post-Keynesian theory

'Keynesian' economics is perhaps the category most prone to confusion and requiring of clarification. Following Coddington (1976), the distinction may be drawn between hydraulic Keynesians, reconstituted reductionists and fundamentalist Keynesians. By investigating the approach to the microfoundations of each, it will become apparent that Coddington's classification referred to difference in methodology and it allows us to identify the third as the approach which differs methodologically from other approaches to macroeconomics.

Hydraulic Keynesian methodology was logical positivist in the sense that it concentrated on empirical relationships between aggregates without concern for microfoundations. 'Keynesian' results of demand failure, based on this approach, relied on observation of particular values of elasticities and assumptions of wage and price rigidity.[12] Challenge from more avowedly neoclassical logical positivists as to the validity of these observations and assumptions played a large part in prompting the development of microfoundations to strengthen the argument. Thus emerged the disequilibrium analysis of the 'reconstituted reductionists', most notably Clower and Leijonhufvud and the analytical distinction between fixprice and flexprice markets (see Hicks, 1974). There is a strong methodological parallel, then, between the addition to hydraulic Keynesianism of microfoundations in the form of reconstituted reductionism and the development of the mainstream approach to span the micro and macro levels. Indeed, since the microfoundations of each were built mainly on neoclassical choice theory, the content also had strong similarities.

A methodologically distinct brand of Keynesian economics was more evident in the work of the 'fundamentalist' Keynesians who

---

[11] Where macroeconomic policies proposed by others are to be analysed, a neo-Austrian would concentrate on the microeconomic composition of the policy (see Lachmann, 1973).

[12] As in the case of modern New Keynesian analysis, another explanation refers to information asymmetry.

concentrated on the vicissitudes of individual decision-making in disequilibrium, and the process of market behaviour. Unlike the neo-Austrians, they concluded that markets could not be relied upon because of information problems (together with divergence between individual and collective interests) so that public sector intervention had a central role to play. Using the term 'Post-Keynesian' to encompass those Keynesians who are neither logical positivists nor employ neoclassical choice theory (a category roughly coincident with 'fundamentalist Keynesian', see Dow and Earl, 1982, ch. 13), we can now discuss a Post-Keynesian paradigm, in the sense that it is methodologically distinct from other paradigms.

While there was a logical inconsistency between 'hydraulic' Keynesian macroeconomics and 'unreconstituted' neoclassical microeconomics, Post-Keynesian theory allowed for the practical inconsistency which defines the difference between the micro and macro levels in the first place. This reflected a distinction between internal consistency and external consistency which influenced the choice of methodology (see further Chapter 4).[13] Keynes's microeconomics, with its basis in Marshall, stressed the behaviour of entrepreneurs and households, not only in responding to change, but also in initiating action themselves.[14] This behaviour might be regarded by some to be utility maximising and even profit maximising, but the elements of the decision function are so hedged about by current, shifting and disparate sets of conventional expectations about future values as to give such terms quite different meanings from the mainstream account. Because individuals' decisions are buffeted by the effects of others' decisions, all the Keynesian paradoxes emerge: attempts to increase saving are thwarted by the effect on aggregate demand and reductions in nominal wages fail to increase employment because of the effect on aggregate demand, while attempts to reap capital gains or avoid

---

[13] Crotty (1980) suggested that Post-Keynesians should, if anything, search for macrofoundations of micro. More recently, King (2009) argues that the whole idea of microfoundations is inappropriate to Post-Keynesian analysis, which deliberately chooses a series of partial analyses as a preferable way to understand a complex reality than one overarching analysis (as in general equilibrium theory). This pluralist methodology is discussed in Chapters 4, 8 and 10.

[14] Marshallian theory was later developed by Townshend (1937), Andrews (1949), Richardson (1960) and Shackle (1979), in a manner which adapted well to the Post-Keynesian framework. The ability of some neo-Austrian theory also to encompass action, as well as reaction, was highlighted by Loasby (1983).

capital losses are thwarted if the majority of the market acts on the same expectations.

Because of historical experience of such potentially destabilising developments, the result was the development of institutions designed to promote as much stability as possible, in particular relatively inflexible nominal wages and prices (see Richardson, 1960), the very elements singled out by general equilibrium theorists as perpetuating disequilibrium. The general policy stance which emerged from this analysis thus countenanced the perpetuation of wage and price rigidity as a means of promoting stability, while relying on government intervention to counteract the implications of individual behaviour for aggregate demand.

Equilibrium

Much of the difference in method and outlook employed in constructing microfoundations resulted from the different use of the equilibrium concept: whether equilibrium is general or partial, which variables are exogenous and which endogenous, and how the economy is modelled out of equilibrium.

Mainstream theorists chose as the point of reference of their analysis the situation in which all markets are cleared simultaneously and with no tendency for prices or quantities to change, some on the grounds that it posed the most interesting questions, others (see Hahn, 1973, 1981) on the grounds that it was the only feasible basis for answering interesting questions. The theory was embellished by extensive work on situations of unstable market-clearing equilibrium (temporary equilibrium; see Grandmont, 1977) and of non-market-clearing, primarily with reference to problems of information flows (see Weintraub, 1979).[15] But, in order to explain systematic economic fluctuations, some variables must be defined as exogenous, capable of shocking the system from one equilibrium position to another. The money supply was singled out as the most important short-term exogenous variable,[16] although productivity changes arising from new technology or changes in government behaviour also shock the system in the long-run as well

---

[15] Since the original paper was written, rational expectations theory developed the notion of equilibrium as one in which all agents optimise, such that all situations are identified as being equilibrium ones.

[16] See, for example, Friedman and Schwartz (1963), in which the business cycle was presented as the result solely of money supply shocks.

as the short-run.[17] As long as everything else, like labour market behaviour, is treated as endogenous, then all relevant markets must clear in general equilibrium, even if after some period of adjustment.

The mode of adjustment depends on market conventions (particularly whether prices are slow to adjust) and on the formation of expectations. Laidler (1981) drew a strong distinction between adaptive-expectations monetarists and rational-expectations monetarists in terms of their treatment of economies away from long-run equilibrium. The former allowed for non-clearing while the latter defined every position as one of market-clearing, maximum use being made of all available information. The results of the two approaches differed only insofar as reactions to random shocks were modelled differently. But, as long as the model was stable, then rational expectations must adapt to random shocks in order to produce the same long-run outcome as adaptive expectations. As soon as a general equilibrium framework was employed, the range of possible adjustment processes was defined if the system was to be dynamically stable. This was not to say that adaptive expectations monetarists did not have more confidence in the ability of the monetary authorities to influence relative prices, or more concern that account should be taken of the social implication of short-run disequilibrium. But these were differences on empirical matters and on social preferences, respectively.

Post-Keynesian analysis adopted a range of adjustment processes for attention and then employed the equilibrium concept only insofar as it was consistent with the process analysis. At any one point in time, markets may be moving towards some equilibrium position (long run or even temporary), either through price adjustment, quantity adjustment, or a combination of these. But the search for a market-clearing set of prices takes time, in the historical sense, during which other variables can change, pushing the economy onto another path. Where the equilibrium concept was employed it was as a 'state of rest' with no presumption as to utility and profit maximisation. But if the essence of the economy was viewed as being its susceptibility to change (particularly with respect to expectations), then it was not surprising that the equilibrium concept was not regarded as central.[18]

---

[17] Real business cycle theory has developed on the basis of technology shocks as the source of instability, with the money supply as endogenous. Meanwhile, as an alternative explanation for the cycle, New Keynesians have explored the implications of self-fulfilling beliefs which are similarly represented by stochastic disturbances.

[18] It was possible to interpret *The General Theory,* as Kregel (1976) did, as emphasising the possibility of the economy arriving at a state of rest which

This approach did not need to make such clear-cut distinctions between exogenous and endogenous variables since it was not constrained by the necessity for endogenous variables to clear markets. Rather, the distinction was made with respect to particular lines of argument (so that a variable may be exogenous to one line of argument while endogenous to another), or on disciplinary grounds.[19] Thus, to the extent that wage levels were explained by sociological factors, they might be treated as exogenous to a partial economic theory.[20] Most notably, the money supply was treated as endogenous, albeit influenced by the actions of the central monetary authority.

Among neo-Austrians there was a range of views from Kirzner, who discussed general equilibrium as having objective existence, to Lachmann, who like Shackle viewed it as an artificial construct referring to static conditions (see Loasby, 1983; and Lachmann, 1973). But, by concentrating their analysis almost entirely on individual decision-making and the generation of information, using case study methods rather than mathematics, neo-Austrians avoided use of the general equilibrium concept.

Within a discipline dominated by general equilibrium analysis, it was sometimes difficult to grasp the implications of analysis which did not rest on the general equilibrium concept. Yet many of the debates and misunderstandings in economics could be seen to stem from conflicting uses of it.

The correspondence between Keynes and Harrod on Harrod's (1939) growth model was a case in point (see Kregel, 1980). While Harrod's theory was regarded by many as an extension of Keynes's theory to the long run, Keynes himself found that it conflicted with his view of the economy as being cyclical, but generally dynamically stable. The instability in Harrod's model arose from the cumulative effects on investment demand of a disparity between the growth of demand and the 'warranted rate of growth'. But Harrod expressed this divergence as occurring in a general equilibrium snapshot, not as a process in historical time. Indeed Harrod showed how the warranted rate of growth,

---

involves socially-unacceptable levels of unemployment. In this case, equilibrium played a central role in the analysis.

[19] See Wiles (1979-80) for a discussion of the implications for economics of the disciplinary divide between it and the other social sciences. See further the discussion of pluralist methodology in Chapters 4, 8 and 10.

[20] See Weintraub (1978-79) for a discussion of the extent to which economics can explain nominal wage levels.

while fixed in each snapshot, would change from snapshot to snapshot, altering its position relative to the actual rate of growth and thus the tendency towards cumulative expansion or decline; this formed the basis of his theory of the trade cycle which does refer to historical time. But Keynes's concept of equilibrium was notional, and secondary to the temporal process of evolutionary change in the economy, so interpreting Harrod's model in those terms inevitably led to confusion (which continued to be mirrored in many textbooks). Precisely the same confusion was recognised in the capital theory debates.[21]

Another expression of Keynes's ideas which led to confusion as a result of translation into a general equilibrium framework was Tobin's (1958) theory of portfolio choice (see Chick, 1977; and Dow and Earl, 1982). Tobin explained the choice between bonds and money in terms of the trade-off between risk and expected return. But Tobin required individual decision-makers to be able to form expectations and assess risk with confidence. This contrasts with Keynes's view that uncertainty and the inability to assign probability distributions to risk, as well as to specify preferences and identify the choice set, are important determinants of portfolio selection (see Keynes, 1937).

But, in addition, there was the same difference in treatment of time as that which arose with Harrod's growth model. Tobin's financial investors were depicted in equilibrium at an instant in time. Once such matters as brokerage costs were taken into account, the implication was that actual portfolios were optimal for the particular configuration of risk and return perceived to prevail at each instant in time. Keynes's view of portfolio choice emphasised rather the change in expectations and in the degree of certainty with which expectations were held, over historical time (see further Chapters 5 and 12). In particular, by endogenising expectations to some extent as the outcome of market developments over time, Keynes's framework allowed dynamic analysis of financial instability, most notably that of Minsky (1976).

As with growth models, then, models of financial market behaviour performed different functions, depending on the framework employed. Once a framework was chosen, however, the range of the model was restricted. *The General Theory* did not provide sufficient specifications

---

[21] See Robinson (1953-54) and Harcourt (1972, ch. 1). While a Keynesian Cambridge economist would say, for example, that the rate of interest goes up as the money supply goes down (indicating movement in time), a neoclassicist would use that expression in the sense only that a high interest rate is associated with a low money supply, and vice versa.

to model simultaneous clearing of all markets as the result of optimising behaviour, just as general equilibrium analysis could not explain the process of market adjustment out of equilibrium (other than as movement towards equilibrium). Tobin succeeded in dealing with the problem posed for general equilibrium theory by Keynes's theory of liquidity preference. Success, however, required transforming it into a theory which was no longer Keynesian.

Expectations

Until the 1970s, Keynes's original theory was distinguished from the neoclassical synthesis by the importance given to expectations (see Coddington, 1975). During a period of relatively stable growth, it was natural that the future should be regarded as an extrapolation of the past and the present; so expectations, if modelled at all, could be subsumed in the actual values of variables. Further, general equilibrium analysis did not encourage modelling of decision-making on the basis of expectations which might prove mistaken.

Analysis of expectations, however, experienced a revival with the instability of the 1970s. In particular, lags in expectations formation were invoked to explain labour market behaviour in times of inflation. There were in the 1970s and 1980s three main approaches to modelling expectations: the *General Theory* Keynesian approach, adaptive expectations and rational expectations. These approaches will be discussed in turn, in the chronological order in which they assumed importance.

Keynesian expectations

Keynes (1936, ch. 12) distinguished between expectations about the long run and the short run, the former being dominated by 'entrepreneurs' and the latter by 'speculators'. Entrepreneurs, making decisions about long-term physical investment, financed by financial investors, must form expectations about the values of variables over the life of the project. Given the degree of ignorance about the future, there were no decisive rational grounds on which a decision to invest could be reached, other than passively following conventional judgement. The decision must thus ultimately rest on 'animal spirits' (see further Chapter 3). They were the result of what Shackle called an originative process, requiring the use of imagination.

The provision of finance for investment involved a less long-term commitment, since financial assets are more readily traded than real assets. Formation of expectations was more straightforward since investors could concentrate on the financial market in question; in contrast, the 'entrepreneurial' investor must form explicit expectations about the markets for labour, capital goods and output, as well as financial markets. This distinction becomes greater, the more easily traded the financial asset.[22]

The choice of financial assets to hold depends on their expected relative yields. No matter what the long-run equilibrium yield of an asset, it is short-run fluctuations in that yield which are important (once brokerage costs are taken into account). Thus, if a rational investor expects an asset's price to fall in the short run and rise in the long run, she will sell for capital gain before the price falls, and buy again before the price rises. These short-run fluctuations can occur quite independently of any long-run trend, and they are strongly influenced by the conventional short-run expectations of operators in the market. If the expectation is, on balance, for a fall in price, then sales will be large and the expectation will be proved correct.

Neither long-run nor short-run expectations, as described, can easily be modelled (for reasons explored further in Chapters 5 and 12). If there is no dominant expectation, then a large proportion of expectations will, by definition, be disappointed. In the case of physical investment, the consequences of disappointed expectations can have major and long-lasting effects. If, however, there is a dominant expectation, whether or not it is reasonable *ex ante,* it can prove to be self-fulfilling *ex post.* A major investment expansion will produce the expansion of effective demand to justify it, just as a wave of buying on the stock market causes share prices to rise.

Adaptive expectations

Once the analysis of the macroeconomy was conducted in terms of a mathematical model by which theories are tested empirically and predictions made, some means had to be found of modelling expectations formation. The method of modelling adaptive expectations made expectations quantifiable by expressing them as weighted functions of previous values of the same variables (a method first established in investment theory). Thus, it was assumed that in each period the decision-maker notes the disparity between the expected value of a variable and its actual value, and adapts her expectations by a fixed proportion

---

[22] Entrepreneurs must of course also form short-run expectations in order to reach decisions on output, price and employment in the short-run.

of that disparity; eventually the expected value approaches the actual value asymptotically, as long as the actual value remains constant.[23]

It is important to explore the differences between adaptive expectations and Keynesian expectations, because of their superficial similarity. Conducting his discussion outside of any general equilibrium framework, Keynes depicted expectations being formed uncertainly, with imperfect information, and differently by different people (and thus often disappointed), although influenced by crowd behaviour. He did conclude (Keynes 1937, p. 214) that in practice, expectations are formed largely assuming that the present is a better guide to the future than it actually is, and that the existing state of opinion is a correct assessment of the future, all with reliance on conventional judgement.

This pointed forcefully towards a model of adaptive expectations. But the adaptive expectations model presumed that economic agents are always on a path to general equilibrium and thus always moving in the 'right' direction, if not at optimal speed. The economy is in general equilibrium when all expectations are fulfilled. Adaptive expectations provided the mechanism, previously lacking, to describe the process of adjustment from disequilibrium to equilibrium.

The essence of Keynes's theory was that perpetual adjustments in expectations propel the economy round the business cycle without a benchmark of 'correct' equilibrium prices. More rapid changes in expectations can make the fluctuations more violent; only physical constraints on expansions and contractions can necessarily force a stabilising correction in expectations as to the values of assets. Keynesian expectations could be regarded as adaptive, but outside a general equilibrium framework the consequences were quite different from the conventional adaptive expectations model.

The behaviour represented by adaptive expectations – only a gradual adaptation towards 'correct' expectations – could be explained by institutional considerations (finite contract periods during which information changes) or by money illusion. Alternatively, such behaviour might be explained by irrationality, an absence of utility maximising behaviour. While this 'irrationality' may result from poor information, the ever-increasing availability of information implies that behaviour is

---

[23] Since the 'expectations' variable now appeared in the equation as a distributed lag on the past values of the variable, it did not provide a watertight means of testing the validity of the adaptive expectations hypothesis. A distributed lag is open to alternative interpretations. However, this problem of identifying causality is common to all economic theory.

becoming more 'rational'.[24] This view underlies the rejection of adaptive expectations and its replacement by rational expectations.

Rational expectations

The rational expectations view that individuals made the best possible use of information at any one time (while excluding the concept of bounded rationality) had some of its roots in neo-Austrian economics (see Kantor, 1979; Colander and Guthrie, 1980-81). The neo-Austrians emphasised the poverty of information and concentrated on the process by which information was acquired and incorporated in decision making. In contrast to adaptive expectations, it was assumed that all available information was used to form predictions. But rational expectations models, assuming that correct information was available (with qualifications for stochastic disturbances), in effect assumed knowledge of the long-run outcome of the process on which the neo-Austrians focussed. The coincidence of individual rationality and collective rationality, as of subjective observations with objective facts, was assumed – given the structure of general equilibrium models – rather than proved.[25]

In the neo-Austrian sense, rational expectations were 'reasonable' expectations, which varied from person to person, and accorded also with Keynesian expectations, not least in not being amenable to deterministic (even if stochastic) mathematical modelling. However, in neo-Austrian theory, 'reasonable' expectations promoted individual action which ensured the beneficent working of markets, while in the Post-Keynesian sense, 'reasonable' expectations propelled markets along unstable courses. The nature of expectations formation under uncertainty determined the Post-Keynesian and neo-Austrian approaches to macroeconomic theory, the differences between them stemming from their different views on microfoundations.

In the case of general equilibrium analysis, the formal model was the starting-point. This was, as Colander and Guthrie put it, a case of 'the model determining expectations', the reverse of the situation in the neo-Austrian and Keynesian models. Once analysis referred to a position of general equilibrium, then there was no scope for expectations which were incorrect (or at least not becoming 'more correct') or

---

[24] However, this rationality was viewed by behaviouralists as being bounded by the human capacity to process information (see Simon, 1955).
[25] See Hayek's (1931, 1945) seminal contributions. See also Evans (1983) for an analysis of the conflict between individual rationality and collective rationality.

formed with uncertainty (defined as unquantifiable risk). If the economy is subject to random shocks, then the path to long-run equilibrium will differ, but that equilibrium will be common to both models.

As such, the difference between rational expectations and adaptive expectations was not fundamental within a general equilibrium framework, but rather only a question of paths of adaptation to random shocks. Both Laidler (1981) and Colander and Guthrie suggested, however, that the difference in policy prescription was fundamental, rational expectations theory implying that any systematic policy intervention (other than systematically random intervention) could not alter real variables; adaptive expectations theorists only argued that this was true in the long run. Therefore, just as the difference between monetarist and non-monetarist neoclassicists centred on the size of the interest-elasticity of the demand for money, so the difference between rational and adaptive expectations theories centred on the size of the coefficient of adaptation, except in the case of random shocks. Given the same underlying theoretical framework, the policy argument then was whether monetary policy worked somewhat (in terms of altering output and employment) for a short time, or not at all. There was, however, complete agreement, within this framework, on the long-run policy outcome.

Conclusion

The purpose of this chapter has been to demonstrate that different schools of thought can be understood usefully in terms of their methodological approaches. This argument was illustrated by considering the different conceptualisations which characterised the mainstream, neo-Austrian and Post-Keynesian frameworks in the 1980s. The distinctiveness of the frameworks they employed implied that the meaning and justification of the theories and policy advice of each should be treated as distinctive.

Having said that, how should policy-makers choose between paradigms? At one level, the choice is simple if the worldview of any paradigm corresponds to that of the government in power. Beyond that level, a decision must be made as to which approach is most useful for current problems and conditions, using information on the past performance of policies. General equilibrium analysis' *forte* is in questions of interrelationships under relatively stable conditions with given behavioural and institutional relationships. Post-Keynesian analysis, by concentrating on the potential for change, both in economic variables and behavioural and institutional variables, is more suited to unstable conditions, and particularly to situations in which institutional change is contemplated. It was ironic, then, that in 1979 both the UK and the US governments should have adopted monetarist policies based on a framework which presumed stability to address economic instability. Further, this framework required a change in financial institutional arrangements which would alter the economic structure on which the models were predicated. Monetarist analysis could not then cope with the adaptation of market behaviour, and indeed the adaptation of the range of assets performing money functions.

But we also saw in the discussion of expectations the dangers inherent in concentrating on only one school of thought at a time (even if in principle being prepared to change the approach as circumstances change). A theory of expectations under uncertainty had been central to Keynes's analysis. But this had been set aside and forgotten during the stable decades before the 1970s, such that rational expectations theory could be launched as the only theory taking expectations seriously in the 1980s. Keynes's theory of expectations had been continued in Post-Keynesian economics, but it was not more widely recognised in the 1980s since it did not make sense from a mainstream perspective. It would have made for much more informed debate if the range of extant methodological approaches had been more widely acknowledged and understood.

We conclude, then, that the economics profession should not suppress its ability to provide a menu of theoretical and policy approaches. It would be a sad day when any one paradigm held an absolute monopoly on ideas. But let us guard against the temptation to treat all paradigms as one, the only result of which can be fruitless argument and misunderstanding, and an unnecessarily limited capacity to address new problems.

3
Animal Spirits and Rationality

Jointly authored with Alexander Dow

The concept of animal spirits, which has recently attracted renewed attention, is a good example of the importance of a methodological approach for meaning. In the 1980s, as now, there was a contrast between understanding animal spirits as irrationality on the one hand, and as an integral element of decision-making under uncertainty on the other. The 'irrationality' interpretation relegated animal spirits to mainstream oblivion until the new interest in behavioural economics. But the importance of uncertainty in the recent crisis means that Keynes's interpretation warrants renewed attention.

Introduction

The notion that 'animal spirits' govern investment decisions can be viewed as being central to Keynes's theory of aggregate demand and, at the same time, as being its weakest point. An autonomous shift in long-run expectations among entrepreneurs can drive a wedge between effective demand and full employment output, requiring government stabilisation policy if full employment is to be achieved. That shifts in long-run expectations may occur autonomously is, however, regarded by many as cause for concern. If Keynes's theory can neither explain nor predict these shifts, then it appears to be lacking a crucial element.

If individual entrepreneurs are viewed as acting according to reason, that is, that they are rational in the broadest sense of the term, then 'in

The original version of this chapter was published in T. Lawson and H. Pesaran (eds), *Keynes' Economics: Methodological Issues*, London: Croom Helm, 1985, pp. 46–65; reprinted in 2009 by Routledge.

principle' it may be possible to capture that reasoning in a complete theory of long-run expectations, endogenising animal spirits. Some argued that Keynesians should attempt to develop Keynes's theory of long-run expectations in this way (Tarshis, 1980, and Kenyon, 1980, for example). Animal spirits would then lose their special status. Coddington (1982) pushed the argument further. If long-run expectations formation by entrepreneurs *cannot* be explained by rational behaviour which can be modelled, he argued, then this must be true for all the expectations of agents in all sectors. But then, if all decision-making is subject to the exogenous influence of expectations shifts, economists must retreat into nihilism.

The purpose of this chapter is to re-examine the concept of animal spirits in the light of these charges. The first task is to go back to the origins of the concept of animal spirits in Keynes's early work on probability theory and its development in his theory of entrepreneurial behaviour. This textual analysis allows us to assess Keynes's own views as to the significance of animal spirits as an influence on expectations formation. The third section is devoted to considering why the concept of animal spirits should subsequently have fallen into such disfavour. Our conclusion is that the mainstream critique of animal spirits is the natural outcome of attempting to understand it within the mainstream framework. In particular, the narrow use of the rationality concept employed within the mainstream rules out the possibility of the type of indeterminacy implied by animal spirits. Indeterminacy in the formation of expectations does, however, make sense within the methodology which Keynes employed, which is outlined in the fourth section. Indeterminacy still poses problems, particularly for empirical work. But within the Keynesian framework the solution lies in being alert to a change of mood within an economy, and understanding its significance, rather than in ruling it out of order in academic debate.[1]

Keynes on uncertainty and confidence

A textual analysis of Keynes's own writings clarifies his notion of animal spirits and confirms the importance he attached to confidence factors in determining the level of investment, and so of aggregate demand. Keynes's definition of animal spirits is in his discussion of long-term

---

[1] Dow and Dow (2011) also consider mechanisms for influencing animal spirits.

expectations in Chapter 12 of *The General Theory,* although the ideas on uncertainty and confidence denoted by the term had surfaced much earlier in Keynes's career in his *Treatise on Probability*.

In *The General Theory,* Keynes drew a fundamental distinction between speculation, or the buying and selling of assets (real or financial) in anticipation of capital gains from changed asset prices, and enterprise, a synonym for new investment in real assets. Keynes declared:

> Even apart from the instability due to speculation, there is the instability due to the characteristic of human nature that a large proportion of our positive activities depend on spontaneous optimism rather than on a mathematical expectation, whether moral or hedonistic or economic. Most, probably, of our decisions to do something positive, the full consequences of which will be drawn out over many days to come, can only be taken as a result of animal spirits – of a spontaneous urge to action rather than inaction, and not as the outcome of a weighted average of quantitative benefits multiplied by quantitative probabilities. Enterprise only pretends to itself to be mainly actuated by the statements in its own prospectus, however candid and sincere. Only a little more than an expedition to the South Pole, is it based on an exact calculation of benefits to come. Thus if the animal spirits are dimmed and the spontaneous optimism falters, leaving us to depend on nothing but a mathematical expectation, enterprise will fade and die; —though fears of loss may have a basis no more reasonable than hopes of profit had before. (Keynes, 1936, pp. 161–2)

The implications of this psychological factor were introduced a few paragraphs later:

> We should not conclude from this that everything depends on waves of irrational psychology. On the contrary, the state of long-term expectation is often steady, and, when it is not, the other factors exert their compensating effects. We are merely reminding ourselves that human decisions affecting the future, whether personal or political or economic, cannot depend on strict mathematical expectation, since the basis for making such calculations does not exist; and that it is our innate urge to activity which makes the wheels go round, our rational selves choosing between the alternatives as best we are able, calculating where we can, but often falling back for our motive on whim or sentiment or chance. (ibid., pp. 162–3)

A very few scholars insisted that Keynes's ideas on uncertainty were central to his vision (Davidson, 1978; Shackle, 1974, pp. 35–45; Minsky, 1975, pp. 64–8).[2] For the most part, economists have regarded them as peripheral, as do, for instance, Patinkin (1982, p. 61) and Eatwell (1979, pp. 39–41).[3] Though doctrinal matters are not our main concern in this chapter, we contend here, not only that Keynes viewed expectations under uncertainty as vital, but also that entrepreneurs' expectations, a prime determinant of the level of investment, were of particular importance to his theory.

The evidence that Keynes thought animal spirits to be an important part of his contribution comes from his discussion of long-term expectations in *The General Theory,* the emphasis taken in the article (a sort of 'reply to the critics') published in the *Quarterly Journal of Economics* in 1937, and from observations by his contemporary, Bertil Ohlin (Patinkin and Leith, 1977). Furthermore, the criterion adopted by Patinkin (1982) for such doctrinal judgements, that those themes which are important in a scholar's work resurface like themes in an orchestral work, is seen to support the centrality of uncertainty to Keynes.

In *The General Theory,* it is obvious that Keynes placed enterprise in an important social role. As Keynes re-drafted the 'pre-first proof index version', little in Chapter 12 changed. However, later versions substituted the term 'enterprise' for 'investment' (Keynes, 1973b, p. 468). In writing of enterprise, Keynes sought to distinguish investment in real assets from the alternative meaning of purchasing financial, or other, liquid assets. (Investment in the latter sense plays an equally important role in the theory of aggregate demand, but it is not our concern here.)

The following passage also appeared in the 'pre-first proof index version', and it was rearranged and expanded subsequently:

> There is much of great importance which can be said, quite independently of the rate of interest, concerning the state of long-run expectation and the methods by which the prospective yield of investment is estimated by the market, as distinct from the methods by which this prospective yield is capitalised or converted into present value. It is a subject to which practical men always pay the closest and most anxious attention under the name of the *state of*

---

[2] This argument has gathered force since the 1980s; see Runde and Mizuhara (2003) for a collection of contributions and Skidelsky (2011) for the argument made in relation to the current financial crisis.

[3] More recently see Stiglitz (2010) and Krugman (2011, pp. 2–4).

confidence. But economists have not analysed it carefully and have been content, as a rule, to treat it in general terms. (ibid., pp. 464–5, emphasis in original)

A comparison of the above with the final version (Keynes, 1936, pp. 148–9) shows little change of sense, and we conclude that clarity in drafting rather than modification of meaning motivated the revision. The earlier version had the virtue in retrospect of emphasising concisely Keynes's opinion that long-run expectations, and the state of confidence they dwelt on, were important both to transactions of a speculative sort and to investment decisions involving real assets, or more precisely in the latter case, to assets whose value to the enterprise is given by converting the prospective yield into a present value.

Further evidence of the importance Keynes placed on this matter comes from his article in the *Quarterly Journal of Economics* in 1937, which Joan Robinson (1973, p. 3) describes as a summing-up of *The General Theory*. Keynes himself presented this article as 'a discussion as to certain definite points where I seem to myself to be most clearly departing from previous theories' (1937, p. 112). Keynes went on to discuss at length the economic implications of our having 'only the vaguest idea of any but the most direct consequences of our acts' (ibid., p. 113).

Defending *The General Theory* in this article, Keynes asserted with respect to investment:

> This does not mean, of course, that the rate of interest is the only fluctuating influence on [the] prices [of capital assets]. Opinions as to their prospective yield are themselves subject to sharp fluctuations, precisely for the reason already given, namely, the flimsiness of the basis of knowledge on which they depend. It is these opinions taken in conjunction with the rate of interest which fix their price. (ibid., p. 117)

It is hard not to conclude that Keynes, in the 1937 article, nailed his colours firmly to the mast.

A final piece of evidence in this brief attempt to demonstrate the central importance of confidence and animal spirits in Keynes's eyes comes from Bertil Ohlin. Writing in 1977, he remarks:

> I now turn to other important aspects of Keynes' theory. In the *General Theory*, he emphasises *the uncertainty of the future* and the importance of opinions about the future as a basis for action by businessmen and

consumers. When he came to Stockholm in the autumn of 1936 and gave a lecture to our little Political Economy Club he – to our surprise – emphasised the analysis of this aspect of the *General Theory*. His opinion was that its vital importance had been underestimated. (Patinkin and Leith, 1977, pp. 159–60, emphasis in original)

There can be no doubt that Keynes saw his treatment of uncertainty and confidence as central to his new approach.[4] However, he acknowledged that his discussion had an inductive basis of 'actual observation of markets and business psychology' which placed it on a different level of abstraction from the rest of *The General Theory* (Keynes, 1936, p. 149). The impact of Keynes's approach to uncertainty was to make suspect mathematical calculations of an exact sort respecting real asset values.

Keynes argued that a precise value for real assets could not be ascertained because of the uncertainties involved. No probability statistic can be derived as to the likely returns, as no adequate information exists on certain possible events. Yet these possibilities are often of substantial importance to the decision-maker. The valuation of capital assets is affected in two ways:

(i) Liquidity preference alters as confidence in the future waxes and wanes. An optimistic outlook leads portfolio holders to value liquidity less, making the interest rate fall as bonds and other long-term securities are substituted for money balances. The falling interest rate directly increases the present value of investment goods.

(ii) Future revenues and costs are anticipated values. Not only is there a risk, quantifiable in probability terms, that estimates will be in error, but there is also uncertainty of a non-quantifiable type. For instance, there is no sensible information in the statement that the price of copper will be between £1 and £1,000 in ten years' time.[5]

---

[4] Further evidence is found in a letter from Keynes to Hugh Townshend dated 7 December 1938. Keynes remarked there: 'Generally speaking, in making a decision we have before us a large number of alternatives, none of which is demonstrably more "rational" than the others, in the sense that we can arrange in order of merit the sum aggregate of the benefits obtainable from the complete consequences of each. ... [W]e fall back, therefore, and necessarily so, on motives of another kind, which are not "rational" in the sense of being concerned with the evaluation of consequences, but are decided by habit, interest, preference, desire, will etc.' (Keynes, 1938, pp. 294).

[5] This point was missed completely by Coddington (1976). Keynes explained his meaning clearly in the *QJE* article of 1937: 'The sense in which I am using

Thus, present value is undefined over a very wide range in many realistic investment situations.

Animal spirits relate to the latter set of decisions, judgements concerning revenues and costs in the future as well as the scrap value of the asset through time. Because uncertainties cannot always be reduced to probability statements (not even to a mean expected value, far less other moments), the rational investor, by which Keynes means the entrepreneur, will resort to alternative sources of guidance. Hope, perusal of the general opinion, or satisfaction in the enterprise for its own sake can replace, or supplement, detached assessments of present values.

Thus in Keynes's thought, animal spirits play their part in determining investment, along with the rate of interest, technological advance, and other variables. Changes in confidence, by altering investment levels, expand or contract aggregate demand and the level of income and employment. The individual is subject to the emotions of the herd. Nor is this wholly undesirable; without such psychologically determined motives for investment there would probably be inadequate private entrepreneurship as individuals recognised the significance of the uncertain hazards on which their judgements were exercised.

How did Keynes come to these views? The great work of the early part of Keynes's scholarly life was the *Treatise on Probability,* published in 1921 after 15 years of study and revision. Braithwaite (1973, p. xxi) explains Keynes's concern there as 'to explain how a degree of belief could be rational, and thus not merely a matter of the believer's psychological make-up but one which all rational men under similar circumstances would share'. That such a task should have preceded the development of Keynes's views on uncertainty in economics gives pause for thought to those who interpret Keynes's views on animal spirits as involving irrationality on the part of entrepreneurs.

His study of probability, Keynes acknowledged, was encouraged by the moral philosophy of G. E. Moore, and by Bertrand Russell's work in *Principia Mathematica* (Keynes, 1972c, p. 445). Keynes maintained that certain rational belief arises only from knowledge, which (apart from the direct knowledge obtained, for instance, by sensation) takes the

---

the term [uncertain] is that in which the prospect of a European war is uncertain, or the price of copper and the rate of interest twenty years hence, or the obsolescence of a new invention, or the position of private wealth owners in the social system in 1970. About these matters there is no scientific basis on which to form any calculable probability whatever' (Keynes, 1937, p. 213).

form of propositions. However, some propositions, in which rational belief is possible, are those which, given the evidence, are probable rather than certain (Keynes, 1921, pp. 12–6). Probability then, was defined by Keynes as being 'concerned with *degrees* of rational belief' (ibid, p. 21, emphasis in original).

Keynes concluded that the probability underlying a rational belief, deriving from the evidence, differed from the weight to be attached to that belief. Only the accretion of evidence could increase the weight of the belief, though such an accretion might increase or decrease the probability involved (ibid, pp. 77–85). Keynes made explicit reference to this distinction in order to clarify his meaning when he asserts in *The General Theory* that it is foolish 'to attach great weight to matters which are very uncertain' (Keynes, 1936, p. 148).

If evidence is scant for the propositions put to business decision-makers, then they may legitimately weigh them lightly as offering little in the way of prescience. This behaviour is wholly rational, as is the use of business intuition in such circumstances. Knowledge of the present, or of the past, may be quite a poor guide to the future, but if such is the only available knowledge then an enterprise must use it. Even if enough evidence exists to make some probabilistic statements about the future, if widespread uncertainty is still extant (that is to say the evidence is seriously incomplete), then once again experience, habit and other modes of decision irreducible to a calculus must be relied upon for guidance.

Just as in a symphony, the theme of decision-making in the face of an unknowable future resurfaced in *The General Theory* after its introduction in the *Treatise on Probability* composed some two decades earlier. Once again, according to Patinkin's criterion, these ideas are central to Keynes's vision.

What became of animal spirits?

It is revealing to trace subsequent thought on Keynes's concept of animal spirits. The term itself is rarely used, even by Keynesians.[6] At an early stage in the development of the neoclassical synthesis, much of the source of investment variability was believed to have been captured by the accelerator principle; what remained of animal spirits was absorbed

---

[6] The financial crisis and Akerlof and Shiller's (2009) book have encouraged new interest in the concept; see further Dow and Dow (2011).

into the residual term of investment equations (see Cuthbertson, 1979, p. 15). One is left with the inescapable conclusion that 'animal spirits' have been regarded simply as another slightly embarrassing example of Keynes's purple passages, to be excluded from scientific enquiry.[7]

While the mainstream representation of investment behaviour left scope for non-random changes in long-run expectations to shift the autonomous component of investment demand (see Hicks, 1980-1, p. 140), attention was focused on those conventional variables which could explain at least some investment demand. Indeed, the main thrust of investment theory was to explain as much investment demand as possible by quantifiable variables such as interest rates and income levels. The remnants of Keynes's theory which were preserved in the neoclassical framework built on IS-LM analysis took the form of behavioural assumptions, of inelastic expectations, rigid money wages and so on. Lacking any explanation within this framework, it is no wonder that these assumptions smacked of *ad hoc*ery and irrationality (see Loasby, 1976, pp. 14–15).

These behavioural assumptions further posed the problem that successful empirical testing was predicated on the stability of institutional parameters. If a model failed to predict, it was not possible to say whether the failure resulted from the model itself or from a change in these parameters. The next step was thus to endogenise as many behavioural parameters as possible, first with adaptive expectations, then with rational expectations which were more directly derived from neoclassical microfoundations.[8]

Lucas (1980, p. 708) was quite explicit in claiming to have progressed beyond Keynes by developing a framework within which animal spirits could 'play a well-defined role' (see also Begg, 1982a). Within this rational expectations framework, long-run expectations are based on an assessment of all available information, using the 'true' predictive model of the economy. Expectations only shift when new information becomes available which could not have been anticipated. The response to new information pushes the economy onto another path, but one which leads to the same long-run equilibrium as before. In contrast, shifts in long-run expectations were, in Keynes's theory, themselves capable of changing the long-run outcome.

---

[7] Meltzer (1981), however, attempted to revive interest in the marginal efficiency of capital as a major innovation of *The General Theory*.

[8] See Begg (1982b) for an account of these developments in expectations theory.

Before considering directly whether these developments in expectations theory did actually constitute a progression from the animal spirits concept, it is worthwhile considering further what lay behind the urge to endogenise long-term expectations in the first place, an urge common to economists across the spectrum. First, why does the treatment of animal spirits as exogenous constitute a problem? It is the business of economists, certainly, to explain or predict economic events, so it is natural to try to extend that capacity to a major determinant of investment demand. But the explanation must go further. It must lie in what is *conventionally* acceptable as exogenous. Thus, while attempts are made to endogenise technological change, for example, the difficulties in doing so encouraged the convention of treating it as, at least in part, exogenous.

Among those concerned with endogenising long-term expectations there was a contrasting lack of concern to endogenise the money supply process. Indeed, the parallel between the roles of these two potentially exogenous variables was explicitly drawn in the Friedman-Meiselman (1963) controversy. Just as general equilibrium theorists charged Keynesians with neglecting to endogenise the crucial long-run expectations variable, so Keynesians charged Walrasian general equilibrium theorists with neglecting to endogenise the crucial money supply variable. The two concepts are also similar in involving problems of definition and thus of measurement. Particular money supply aggregates can be measured, as can surveyed business attitudes and intentions, but there must be doubt as to whether any one measure of either variable is what *actually* influences expenditure.

There is nevertheless a difference between the two variables in terms of scope for government influence: the money supply, by some definitions, can be influenced by the central monetary authority. Long-run expectations, on the other hand, are primarily cognitive – they are the product of entrepreneurs' or managers' minds, and as such they are subject to indeterminate influences, given the uncertainty surrounding the future.[9] Herein lies the root of much of the anxiety expressed by Coddington (1982). If long-run expectations are generated by a conventional optimising procedure using 'rational' criteria, then it is simply a question of finding the appropriate technique with which to model them. The only other possibility considered is that the process is

---

[9] This difference is only one of degree. There is now more widespread understanding of the money supply as being endogenous while monetary policy operates substantially through signalling on the one hand, while animal spirits may be managed, to some degree, by the government on the other.

irrational. But irrational in this context can only mean not susceptible to modelling; rationality in general requires the application of reason, which may nevertheless elude modelling.

Joan Robinson (1973, p. 3) was using the narrow concept of rationality when she explained, 'the [Keynesian] revolution lay in the change from the principles of rational choice to the problems of decisions based on guesswork and convention'. The need to rely on guesswork and convention stems from the uncertainty with which any view is held about reality, but particularly views about the future. Coddington suggested that, since expectations in all sectors must similarly reflect resort to guesswork and convention in the face of similar uncertainty, economists therefore must relinquish the capacity to model any behaviour, not just that of investors. With such a prospect in view, it was not surprising that the alternative of presuming animal spirits to be 'rationally' based and thus potentially predictable was appealing.

It must be emphasised further, however, that the standard economist's definition of 'rationality' is a very particular one. The definition of consumer rationality employed is that consumers have 'consistent preferences' and know their current and future budget constraints (see, for example, Laidler, 1974, p. 140). For producers, the equivalent requirement is that the cost and revenue functions are known for production of all different amounts and using any of the entire range of different production processes.

The existence, far less the ordering, of consumer preferences and information on production processes requires a degree of knowledge which common sense tells us is impossible. Even if our lack of knowledge about existing commodities and processes could be explained by information costs, we have no means of knowing about commodities and processes to be developed in the future. Herein lies an important distinction between consumption and investment (where consumer durables are included in the latter category), and thus between short-run consumers' expectations and animal spirits. Current consumption is not generally profoundly affected by surprises such as the emergence of new products (if only because the scope for such surprises is limited within the short run), whereas investment and the estimation of its rate of return *are* profoundly affected. New processes may render the planned process obsolete, as may the design of new products by rival producers. The decision-making process under uncertainty is the same for the consumer as for the producer (see Earl, 1983b, 65–7, p. 134) but the scope for surprise is so much greater for the latter that it is quite appropriate for expectations formation to be analysed separately.

Using the mainstream definition of rationality, investors do not have access to the information which would allow them to be rational. This definition of rationality is clearly too restrictive to cope with the unknowable future, and thus with any decision-making involving expectations, as all decision-making must.

As long as it was apparent that investors' behaviour necessarily contained 'irrational' elements (by the mainstream definition), there was still a role for animal spirits as an exogenous variable within general equilibrium models. But this role was eroded by the introduction of rational expectations. The general proposition of rational expectations is that all *available* information is brought to bear on decisions, so that expectations are arrived at 'reasonably'. This proposition is consistent with the broad definition of rationality. At this level of generality, Keynes and the rational expectations theorists have something in common in their view of expectations-formation (see Colander and Guthrie, 1980-81).[10]

By further defining expectations to be rational if their probability distribution is the same as the probability distribution of the forecast variable (see Muth, 1961, and Lucas and Prescott, 1971), the rational expectations theorists parted company with Keynes and the broad definition of rationality. Keynes's own work on probability and Shackle's work (see, for example, Shackle, 1955, and Bausor, 1983), have shown the limitations of probability theory in generating predictions among economists, let alone the general population. It is indeed widely acknowledged that the rational expectations model does not reflect actual behaviour. But lack of realism was freely admitted by Lucas (1980, pp. 696-7) on grounds similar to those used by Machlup (1967) to justify 'as if' models of individual behaviour.[11] If deterministic models are to represent individual behaviour then unrealistic assumptions must be made. The question now to be addressed, then, is whether this 'as if' method of endogenising long-run expectations constituted progress relative to Keynes's use of animal spirits. While not reflecting actual investment behaviour, did it capture the essence of the situation for either predictive or explanatory purposes?

---

[10] Simon's (1955) concept of bounded rationality which refers to decision-making with incomplete information is also consistent with this definition. His concept of procedural rationality is used to explore the process by which decisions are arrived at when information is incomplete, contrasted with substantive rationality when complete information is available (see Simon, 1976; Garner, 1982).

[11] By no means do all general equilibrium theorists accept that their microfoundations are unrealistic (see Hahn, 1973).

The answer lies in Colander and Guthrie's (1980-81, p. 230) observation that, within mainstream theory, 'the model determines expectations', while the reverse was true for Keynes. In other words, once the general equilibrium framework was adopted, the way in which expectations might be incorporated was severely constrained. Hahn (1952) at an early date anticipated the necessity for general equilibrium models when attempting to deal with time, to specify the procedure of expectations formation. He then spelled out the limits to be imposed on that specification if a stable equilibrium were to be maintained. Hahn (1973) later limited the relevance of Walrasian general equilibrium theory to those commodities with futures markets, since only in these cases could actual expectations conform at all closely to the limitations imposed by the general equilibrium framework. In general, the acceptability of any form of expectations modelling (whether rational or adaptive expectations), depends on the acceptability of the framework in which it is incorporated.[12]

A general equilibrium model cannot incorporate surprises in the form of new products or processes other than as exogenous shocks. The economic system, as modelled by general equilibrium principles, must be either dynamically stable or dynamically unstable. The observed general absence of chaos encouraged the presumption that economies are dynamically stable, that there is an automatic tendency for economies to approach an equilibrium position. The only reason for the economy to depart from such a position in the first place is a shock from a variable exogenous to the model.

But it was unacceptable for entrepreneurs' long-term expectations to constitute such an exogenous variable since the behaviour represented by the 'as if' model was put forward as being *uniformly* motivated. It has been regarded as one of the achievements of the marginalist revolution that it allowed economists to abstract from groupings of individuals by function, class, location of residence and so on, and concentrate on the universal principles governing individual behaviour itself. It is from this standpoint that Coddington (1982), for example, insisted that if entrepreneurial expectations could not be explained within the model in question, then, on grounds of consistency within a universal theory of human behaviour, neither can any other form of expectations. If rational expectations are imposed with respect to the price level, investors' expectations must be treated likewise.

---

[12] Boland (1981) makes the similar argument that a model such as that based on the neoclassical maximisation hypothesis ultimately can only be judged on the grounds of its own 'metaphysics'.

In summary then, once a Walrasian general equilibrium framework is chosen, and decision-making is included which refers (as it must) to the future, then expectations must be endogenised in such a way as to drive the economy along an adjustment path which leads to the long-run equilibrium position. Within such a framework it is logically difficult, as well as antithetical, to leave one set of expectations outside the model. Indeed, it is an inherent property of closed, deterministic models, which are designed to represent a complete system, to enforce a strict dualism (between endogeneity and exogeneity, as between rationality and irrationality) which is consistently upheld throughout the system. Either a variable can be explained by other variables or it cannot. It is within this particular framework, rather than in Keynes's framework, that classifying a variable as exogenous constitutes a throwing in of the explanatory towel.

Animal spirits in their spiritual home

Animal spirits, insofar as they survived the neoclassical synthesis, have taken on a meaning quite different from that intended by Keynes. It is the difference in methodological framework which is crucial.[13]

But then how should animal spirits be dealt with in the Keynesian framework? It is significant that concern over reliance on animal spirits has been expressed among Keynesian sympathisers as well as by critics. Is it sufficient to regard animal spirits simply as an exogenous variable? In terms of empirical modelling, there appears to be no alternative, although the difficulty of identifying a quantifiable proxy for expectations is of no small importance for predictive work. As long as it is accepted that some sets of expectations, such as price-level expectations, can be captured reasonably well by other variables while others, like animal spirits, cannot, then the former can be treated as endogenous and the latter as exogenous, on operational rather than logical grounds (see Lawson, 1981). That need not prevent judgements being formed as to trends in animal spirits, on the basis of detailed observation of the economy, and of business attitudes in particular. For example, any receptive observer of Western economies in the early 1980s could detect

---

[13] Rational expectations have been the subject of a range of critiques from the Keynesian perspective; these critiques have demonstrated the inability of rational expectations to deal with historical time (Bausor, 1983), with crucial experiments (Davidson, 1982-83), with conflicts between individual and collective rationality (Evans, 1983) and with observed facts (Pesaran, 1982).

a pervasive air of pessimism (except in a few readily identifiable indus-tries). By allowing that factor to be incorporated exogenously into pre-dictive models, the effect of animal spirits could be captured. Rational expectations models can only incorporate expectations in the form of the model's own predictions.

At the theoretical level, also, there is a range of approaches to ana-lysing confidence shifts: these include Shackle's (1955) concept of sur-prise, Leijonhufvud's (1981, ch. 6) corridor theory or Harris's (1979) use of catastrophe theory. Such theoretical work can be justified by the fact that, while animal spirits cannot easily be quantified *ex ante,* evidence can be interpreted as measuring the effect of animal spirits *ex post.* Thus, for example, Andrews's (1982) study demonstrates the degree to which conventional economic variables failed to explain the cutback in private sector investment in the United States prior to and during the Great Depression. The results are consistent with the explanation that a wave of pessimism (a collapse of animal spirits) initiated the contraction in the capital goods sector which played such a signifi-cant role in the general contraction in aggregate demand during the Depression.

It is unfortunate, however, that in econometric work animal spir-its of necessity fall within the residual term. This fact encourages the view of animal spirits as being of residual importance, or as something which should, if possible, be brought into the body of the equation. Furthermore, it encourages the conceptual separation between the past values of variables and expectations as to their future values.[14] In its turn, the residual, being stochastic, gives every appearance of being irrational according to the narrow definition of rationality, equated with 'ability to be modelled'. These implications are not a logical con-sequence of stochastic formulations, nor necessarily the intention of the econometrician, but they are of considerable rhetorical significance, that is, they influence interpretation, communication and future chan-nels of thought and investigation.[15]

---

[14] As Keynes put it: 'There are not two separate factors affecting the rate of investment, namely, the schedule of the marginal efficiency of capital and the state of confidence. The state of confidence is relevant because it is one of the major factors determining the former, which is the same thing as the invest-ment demand schedule' (Keynes, 1936, p. 149).

[15] McCloskey (1983) makes the case that language (including mathematical and statistical language) is of fundamental significance to the development of economic thought.

In contrast, 'Chapter 12 Keynesians' view animal spirits as being of central significance, and the epistemological problems associated with long-term expectations as being a more serious version of those facing all decision-makers (see Loasby, 1976, ch. 9). Indeed, from this view of decision-making stems the explanation for money's (non-neutral) role in the economy as the refuge of uncertainty, and, more generally, the necessity to conduct analysis within the context of historical time and thus to eschew any focus on general equilibrium. In short, this view of expectations is integral to the entire Keynesian theoretical framework.

It is possible to take this analysis further, however, by looking at the epistemological basis both of the view of expectations and of the theoretical framework. Perceptions of how expectations are formed are themselves not objective, but the product of a particular way of looking at the world. Indeed, it is at this level that we must look for the difference in methodological framework which underlies differences in analysing expectations. The mode of perception and analysis on which Keynesian theory is built is quite different from the all-encompassing closed system derived deductively from a set of axioms which is the basis for orthodox theory. This latter approach has been dominant or perhaps, more significantly, aspired to in Western thought since the ancient Greeks (see Dow, 1980). Given the difficulties of identifying appropriate universal axioms, an alternative theoretical structure can be built using a variety of logical chains (expressed with varying degrees of formality depending on the content) with different starting points, and taking different parts of the system as exogenous. As a result, the duality of endogeneity and exogeneity loses its universal application and becomes specific to the particular chain of reasoning at hand. Stohs (1983) categorised Keynesian methodology as Babylonian, relying on 'several, parallel, intertwined and mutually reinforcing' chains of reasoning.[16]

Keynes himself was in his early years influenced by G. E. Moore to aspire to the orthodox, axiomatic mode of thought, although he later rejected it (Keynes, 1972c, pp. 433–50). It is clear from the style of Keynes's writings, as much as from their content, that in practice he conformed more to what – for want of a better term – we may call the 'Babylonian' mode (see further Chapter 4). In line with this view, the 'purple passages' in *The General Theory*, including the term 'animal

---

[16] See Dow (1985) for a detailed discussion of the origins, character and significance of these differences in modes of thought. See further Dow (2003a) and the forthcoming second edition.

spirits', were an integral part of his attempt to communicate and persuade. Thus, it was in a sense from the traditional Western mode of scientific thought that he had his 'long struggle to escape'.

One implication of the non-dualistic Keynesian approach is that, while there are objective facts, perceptions of these facts are not objective. Information is thus not always an absolute of which one has knowledge, or absence of knowledge.[17] On this epistemological basis, rationality takes on a different hue. Decision-makers organise their perceptions and their expectations around worldviews or paradigms. Such behaviour is rational in the sense of reasoned, according to the theories adopted by each decision-maker.

Indeed, long-run expectations can be viewed as 'theories' about how the future will unfold. What will shake one investor's theory poses questions as complex as those which arise in discussions of what constitutes an effective falsification of an economic theory, that is, one which will persuade an economist to switch theories. Further, since members of a group (of consumers, or investors, say) tend to share ways of perceiving and analysing the world, they can also be expected to share expectations to a considerable degree. Again, it seems legitimate to consider expectations by group: for example, the animal spirits of investors, the short-term expectations of consumers of non-durable goods and those of purchasers of financial assets.[18]

Finally, the notion of what is 'central' to a theory is inherent in the theory's own methodological framework. The dualism of orthodox theory requires certain variables to be exogenous to explain change other than movement along a steady-state path.[19] What these variables are is then of central importance. Thus isolated, these variables become the subject of uncomfortable scrutiny; only the caprices of government survived this scrutiny, remaining exogenous (and, by implication, irrational according to their narrow definition of rationality) in the rational expectations framework.

Within a non-dualistic Keynesian framework, the centrality of the animal spirits concept takes on a different significance. It does not make sense to say that, if only investors were rational in the narrow

---

[17] Coddington (1976) identified this subjectivist view of knowledge as being an identifying characteristic of fundamentalist Keynesians. It is at least a feature of what might be called Keynesian microfoundations, as developed for example by Earl (1983b).

[18] This is developed in Dow and Dow (2011).

[19] See Chapter 4 for a discussion of dualism.

orthodox sense, there would be no unemployment. Rather, implicit in the choice of a framework designed for studying economies in historical time is the judgement that this framework allows analysis of the most important features of the economy. The framework requires that attention be paid to decision-making under uncertainty. The area of decision-making in which that uncertainty impinges most, with the most widespread implications for employment and incomes, is in the purchase of new capital goods. This accounts for the importance of the animal spirits concept. It epitomises the methodological framework from which it arises; ultimately, it is that methodological framework which frames the content of Keynesian theory.

Conclusion

We have attempted to show that the animal spirits concept was significant within Keynes's own thought and considered why it should have become so peripheral to the subsequent development of macroeconomics. The formation of expectations in conditions of uncertainty, as something beyond probability analysis, was a theme which recurred in Keynes's work throughout his life. The scope for those expectations to be volatile and to affect profoundly the level of investment, and thus of income and employment, was for Keynes a serious concern.

We suggest that this feature of Keynes's theory failed to hold the attention of later macroeconomists for methodological reasons. The prevailing mainstream mode of thought in macroeconomics sought a uniform behaviour pattern in all economic agents, which is rational in the narrow sense of 'capable of being modeled', and which is consistent with a modelling system which is not dynamically unstable.[20] Entrepreneurs' long-run expectations must thus be treated consistently with other forms of expectations. Thus endogenised, there is no scope for sudden shifts in these entrepreneurial expectations other than those resulting from the emergence of unanticipated objective information; long-run expectations lose their capacity to have any independent effect on the economy. The only alternative, that they be exogenous, renders them unsatisfactorily arbitrary.

---

[20] This common behaviour pattern is determined by the hard core of the mainstream approach, as explained in Chapter 1. There have been significant developments in heterogeneous agent models. But the heterogeneity refers to endowments, preferences and information sets rather than to rational optimisation.

Within Keynes's methodological framework, however, animal spirits are no longer arbitrary, but follow logically from his epistemological stance. Keynes's methodology reflected the judgement that no one method can satisfactorily explain or predict within a social science such as economics. Rather the preferred approach was to tackle each question from a variety of angles, with a variety of methods, in fact just as an entrepreneur in reality forms long-run expectations in the face of uncertainty. Thus, what is exogenous within one approach or line of reasoning, is endogenous within another. For example, long-term expectations must be exogenous to predictive econometric models, but they can be explained by a questionnaire method combined with historical analysis of the economy in question.[21] Indeed, this methodology was adopted by Keynes following his work on probability theory, which indicated the limited ability of the probability calculus to deal with economic decision-making.

In conclusion, then, the question of whether or not animal spirits should be singled out for special theoretical treatment must first refer to the methodological framework to be employed. Within the mainstream framework, it makes no sense to single out animal spirits from expectations formation more generally. Within a Keynesian methodological framework, however, the behaviour of different groups, as groups, is the focus of attention. The means are available for analysing the behaviour of the entrepreneurial group, with the particular epistemological problems involved. Any judgement as to the value of the animal spirits concept thus requires a judgement as to the relative value of these two methodological frameworks.

---

[21] There is now much wider use by economists of the questionnaire method, as advocated by McCloskey (1983).

4
Beyond Dualism

A major factor influencing the meaning of terms and the way in which theory is constructed is dualism, an important example being the either/or categorisation of rationality/irrationality. The dualistic habit of thought is something deep rooted, continuing to influence what many economists regard as good arguments and good theory. This chapter explores the meaning and significance of dualism and explores other possibilities which might guide new economic thinking. The focus is on the level of mode of thought.

Introduction

A growing sense of unease with the current state of economics has encouraged an increased interest in methodology. This interest reflects both a concern to examine fundamentals, and a wish to understand criteria for appraisal. If it were possible for economists to agree on appraisal criteria, then the settlement of debates within economics would be a relatively straightforward matter. But such agreement has not proved to be possible, so that it is necessary also to address the issue of methodological differences. This requires analysis at yet another level: the level of mode of thought, which determines the way in which competing methodologies are understood.

The original version of this chapter was published in the *Cambridge Journal of Economics*, 14(2), 1990, 143–58. It benefited from the comments and suggestions of Bruce Caldwell, Tony Cramp, Geoff Harcourt, Arjo Klamer, Peter Kriesler, Tony Lawson and two anonymous referees.

The purpose of this chapter is to discuss a mode of thought which I have termed elsewhere 'Babylonian' (see Dow, 1985). It is one possible alternative to the Cartesian/Euclidean mode of thought which underlies much of mainstream economics and the methodological principles on which this economics is based. Two particular features of Cartesian/ Euclidean thought which have far-reaching methodological implications are atomism and dualism.[1] Although these two features are not unconnected, the focus here will be on dualism: its presence or absence is influential in any methodological discussion, given the frequency with which dualistic arguments are invoked in the philosophy of science. The use of dualism in economics will be analysed primarily in conceptual terms; a more historical approach may be found in Dow (1985).

Dualism is the practice of organising thought by means of all-encompassing mutually exclusive categories with fixed meanings. It is a particular means of imposing order on ideas, or on perceptions of reality or indeed of drawing distinctions (as between ideas and reality, for example). Dualism has been endemic to a particular stream of Western thought since the Platonic distinction between mind and matter. In classical logic, it appears as the principle of the excluded middle: given a category x, any entity must fall either into the category x or into the category not-x.

Understood as a means of labelling or categorising, dualism would seem to be necessary to any attempt at theorising. Thus, for example, the category 'dualism' itself implies its opposite, 'not-dualism'. But, in this sense of labelling, dualism loses significance owing to its universal applicability. Here the term is being used rather to categorise a particularly restrictive use of labelling.

First, dualism treats the categories x and not-x as being both all encompassing and mutually exclusive; there is no additional or middle category. Yet there have been direct challenges to the principle of the excluded middle. Hegelian dialectics constitute precisely such a challenge in terms of the evolution of ideas. There is a notion of opposites in the thesis and antithesis, but then this opposition coalesces to form yet another category, the synthesis. Categories are thus employed, but change in their application over time, at changing levels

---

[1] The contrast between atomism and organic thought is drawn out by Brown-Collier and Bowser (1988), Carabelli (1988) and Winslow (1986b). Dualism and atomism are not presented here as fully defining Cartesian/Euclidean thought but as particularly interesting features of it.

of consciousness. More generally, Hegel rejected Kant's dualistic analysis of human nature in favour of an evolutionary, historical analysis of human nature, which might be subject to different divisions in different historical contexts. Further, in his theory of logic, Hegel used the notion of opposites in a particular, non-dualistic way; far from being mutually exclusive, opposite categories obtain their meaning partly from each other.

Intuitionist logic also poses a challenge to the principle of the excluded middle, in the context of number theory. Here the distinction is drawn between categories which are known in practice and those which can only be known 'in principle'. Thus, it is possible in principle to define a natural number l according to the following dual: either l is the greatest prime such that $(l - 2)$ is also a prime, or $l = 1$ if such a number does not exist. But if we do not know if there is a prime such that $(l - 2)$ is also a prime, l cannot in practice be defined. We need another category 'l, undefined'. Thus, here it is in practical application that the dual breaks down (see Heyting, 1971, p. 2).

The intuitionist argument poses particular problems for the practical application of a dualistic theoretical structure. One possibility is to specify three categories rather than two to cover all possibilities. Ziman (1978, pp. 26–7) suggests 'true', 'false' and 'undecided'. But these three categories, when applied to empirical questions, are not in fact mutually exclusive. The problem of induction, combined with the Duhem-Quine thesis (concerning the difficulty of identifying what is falsified by evidence), provides the basis for the endless arguments over what is true, false or undecided so familiar in the economics literature.

Further, specification of three categories, where one is 'undecided' or 'uncertain', is more a statement of a problem than a solution. Thus, the development of quantum mechanics can be understood as a *gestalt* shift from the dualism of classical mechanics: empirical observations are shown to be probabilistic, but, being observer-dependent, they are also uncertain. All observations, therefore, fall into the 'undecided' or 'uncertain' category. But to conclude simply that all results are 'uncertain' is to apply the mutually exclusive reasoning of dualism to the categories 'certain' and 'uncertain'. Rather, quantum mechanics progressed by developing theory to deal with uncertainty of different kinds and different degrees (see, for example, Capra, 1975, ch. 4), that is, it moved beyond dualism.

The developments in philosophy of science which followed these developments in physics involved also the rejection of the third feature of our definition of dualism: fixity of meaning of categories. Kuhn

(1962) demonstrated that paradigmatic shifts in scientific activity brought new meaning to scientific terms which impedes cross-paradigm appraisal. Hegel's dialectics similarly involve a change in meanings over time as consciousness changes. Once categories are no longer fixed, their theoretical power is diminished.

Just as developments in philosophy, mathematics and physics can be understood in terms of reliance on dualism or its absence, an understanding of what is entailed in dualism or its absence can illuminate developments in economics. In what follows, I shall discuss dualism in relation to economics at several levels, and explore the possibilities for moving beyond dualism, focusing particularly on one possible non-dualistic mode of thought, labelled 'Babylonian'. The next section starts at the level of mode of thought, with an explanation of the Babylonian mode. The third section shifts the discussion to the levels of methodology and philosophy of science, with a particular focus on the rationalism-relativism dual. It is argued that interpretations of Kuhn as relativist rely on dualism, whereas Kuhn's thought is explicitly non-dualistic.

The fourth section approaches the issue rather differently, in the form of a case study of economic thought; the political economy tradition is considered as a possible example of Babylonian thought in economics. The concluding section considers explicitly the usefulness of the foregoing analysis for economists in general, and applied economists in particular.

Modes of thought

Economic analysis can be understood in terms of a hierarchy. The end product (for most, though not all, economists) is statements about the real world and, possibly, policy prescriptions. This level is based, explicitly or implicitly, on the next, theoretical level. Economic theory, in turn, is based on a further methodological level; methodology is understood in terms of the fourth level of mode of thought. While the theoretical and methodological bases for policy statements are sometimes made explicit, the underlying mode of thought is almost universally left implicit. Yet, since it influences the initial choice of methodology, which in turn influences the admissible range of statements about the real world, mode of thought is of crucial importance. The nature and direction of influences within this hierarchy are complex. But, once a mode of thought has been acquired, owing to whatever influences, its influence on the other levels of the hierarchy is pervasive.

The terms theory and methodology are subject to variable usage. The term theory is being used here in the relatively narrow sense of propositions: examples would be the theory of liquidity preference or the quantity theory of money, as statements about the relationship between sets of specified variables. 'Methodology' is the term used here to capture the basis on which these statements are made: the underlying worldview (in the above examples, the view of the way in which the financial sector fits into the workings of the economy, and how those workings themselves are perceived and analysed) and the admissible range of techniques by which propositions may be expressed and assessed (in the above examples, contingent on contextual institutional arrangements, or as universal formal statements, respectively). This definition of methodology corresponds closely to Kuhn's definition of paradigms to be discussed in the third section.

Mode of thought refers to the level at which a particular worldview and technique of analysis are appraised. It is possible to push the analysis even further back, to consider what determines modes of thought. This requires consideration of the influences in turn of methodology, theory and perceptions of reality on the adoption of a mode of thought. An attempt will be made in that direction in the case study analysis in the fourth section. But it is sufficient at this stage simply to describe modes of thought and analyse their methodological consequences.

The need for theorising arises from the complexity of the economic system; we do not in practice have complete knowledge, and even so, we may have too much information to assimilate effectively. In such circumstances, a particular mode of thought enables an economist to order observations and ideas in such a way as to form a basis for theorising. One possible mode of thought is the Cartesian/Euclidean mode, which achieves its most consistent expression in pure general equilibrium theory, but which is implicit also in much of the rest of mainstream theory. A Cartesian/Euclidean theoretical system is a closed system, based on classical logic, derived from axioms, with universal application. Categories are employed as being all-encompassing, mutually exclusive and with fixed meanings, that is, Cartesian/Euclidean thought is dualistic.

If it is to be an applied social science, Cartesian/Euclidean economics must presume some correspondence with reality, that is, reality itself must be dualistic, either in principle or in practice. If it is only dualistic in principle, the question remains as to how practical application is to be achieved. Two possible methods of dealing with this correspondence problem are evident in Johnson (1973) and Hahn (1983). In the context of the capital theory debates, Johnson argued that, while aggregate capital is not measurable in practice, it is measurable in principle and so theorists may proceed confident in that knowledge. In the context of general equilibrium theory as such, Hahn displayed less confidence, simply admitting that there was no correspondence with reality; economics then was presented as a pure discipline.

Applied economists in the mainstream, however, must deal with the correspondence problem: variables must be measured in practice, and correspondence between dualistic theory and reality must be presumed. The problem is limited by testing only reduced-form relationships, so that many of the measurements, and correspondence with reality of interior relationships can be retained 'in principle'. But the problem is ultimately still unresolved. For example, Casson (1981, p. 33) stated that 'the typical market spends more time out of equilibrium than in equilibrium'.[2] This is the application to the reality of the dual 'in equilibrium'-'out of equilibrium'. These are the only two possibilities, they are mutually exclusive, and they have a fixed meaning. Lipsey imposed a similar dualism on reality when he discussed two possibilities for any market: that it 'works' or 'doesn't work' (Lipsey, 1983, p. 459).

To the extent that applied mainstream economists adopt a dualistic theoretical structure, while regarding reality as being non-dualistic, an unresolved problem is inevitable with their work. A conflict between methodology and practice was expressed by Blaug (1980) as a failure to live up to principle; perhaps, rather it is the result of conflict between 'in principle' dualism and a non-dualistic reality.

The Babylonian mode of thought is another attempt to theorise about a complex reality, but one which does not aim at a complete, closed, theoretical structure.[3] The complexity of reality is regarded as being beyond complete understanding, and thus endemically uncertain. If we do not comprehend the extent of the universe (entities are not finite), and if we cannot with certainty categorise in a complete way, with labels which have fixed meaning, then reality cannot be understood dualistically. The Babylonian approach, then, is to construct theory in a non-dualistic manner in order to promote correspondence with reality.

---

[2] The rational expectations approach subsequently resolved the issue by defining all observations as referring to equilibrium states.

[3] The term was used in this sense with reference to the Babylonian approach to mathematics by Feynman (1965). It was developed by Wimsatt (1981) and applied to economics by Stohs (1983). See further Dow (2003a).

In practice, this mode of thought involves approaching any issue from a variety of starting points, using a range of partial analyses in order to build up a picture. Each chain of reasoning may be said to start from axioms, but the axioms of one chain of reasoning may be the conclusions of another. One aspect of Babylonian thought is the rejection of formalism in the sense that not all knowledge can be expressed formally. (Formalism is entailed by dualism, although not coextensive with it.) For example, Feynman (1965), who applied the term 'Babylonian' to a style of mathematical reasoning, demonstrated that three statements of the law of gravitation which are mathematically equivalent are philosophically and psychologically non-equivalent. To express all economic theory in terms of a common language, as advocated by Hahn (1986), would thus be to eliminate knowledge (see Harcourt 1987, pp. 14–5; see further Chapter 9).

For example, a Babylonian approach to monetary analysis could draw on a formal model which took the interest rate as exogenous, in the sense of being set by the monetary authorities. The behaviour of banks as firms may not, however, be conducive to formal modelling, so that the means by which interest rates are set in a particular context must be analysed on the basis of institutional studies. The requirement of mainstream theory to derive all results formally from common axioms inhibited the emergence of a satisfactory theory of the banking firm which is logically fully consistent with the general equilibrium system,[4] so that the only admissible policy assumption was that of an exogenous money stock (see Gale, 1982, p.182, and 1983).

The most complete example in twentieth-century economics of a move beyond dualistic reasoning which may be described as Babylonian is provided by the work of Keynes. He explicitly recognised the importance of mode of thought for constructing and communicating ideas. An early influence on his thought was Whitehead, a senior member of the Apostles (see Skidelsky, 1983, p. 119), who later elaborated on non-dualistic modes of thought in Whitehead (1938).[5] What is meant by Babylonian thought may be illustrated by means of the approach of Whitehead to the question of consistency, and of Keynes to uncertainty, and to probability and expectations formation.

---

[4] Several valiant attempts have been made to rectify this lack. See, for example, Stiglitz and Weiss (1986) and Anderlini (1986). But, while the theory of the banking firm has developed significantly since the 1980s, it was unable to predict the banking crisis or inform about bank behaviour during the crisis.

[5] Keynes in turn may be seen as an influence on Whitehead (see Skidelsky, 1983, pp. 182–4, and 198), both in turn being influenced by G. E. Moore.

Consistency

While Cartesian/Euclidean thought is generally the implicit or explicit ideal of mainstream economics, influencing the way in which theories are generally presented in print, the formulation of mainstream theories and their informal communication frequently do not conform to this ideal (see McCloskey, 1983). In other words, other modes of thought, including what I call the Babylonian mode, are commonly employed in practice. The Babylonian mode is to approach issues simultaneously with a range of different chains of reasoning (not necessarily all developed by the same person, but used in any one person's analysis). Thus, the Babylonian mode requires a range of methods of analysis, on the grounds that no one method can justify confidence in knowledge about the real world. A question may be addressed by drawing on all or any of historical material, questionnaire data, aggregative data and formal models, for example. (Formal models thus have a role to play, but only as part of a wider approach, and only if the institutional context accords with the assumptions of the model.) More weight is attached to the conclusion of any one chain of reasoning if it is confirmed by the conclusions of other chains of reasoning.

Each part of the analysis may therefore be inconsistent in the sense that it cannot be collected together with the rest into a cohesive formal system. But there need be no logical inconsistency, since each chain of reasoning may start from different assumptions.

Logically, there should be no difficulty with duals specified by unbounded sets. But where such an unbounded set is as complex as the economic process, correct specification of a dual may be extremely difficult, leading to an incorrect perception of inconsistency. As Whitehead (1938, p.75) noted: 'By means of process the universe escapes from the limitations of the finite. Process is the immanence of the infinite in the finite; whereby all bounds are burst, and all inconsistencies dissolved.' Inconsistency is anathema to Cartesian/Euclidean thought, which is specified in terms of the finite. But for theorising with respect to (infinite) processes, the dual of consistency-inconsistency is unhelpful. It is unhelpful as a representation of reality. While each chain of reasoning in a Babylonian system involves abstraction, the fact that these abstractions cannot be contained in a single formal system renders the dual unhelpful also at the theoretical level.

Put another way, a dual is unhelpful if propositions can be classified both as x and not-x. Thus according to the above discussion, propositions may be consistent in one sense although inconsistent in another.

The notion of relativity, to be discussed in the next main section, entails a cohabitation of the absolute and the non-absolute.

The consistency-inconsistency dual also provides an example of a dual which is vulnerable to the criticism that it only has local application, although it is often used as if it had universal application. Whitehead concludes his discussion of consistency as follows: 'Thus inconsistency is relative to the abstraction involved' (Whitehead, 1938, p. 76).

Uncertainty

Babylonian thought may further be explained epistemologically, since its starting point is an assumption that full knowledge is impossible to attain. Knowledge at all levels is treated as being incomplete in a fundamental sense; the use of a range of explicitly partial analyses is designed to deal with that incompleteness as effectively as possible. Information in Babylonian thought, therefore, does not generally fit into the two categories known and not-known; there is a large intermediate category of 'believed to be known, subject to uncertainty of various degrees which are generally non-quantifiable'. As Keynes (1973b, p.2) put it: 'As soon as one is dealing with the influence of expectations and of transitory experience, one is, in the nature of things, outside the realm of the formally exact'.

Insofar as incomplete knowledge is explicitly dealt with in Cartesian/ Euclidean thought (rather than existing outside it) it is treated dualistically. The object of study is categorised according to whether there is knowledge or no knowledge. There may be risk, in the sense that knowledge in a particular context may be subject to a probability distribution, but again, that distribution is known or it is not known. There is no room for Knightian or Keynesian uncertainty (see Lawson, 1985b).

The Cartesian/Euclidean reaction to the possibility of uncertain knowledge in reality is thus to exclude it from the theoretical system as complete lack of knowledge. This explains the elimination of Keynes's concept of animal spirits from the mainstream literature, since it involves decision-making under unspecifiable uncertainty (see Coddington, 1982; Dow and Dow, 1985/Chapter 3). But if knowledge is endemically incomplete, then a dual which excludes the bulk of human knowledge, which is uncertain, must be subject to question; at the very least, alternative modes of thought not founded on such a dual merit serious consideration as a basis for theory construction. More generally, Whitehead noted with respect to the subject matter of theory: 'In the nature of things there are no ultimate exclusions, expressive in logical terms' (Whitehead, 1938, p. 76).

Probability and expectations

One of the notable expressions of a Babylonian mode of thought is Keynes's (1921) theory of probability.[6] This theory was developed in an attempt to find a rational basis for induction. Statistical probability estimates can only be arrived at on the basis of frequency distributions in the case of repeatable experiments with a known set of possible outcomes. Since most phenomena are not in this category, some other basis must be found for estimating probability and thus forming expectations. Keynes described this basis as organic: 'A degree of probability is not composed of some homogeneous material, and is not apparently divisible into parts of like character with one another' (ibid, p. 32). Rather, a view on probability (in the wider sense than the frequency distribution sense) can only be found by an accretion of evidence from a variety of sources which may preclude quantification (ibid, pp. 77–85; Keynes, 1937). Keynes's depiction of individuals' theorising about their economic environment, as well as his view of scientific behaviour in the stricter sense, accords well with our definition of a Babylonian mode of thought.[7] Indeed, this is made clear in Keynes's discussion of organic processes: '[T]here might be quite different laws for wholes of different degrees of complexity, and laws of connection between complexes which could not be stated in terms of laws connecting individual parts. In this case natural law would be organic and not, as it is generally supposed, atomic' (Keynes, 1921, p. 277).

If indeed this organic method of forming expectations is the basis for decision-making, individual behaviour cannot be rational in the particular sense of the term employed by mainstream economics; this latter form of rationality requires numerical estimates as if it is based on a complete formal model of the economy. For Keynes (ibid, p. 124), the imperative of action requires that agents somehow construct hypotheses on which to base that action, in spite of a lack of knowledge. But with Cartesian/Euclidean models, the only alternative, as Coddington (1982) pointed out, is for behaviour to be irrational. Even the most general definition of rational behaviour, which refers to all available

---

[6] See Carabelli (1985), Dow and Dow (1985)/Chapter 3 and Lawson (1985b) for discussions of the implications of this work.

[7] Keynes in fact applied the term Babylonian to Newton in his biographical essay (Keynes, 1972b, p. 364). Here, and in Keynes (1972c), it is argued that Newton's actual scientific method diverged significantly from the positivist, mechanistic methodology normally attributed to him. I am indebted to Victoria Chick for pointing this out.

information being used, still cannot rescue Keynes's decision-makers; the notion of optimising information gathering requires a theory about efforts made to acquire information and the expected benefits, which cannot be formalised in the context of Keynesian uncertainty. Here we have another example of a dual (rational/irrational) being applied according to a methodologically specific sense of the words. This categorisation of rationality was employed quite differently by Keynes, for example, with reference to the goal of monetary accumulation (see Winslow, 1986a). However, the rational-irrational dual in its Cartesian/ Euclidean sense is often applied universally, while it only has application within a Cartesian/Euclidean system of thought.[8]

The analogy between general, human and scientific thought processes is in fact helpful with respect to the important question of what guides the choice of chains of reasoning within a Babylonian system. Just as individuals have habitual sources of information which accord with their general worldview or the conventions of their reference groups (as outlined in Keynes, 1937), so economists are guided by a more or less well-specified view of the economic process. It is this worldview, as applied to the economic process, which binds applications of Babylonian thought holistically, distinguishing it from eclecticism; there is scope for a range of Babylonian worldviews, by which a range of schools of thought can be identified. This form of holism is fundamentally different from the reductionist holism of mainstream theory, which derives from the technical requirements of Cartesian/ Euclidean thought (see, for example, Wiles, 1979–80). It also differs from the reductionist form of holism which creates a dual between the whole and the parts; Babylonian holism rather refers to particular, non-compartmentalised perceptions of the economic process. I will return to this important issue in the fourth section, when I discuss political economy in terms of Babylonian thought. But first I move to the level of methodology, with a particular focus on the distinction often drawn between rationality and relativism.

The meaning of relativism as applied to Kuhn

The modern methodological position most closely associated with the notion of Babylonian thought is Kuhn's (1962) classification of the development of science in terms of paradigms. Kuhn's analysis is more

---

[8] The rhetorical significance of the rational-irrational dual for the rational expectations hypothesis has been noted by Barro (1984).

sociological than epistemological; a more explicitly epistemologically based analysis of particular interest to economists can be found in the writing of Adam Smith (1795).[9] But Kuhn's notion of the paradigm provides a useful focus for the methodological implications of the Babylonian mode of thought.

Kuhn's (1962, 1974) notion of the paradigm accords with our use here of the term methodology. It ranges from worldview to technical apparatus – the disciplinary matrix. A paradigm is identified with a community of scholars or scientists who employ a common disciplinary matrix, that is, who speak the same disciplinary language. Kuhn argued that paradigms are incommensurable in the sense that there is no extra-paradigmatic set of appraisal criteria or meanings by which any paradigm may be judged. Rather, paradigms are subject to revolutionary episodes whereby a new paradigm becomes accepted on the basis of its own criteria.

Kuhn's methodology with respect to the history of science itself constitutes a paradigm. It is thus circular in the sense that past scientific episodes are analysed in terms of that paradigm. It is significant, however, that Kuhn set out to describe rather than to appraise (unlike other approaches to the philosophy of science, including, as we shall see, even amethodological philosophies of science), so that the imprint of his paradigm was limited to colouring perceptions.[10]

Much of the criticism of Kuhn has been expressed in dualistic terms. If there are no common goals of science or appraisal criteria, then science cannot be rational; it must then be relativist or irrational. For example, Popper described Kuhn's argument as a: 'thesis of *relativism*. And *it is a logical* thesis ... [which] is in our time the bulwark of irrationalism' (Popper, 1970, p. 56; emphasis in original). This terminology is also employed by those who argued against traditional methodology, like Feyerabend (see, for example, Feyerabend, 1970, p. 214). The title of his main work was, after all, expressed in the dualistic form, *Against Method*.[11]

---

[9] Smith was influenced in his epistemology by Hume: see Raphael's contribution to the general introduction to the Glasgow edition of Smith (1759, pp. 15–21).

[10] In spite of Popper's (1970) reaction, Kuhn was not attempting to advocate normal science; see Kuhn (1970).

[11] It is likely that Feyerabend (1970) expressed his position dualistically for rhetorical reasons, in order to argue against an orthodox position, but that his true position is much closer to that expounded by Rorty (1979). See for example, Feyerabend (1978, Part 1), in which he responds to reactions to his earlier work.

The notion of revolutions in particular has been criticised dualistically as a complete recognisable break between one paradigm and the next, a representation which conflicts with the actual continuities of thought (as well as those imposed paradigmatically). Similarly, Kuhn explicitly pointed out that incommensurability is by no means complete: some criteria of appraisal, some perceptions of reality (indeed the underlying reality itself) and some techniques of analysis are likely to be common to more than one paradigm. But as long as there are some differences, any exercise of theory appraisal necessarily belongs to only one paradigm at a time. Again, the conventional interpretation forces ideas which may properly occupy a middle ground into one or other of what some would regard as a mis-specified dual.

Of the methodologies which occupy what is seen as the relativist side of the rationality-relativist dual, it is Feyerabend (1970) who provides the clearest account. He wished to divert attention from methodological considerations on the grounds that they are inevitably normative. The injunction not to aspire to universal appraisal criteria is itself normative and constitutes a methodological position. This approach was the inspiration (acknowledged in the preface) for the thesis put forward on the philosophy of science as applied to economics by McCloskey (1986). Economic arguments are portrayed as conversations in which the techniques of rhetoric are employed in order to persuade. This depiction is helpful as a description of actual practice, although the expression 'rhetoric' perhaps conveys most to those embedded in the American academic tradition. McCloskey argued against explicit consideration of appraisal criteria, thus adopting a recognisably relativist position. For McCloskey, not only should philosophy of science be pluralist in the sense of recognising and studying different methodologies, but so also should scientists; preferably these methodologies should be buried in the practice of rhetoric so that they do not constitute a barrier to constructive conversation.

Kuhn's approach did not take this second normative step. His theory of paradigms is an abstraction designed to capture the essence of an actual process of scientific endeavour. In that sense, methodologists have to be pluralist to some degree if they are to recognise and analyse the different methodological positions represented by each paradigm. But the approach is not normative as far as scientists themselves are concerned. Each is functioning within a community which shares a paradigm, including criteria for appraisal. Each scientist then, by belonging to such a community, implicitly or explicitly demonstrates a preference for this set of criteria. When confronted with the criteria of another paradigm, we should expect such a scientist to argue in favour of his/her own paradigm. In other words, the scientist is not necessarily relativist with respect to the actual conduct of science, only, to a degree, if there is some successful communication with practitioners of other paradigms. The implication for scientists themselves of Kuhn's approach is thus that communication between paradigms will be fruitless unless there is some recognition of the practice of scientists which involves choice of paradigm.

While Rorty (1979)[12] argued against epistemological discussion at the philosophical level, he nevertheless recognised that such discussion is inherent at the scientific level. Far from leaving methodology to the philosophers, such a stance favours leaving (prescriptive) methodology to the practitioners. Rorty used the term 'epistemology' to refer to normative theories of knowledge and the term 'hermeneutics' to refer to descriptive theories of knowledge:

> For hermeneutics, to be rational is to be willing to refrain from epistemology – from thinking that there is a special set of terms in which all contributions to the conversation should be put – and to be willing to pick up the jargon of the interlocutor rather than translating it into one's own. For epistemology, to be rational is to find the proper set of terms into which all the contributions should be translated if agreement is to become possible. For epistemology, conversation is routine inquiry. (Rorty, 1980, p. 318)

Epistemology was the proper province of what Kuhn called 'normal science', enquiry within a paradigm; hermeneutics was the proper province of what Kuhn called 'extraordinary science' which involves enquiry outside the ruling paradigm, bringing other than that paradigm's appraisal criteria to bear.

But habitual use of language is drawing the discussion into a dualistic framework. While Kuhn and Rorty inevitably used categories, they were not intended to be dualistic. Thus, to categorise their descriptions of science and meta-science as either rationalist or relativist, or as either prescriptively epistemological or hermeneutic, is to employ a dualistic mode of thought which they both rejected. What they suggested was that successful (normal) science requires a prescriptive theory of knowledge as part of a paradigm, while successful methodology and extraordinary science require openness to different epistemologies and

---

[12] Also noted by McCloskey as a major influence.

paradigms. Scientists and methodologists are necessarily embedded in their own paradigms; the discussion is about the degree and type of consciousness of other paradigms that are required to maintain successful scientific communities and study of these communities.

As with the recognition of endemic uncertainty, this view of methodology states the problem rather than presenting a solution, of which there are many. McCloskey suggested one solution, which is to be relativist or hermeneutic at all levels of enquiry and to eschew epistemology and rationalism in favour of study and application of rhetoric. This choice represents in effect the dualistic alternative to the traditional rationalism-at-all-levels. Babylonian thought makes a different choice: a pluralist approach to methodology is preferred, in the sense of promoting awareness of alternative paradigms (although the preferred paradigm, whatever that is, colours that awareness), while scientific practice is more concerned with establishing rules for theorising within the chosen paradigm and building theory accordingly.

Consistent with a Babylonian style of reasoning, the process of others becoming acquainted with this style of reasoning itself requires several chains of reasoning. So far, an exposition has been presented first at the level of modes of thought, or meta-methodology, and then at the methodological level. It is time now to turn to the level of scientific theory itself, in this case, economic theory.

Political economy as Babylonian thought

Mainstream economic theory, particularly in the form of pure general equilibrium theory, conforms very clearly to the Cartesian/Euclidean mode of thought outlined above. In attempting to identify a body of theory which conforms to Babylonian thought, the general category of political economy seems to provide a possible starting point; political economy is often put forward expressly as an alternative to mainstream theory.[13] However, the prior task is to define what is meant by 'political economy'; in turn, discussing political economy in terms of mode of thought may contribute to that attempt at definition.

Historically, the term 'political economy' was used synonymously with 'economics' (see Deane, 1983; Groenewegen, 1985), but it is often used to distinguish the continuity of classical principles from the emergence of current mainstream economics out of the marginalist revolution.

---

[13] The term 'heterodox economics' is often used now as an alternative to 'political economy'.

The term indeed is used in a variety of ways (see Arndt, 1984). Insofar as it refers to the normative or ideological aspects of a 'moral science', a Babylonian/Kuhnian/political economist would maintain that political economy must still be coterminous with economics: no theory can escape normative or ideological content.

The other major characteristics commonly identified with political economy are interrelated: policy, rather than theoretical, questions as a starting point, and a choice of abstraction which retains as much as possible of the type of realism which would allow theoretical conclusions to generate policy conclusions. By this characterisation, then, political economy has the same starting-point as Babylonian thought – practical problems – and thus the primacy of realism over technique. But the content of Babylonian thought is only one possible avenue to take from this starting-point. A political economist may still be dualistically rationalist at the methodological level or hermeneutic at the methodological level and at the theoretical level. McCloskey is perhaps the most outspoken of this type of political economist, addressing methodological questions in order to dismiss them. There is, however, a large body of applied economists, who would possibly classify themselves as political economists, who implicitly deny the relevance of methodological discussion for the appraisal of their theories within their paradigm (as well as from without).

Babylonian thinkers among political economists, then, I would define as those who incline towards hermeneutics at the methodological level, and epistemology at the theoretical level,[14] insofar as these levels can be distinguished. The corollary of such a mode of thought is tolerance of other paradigms, in the sense of recognition that none has any monopoly on the truth, but coherent, rational advocacy of one's own paradigm, albeit necessarily on the basis of that paradigm's criteria of appraisal.

Since political economy thus appears to be methodologically diverse as an approach to economics, a subset of political economy is required to provide a case study. The Scottish political economy tradition provides a particularly useful example, not only because it provided the grounding for or shared a heritage with many of the subsequent strands of political economy, but also because its key figure, Adam Smith,

---

[14] Whynes (1984, pp. 209–16) identifies political economy with essentialist epistemology. This may in practice require a hermeneutic methodological approach, but need not do so; 'economic man' could be said to reflect a particular essentialism which does not require a hermeneutic methodology.

is frequently misrepresented as the model for Cartesian/Euclidean thought in economics as epitomised by general equilibrium theory (see for example Hahn, 1984, p. 72).[15]

The environment which spawned the Scottish Enlightenment, of which the new discipline of political economy was a product, sheds light on the character of that new discipline. The Enlightenment is generally characterised as rationalist, but in the Scottish case, that rationalism could not be divorced from the pervasiveness of moral questions and a fundamentally historical or evolutionary approach to knowledge. The result, for Smith, was to develop a non-rationalist epistemology based on Humean ideas; this theory of knowledge corresponds to what we have termed here hermeneutics, and anticipated much of Kuhn's work.[16] Nevertheless, Smith is noted for the force with which he advocated his own particular epistemology (see, for example, Dow, 1984); he was Babylonian in being more relativist at the methodological level, but more rationalist at the theoretical level. But the two levels are interwoven, for example as between his discussions of the psychology of theorising, and the psychology of economic agents.

A second major feature of that environment was debates about issues of jurisprudence (in which Smith himself took part). Indeed Scottish law itself demonstrates a non-dualistic epistemology in its offer of three verdicts: innocent, guilty and not proven. Of importance also were the debates concerning the competing considerations of laws of natural justice on the one hand, and moral sense, evolving by social convention, on the other. As a result, individuals were not regarded as isolated atoms, but rather as social and political beings, with behaviour the result of tension between civic, civil and social considerations (see Pocock, 1983). Smith thus did not represent economic man as the atomistic selfish individual of general equilibrium theory, but as one whose self-interest is intrinsically tempered by social convention (see Kregel, 1985).

Third, the education system had a profound influence on the content of disciplines. The Scottish degree was designed to promote breadth within a structure. Thus, most notably (in contrast to English universities of the time) moral philosophy, logic and metaphysics were taught in the first year, encouraging argument from first principles on moral questions of general interest (a development encouraged by the practice

---

[15] See Dow (1987) for a fuller analysis of the Scottish political economy tradition.

[16] See Smith (1795) and Skinner (1979).

of peer review). Further, it was the common practice in all disciplines (including mathematics) to teach first principles in terms of their historical development (see Davie, 1961, II, ch. 1). Indeed, mathematics was deliberately taught in terms of its foundations in order to make it more readily applicable to practical questions: there was a consciousness of the distinction between mathematical (axiomatic) reasoning and ordinary reasoning. Thus, the notion of argument from first principles did not imply an axiomatic, Cartesian/Euclidean structure, but rather a system of thought, drawing on several disciplines, which would be sufficiently adaptable to deal with policy questions. Smith, for example, is sometimes accused of inconsistency (a flouting of Cartesian/Euclidean principles), but Skinner (1979) argued convincingly that Smith's work derived its unity from his overall system of thought, which encompassed a diversity of parts, but which was bound together at the level of first principles.[17]

In short, the work of Smith in particular, but also the mode of thought which he encouraged to prevail in the Scottish political economy tradition, can be identified as an example of Babylonian thought. The emphasis given above to the environment which spawned this tradition was deliberate; the propagation of a paradigm is crucially dependent on a congenial intellectual environment. This type of case study can be pursued further for explanations of the current status of political economy, and for policy prescriptions for improving that status.

Conclusion

The purpose of this exposition has been to draw out the meaning of a mode of thought other than the one conventional in the methodology of orthodox economics. The underlying rationale has been that divisions between schools of thought are deeply rooted in different modes of thought; the criteria by which one school of thought is appraised by another are inevitably the product of a particular mode of thought which may conflict with that underlying the school of thought being appraised.

To argue that schools of thought may be compared (and indeed should be compared) objectively in terms of the common language of classical logic is to employ the Cartesian/Euclidean mode of thought of mainstream economics. Similarly, to argue that any other position

---

[17] This methodology differs fundamentally from axiomatic deductivism (Dow, 2009).

is illogical is to employ the dualistic style of reasoning endemic to that mode of thought. Rather, to explore the source of difference between schools of thought which extend beyond classical logic, and indeed the different ways in which logic itself may be employed to understand complex economic systems, is likely to be more productive in cutting through confusion.

By stepping outside a dualistic framework, this chapter has attempted to map out some of the middle ground between rationalism and relativism. Like an economy, this middle ground is complex and requires a variety of approaches to convey its meaning. The particular mode of thought considered here involves different degrees and meanings of relativism and rationalism for different purposes. The implications are different for methodology and for practical economics: if methodology is to promote understanding and critical analysis of different schools of thought, it should involve a degree of pluralism.[18] Practicing economists may by all means construct and defend their theories on the basis of the principles common to their own paradigm, while retaining a tolerant and open-minded attitude towards members of other paradigms.

The element of rationalism of a Babylonian practicing economist takes a particular form. Since Babylonian thought involves a theory of knowledge which is non-dualistic, theorising about economic agents, institutions and aggregates accords with the same theory of knowledge. The example has been given of Keynes's theory of uncertainty and investment behaviour. A more modern example of exploring the 'middle ground', rather than a dual, is Hodgson's (1986, 1988) advocacy of a study of institutions, rather than any deterministic relationship between individuals and aggregates (with causation running in either direction).

Inevitably, this argument has been presented here from the point of view of a particular mode of thought and paradigm. Implicit, therefore, is an argument not only against the Cartesian/Euclidean mode of thought, but also against other, non-dualistic, modes of thought. But in the spirit of a hermeneutic approach to methodology, this argument is intended to be constructive with respect to other paradigms. Providing accounts of other paradigms and their underpinnings is the first step to constructive dialogue. This involves a hermeneutic approach to

---

[18] The case for pluralist methodological study has been made forcefully by Caldwell (1982), although pure pluralism would seem to represent a logical inconsistency in advocating one methodological position and, at the same time, none.

understanding, but retains a focus on methodological difference as something to be discussed and debated. Difference at the level of mode of thought is usually too ingrained to contemplate change as a result of persuasion (see Chick, 1995). But understanding of differences of mode of thought allows better mutual understanding on which to base debate and persuasion at the level of methodology.

The particular focus here on dualism as an important feature of Cartesian/ Euclidean thought has highlighted a particular problem for applied mainstream economics. If indeed reality involves infinities and uncertainties, and evolves over time, then it is not dualistic. But mainstream methodology and theory is predominantly dualistic. The resulting conflict between theory and reality may account for much of the evident crisis in mainstream economics.

It is a commonplace argument among many economists (both rationalist and relativist) that methodology should be left to the philosophers. The argument presented here suggests rather that it is important to recognise the constructive role that methodology can play at both the philosophical and practical levels. Dualistic mainstream thought has supported a prescriptive role for methodology at the philosophical level, which establishes rules for practicing economists. The mode of thought outlined here, rather, advocates a greater pluralist, hermeneutic content for economic methodology. The aim of such study would then be to ensure that each of the various possible methodologies is consistent by its own criteria and to promote mutual understanding among practitioners of different methodologies. Such understanding provides a basis not only for tolerance, but also for creative cross-paradigm developments. But the *onus* for choosing a paradigm and applying and developing its methodology lies squarely with practicing economists. Such an *onus* cannot be borne responsibly without a conscious recognition of the methodological dimension.

5
Uncertainty about Uncertainty

Corresponding to the different interpretations of such concepts as animal spirits are different sets of interpretations of uncertainty. Discussions in the wake of the recent crisis display different degrees of attention to fundamental uncertainty, and thus a different attitude to incorporating it into new economic thinking. A range of interpretations of uncertainty is classified here in an attempt to clarify discussion of this important concept. The psychological propensity to either acknowledge or ignore uncertainty at different levels is shown to be important for economic agents and also for economists.

Introduction

'To teach how to live without certainty, and yet without being paralysed by hesitation, is perhaps the chief thing that philosophy, in our age, can still do for those who study it' (Russell, 1946, p. 14).

The concept of uncertainty is complex. The more economists delve into Keynes's philosophy and consider alternatives, the more complex it becomes. Furthermore, this work is of profound and far-reaching importance. Mainstream economic theory has adopted a particular range of meanings of uncertainty which requires that it be measurable. But as the economy and our expectations of it become more turbulent,

The original version of this chapter was published in S. C. Dow and J. Hillard (eds), *Keynes, Knowledge and Uncertainty* (Aldershot: Edward Elgar), 1995, pp. 117–27.

the measurability restriction on uncertainty assumes increasing importance.

That this should be so is ironic. The relative stability of Western economies in the 1950s and 1960s was due in large part to the success of stabilisation policies inspired by Keynes. But the instability which escalated from the mid-1970s was also ascribed by critics to Keynesian policies. This made it all the more difficult to attract attention to Keynes's work on uncertainty, which has direct bearing on this instability. Instead, while attention to expectations was revived in the 1980s, it took a form quite different to Keynes's analysis.

It is the purpose of this chapter to attempt an account of uncertainty, drawing on the existing literature, which communicates some of the complexity of the concept in relatively simple form. In particular, an attempt is made to combine results of work based on Keynes's *Treatise on Probability* with work on uncertainty in the Shackle-Loasby tradition. As a result, some conclusions emerge with relevance to the subjectivism-objectivism debate; these conclusions refer to choice (implicit or explicit) as to what degree of uncertainty is recognised or admitted by decision-makers. It follows that the notion of confidence is conditional on the degree of uncertainty which is admitted.

In the next section, some of the literature will be reviewed which defines and categorises uncertainty. This literature is approached from a non-dualistic interpretation of Keynes's philosophy (as is found in Carabelli, 1988 and O'Donnell, 1989). The third section offers a formalised version of a definition and categorisation of uncertainty, including uncertainty as it is understood in the mainstream tradition. While these different types of uncertainty can be discussed in terms of objective logic (that is, in terms of rational grounds for belief), there is a subjective element involved in choosing which types of uncertainty are recognised in decision-making. The fourth section discusses briefly the possibility that decision-makers do not systematically optimise the amount of information they seek on which to found their beliefs; it is suggested in particular, that evidence as to ignorance may deliberately be avoided.

Davidson (1991, p. 67) argued against the notion that Keynes employed uncertainty in different senses. This chapter shares Davidson's view that all uncertainty is unified in that it derives from limitations on knowledge. Nevertheless, the concept of uncertainty can be broken down to refer to limitations on knowledge at different levels; it is on this basis that a categorisation is offered here. Only then can consideration be given to the choice as to the level of uncertainty to be acknowledged.

Definition and categorisation of uncertainty

We start with Lawson's (1988) general categorisation of uncertainty with respect to its range of senses in economics as a whole. Uncertainty is best understood in relation to whether probability and/or uncertainty attach to the material world or to beliefs about the material world (that is, whether they are aleatory or epistemic). Rational expectations theorists understand uncertainty as a property of the material world which can be represented by measurable probabilities. There is a true model in which uncertainty is captured by stochastic terms. Similarly, theories of rational choice may introduce a stochastic element into choice; this too can be understood as aleatory to the extent that actual choice is a feature of the real world.

Other mainstream theorists regard uncertainty as a matter of belief, with no necessary connection with the real world. This is the subjectivist approach, evident in the work of Friedman and the subjective expected utility theorists, for example; here the stochastic aspect of choice is seen as arising from uncertainty in belief about the real world. Individuals are envisaged as subjectively establishing measures of probability.

Keynesian probability is also a matter of belief rather than material reality, since probability changes with new evidence. Uncertainty in general refers to situations in which probability cannot be measured. This immeasurability arises from the nature of the real world. As with most duals, the aleatory/epistemic dual therefore has limited applicability to Keynes. While Keynes certainly understood uncertainty as pertaining to belief, beliefs are uncertain because of the nature of the real world. Nor is it just that our capacity to know about the real world is limited, powerful though the implications of those limitations may be. It is that key aspects of reality are unknowable. Keynes (1972a, p. 262) regarded the economic system as being organic. Not only does this involve complex interdependencies over time and space, but also the entire economic system is seen as being open; once we allow for human creativity and caprice, that is, for indeterminism, there is not a closed system waiting to be known.

Further, the scope for subjectivism in Keynes's logical theory of uncertainty is a matter for some dispute. There is no question that Keynes consistently focused on circumstances in which probability was immeasurable. So in that sense it cannot be maintained that Keynes accepted the view that individuals could always subjectively quantify probabilities, in the sense that they would always take positions on bets. Indeed, liquidity preference can best be understood as unwillingness to place bets. Nevertheless, action is often required, or at least often occurs, whether probabilities can be measured or not. If they cannot be measured, the logical foundations for a decision are by definition weak; reliance is placed on convention, animal spirits or caprice. The objective rational basis of decisions taken with less uncertainty trails into the subjective basis of decisions taken under conditions of greater uncertainty.

Keynes is not subjectivist in the subjective expected utility sense in that the element of subjectivism arises from the particularities of context of the decision-maker concerned. Subjectivity arises because of the absence of cardinally measurable probability. Keynes emphasised the placing of reliance on group conventions, rather than individual conventions; this has been classified as intersubjectivity (see Gillies and Ieto-Gillies, 1991). Reliance on conventions provides some objective grounds for rational belief, but the formation of conventions and the choice of convention involve some element of subjectivity. The question of how to understand that element of subjectivity will be explored further in the fourth section.

Let us now consider some further categorisations that have been put forward with respect to Keynes's conception of uncertainty. Prior to the investigations of the *Treatise on Probability* dating from the 1980s, Keynes's concept of uncertainty was understood almost exclusively in the absolute sense of an absence of measurable probability. This understanding drew primarily on chapter 12 of the *General Theory* and the 1937 *Quarterly Journal of Economics* article, in which Keynes referred to unknowability, in contrast to the mainstream concept of uncertainty as measurable probability.

But study of the *Treatise on Probability* revealed the additional significance of the concept of weight (see Lawson, 1987; O'Donnell, 1989 and Runde, 1990). This concept allows understanding of uncertainty as a relative concept (which was for long an unremarked element of uncertainty in the *Quarterly Journal of Economics* article). More weight can be attached to an assessment of probability the more relevant evidence is available (whether or not it actually makes a proposition more or less probable). O'Donnell (1989) accordingly broke uncertainty down into uncertainty as measured by probability (uncertainty in the mainstream sense), uncertainty measured by weight of evidence, and uncertainty about the probability relation, that is, how the evidence bears on the proposition. He later refined the last distinction to include both irreducible uncertainty – 'we simply do not know' – and unrankable uncertainty, in which probabilities cannot be ordered (see O'Donnell, 1991). Langlois (1983) too, drawing on Loasby (1976), made the distinction between parametric uncertainty (limited availability of evidence) and structural uncertainty (limited understanding of what would be the best model).

Keynes used weight both as an absolute and as a relative concept. According to the former, weight is measured by the absolute amount of relevant evidence. But the latter introduces the notion of relevant ignorance. After referring to probability as depending on the balance of favourable and unfavourable evidence, Keynes introduced the concept of weight as an additional respect in which arguments may be compared: 'This comparison turns on a balance, not between the favourable and the unfavourable evidence, but between the *absolute* amounts of relevant knowledge and of relevant ignorance respectively' (Keynes, 1921, p. 77, emphasis in original).

The introduction of the notion of relevant ignorance opens up possibilities for further refinements. Runde's (1990) addition to Keynes's notion of weight was particularly suggestive. He pointed out that increased evidence, rather than increasing weight, may reduce weight if it reveals new realms of ignorance. In particular, new evidence may reveal that what was understood to be the best model is in fact inadequate. Thus, attempts to reduce parametric uncertainty may actually increase structural uncertainty, in Langlois' terms. For example, a simple consumption function based on the absolute income hypothesis may perform well for significant periods of time, confirming the strong belief that consumption behaviour conforms to this pattern. But new evidence which demonstrates a shift in the consumption function reveals that knowledge of underlying behaviour was inadequate and throws previous work into doubt. Similarly, investment plans based on evidence of a particular range of competing products can be thrown into disarray with the discovery of some totally new competing product.

An attempt is made in the following section to systematise the understanding of uncertainty arising from these different classifications.

A taxonomy of uncertainty

Table 5.1 attempts a taxonomy of uncertainty to encompass a range of the meanings found in different literatures. The crucial distinction is between measurable and immeasurable probability. For probability to be measurable, the range of possible outcomes must be known with certainty and the structure which generates these outcomes must also be known, either by logic or by empirical analysis. Measurable probability can yield three orders of uncertainty. Immeasurable probability yields at least three (overlapping) orders of uncertainty.

Table 5.1 A taxonomy of uncertainty

	p **measurable (K = 1)**	p **not measurable (K < l)**
U_1	$\sigma(\varepsilon)$	–
U_2	$1 - p$	low order of p
U_{3a}	$1/w_1$	$1/w_1$
U_{3b}	–	$1 - w_2$
U_{4a}	–	low order of K
U_{4b}	–	low order of K relat. to I
•	•	.
U_∞	–	K = 0, I = 1

$p = a/h$
$w_1 = h/K$
$w_2 = [h/(h +i)]/ K$
$K = K [R (h,i)]/h$
$I = I[R (h,i)]/ h$
where p = probability
a = argument
h = evidence
i = ignorance of evidence
R = relevance
K = knowledge of R, $0 < K \leq 1$
I = ignorance of R, $0 \leq I < 1$
w = weight of evidence

Each type and order of uncertainty can be illustrated with respect to a demand for money function, that is, the uncertainty in the example is that of the economist. (Uncertainty could be equivalently illustrated with respect to knowledge of the economy on the part of actors in the economy.) We start with a simple money demand equation:

$$M/P = \alpha + \beta y + \gamma r \qquad \alpha, \beta > 0, \gamma < 0$$

where P is the general price level, M is the money supply, y is real income and r is the rate of interest; α, β and γ are parameters.

The first category of uncertainty U_1 refers to the rational expectations view that uncertainty is inherent in reality and is thus captured in the stochastic term, ε. The equation would then be expressed as:

$$M/P = \alpha + \beta y + \gamma r + \varepsilon$$

The degree of uncertainty might then be measured by the variance of the stochastic term. The economist is not portrayed as uncertain, only as acquiring ever-better skills in identifying real relationships (see for example Lucas, 1980).

A second order of uncertainty, U_2, is associated with the notion of probability as a matter of belief. In the case in which probability is measurable, uncertainty of this order is greater the lower the probability measure; it can be measured by $(1 - p)$, where p is the degree of belief in the proposition of argument a, conditional on the evidence h: $p = a/h$.

Thus, for example, a money demand equation of the type set out above might be estimated with evidence h, yielding an estimate of the parameters within a certain confidence interval. If that confidence interval were 5 per cent, then that would define the dimension of the uncertainty attached to the proposition that a particular fall in the rate of interest would yield the predicted change in the demand for real balances. This indicator of uncertainty requires that the underlying relationship be known, which can be represented as $K(R) = 1$; otherwise account has not been taken of type II error, so that the confidence interval would be an inadequate measure of uncertainty. Since the structural relationship must be known for p to be measurable in this way, the mean of the error term in the estimation must be zero; but the variance of the error term can be an indicator of the economist's uncertainty about the estimation. More generally, the degree of uncertainty of the economist can be quantified in terms of the standard diagnostic tests.

Keynes's judgement that the economic process is organic would suggest that it is in general impossible to specify correctly the structure of relationships of the sort illustrated above: financial innovation and the changing moneyness of assets, for example, can account for an evolution of structural relationships. Goldfeld's (1976) case of the missing money revealed an exercise in which evolution of financial structure was not being picked up by econometric models of the demand for money. To the extent that models now explicitly incorporate proxies for innovation and evolution of financial behaviour, the models perform better by standard econometric criteria; in that sense, there can be said to be less uncertainty attached to grounds for belief in the propositions represented by the models. Probability is still given as a/h, and it may be capable of ordering; greater uncertainty, then, would be associated with a lower order of probability. Keynes took great pains to point out the rational basis for belief built on such evidence as is available.

The third order of uncertainty refers to the completeness of the evidence on which the judgement of probability is reached. Weight is a measure of completeness of relevant evidence; greater uncertainty would prevail the lower the weight of a probability estimate (measurable or immeasurable). Uncertainty of the third order may thus be measured by the inverse of weight. Keynes used the measure in two senses: absolute completeness and relative completeness. In the case of absolute completeness, uncertainty is measured as the inverse of w_1, where w_1 is a measure of the absolute amount of relevant evidence. In the second case, uncertainty may be measured by $(1 - w_2)$, where w_2 is the ratio of relevant evidence available (h) relative to the total of relevant evidence and ignorance ($h + i$).

Measurement of either absolute or relative completeness requires knowledge of what constitutes relevance and that knowledge and ignorance are of the same dimensions. Knowledge of the complete range of evidence which is relevant depends on knowledge of structure. This is not an issue for measurable probability; if probability is measurable, then the structure must be known. Then, for example, the weight, w_1, of the simple argument represented by the money demand equation above would increase (and uncertainty decrease) the more case studies confirmed the posited demand for money function. In the case of known structure, econometric tests are like repeated experiments. As long as data on the variables in the equation are available, the notion of relevant ignorance has applicability only in the sense that there is no pre-assigned limit to the number of experiments that could conceivably be performed. Nevertheless, in practice there is a limit beyond which significant further information would not be expected. The weight measure relevant to situations of known structure and so measurable probability is w_1.

For immeasurable probability, therefore, uncertainty moves readily into a further order, that of the degree of belief in a hypothesised structure on which to base an estimate of weight. Now K itself becomes subject to uncertainty. K is clearly not measurable, since it refers to knowledge about immeasurables. But it may be possible to rank order K, such that higher uncertainty of the fourth order is entailed in a lower ranking of K. In terms of the absolute concept of weight, uncertainty about K must be captured in the (measurable) amount of evidence relevant to knowledge of the structure of economic relationships. For the relative concept of weight, higher uncertainty is implied by a lower order of K relative to ignorance of the relevant h and i, I [R(h,i)]. Ordering this type of uncertainty is clearly more difficult than ordering uncertainty about knowledge of structure: knowledge of knowledge and ignorance is easier to establish than ignorance of knowledge and ignorance. Yet some degree of belief in knowledge of structure is required for estimation of weight, that is, for estimation of uncertainty in terms of weight.

Logically, this progression into ever-higher orders of uncertainty about uncertainty can continue indefinitely. The limiting case could be characterised as one in which knowledge of structure is completely absent and ignorance is absolute. Then, literally, we simply do not know. But this absolute state, like that of complete certainty, is not feasible. As uncertainty is compounded at higher recursive levels, our necessary conceptual structures become complex, counterintuitive and involuted to the point that they collapse under their own weight. Put another way, absolute ignorance is incompatible with knowledge of absolute uncertainty.

Yet the limiting case is of lesser relevance anyway to economic decision-making than Keynes's 1937 *Quarterly Journal of Economics* article might imply. Decisions are taken and action undertaken even in situations in which we might be said simply not to know. We may well have no idea of what the price of copper might be 20 years hence, but investment decisions are taken with respect to copper mining which rely on particular outcomes 20 years hence. In such circumstances, the extent of ignorance may not be acknowledged, and investors may act as if uncertainty is only of the second or third orders, for example. In other words, there is an important distinction between rational argument and rational decision-making. In the next section, we explore the positioning of decision-makers in relation to the different orders of uncertainty.

Decision-making under uncertainty

There has been much analysis of decision-making under uncertainty. Here we wish to explore the particular implications of considering uncertainty of different orders. In particular, we will reconsider the implication of Keynes's theory of probability in terms of grounds for rational belief that all relevant information is employed by decision-makers. This train of thought is prompted by a suggestion in Loasby (1976, p. 158), that 'confidence may be the direct result of ignorance'. This goes against the suggestion, such as that by O'Donnell (1989, ch. 4), that confidence is inspired by weight of argument, that is, by the degree of evidence relative to ignorance. The two positions can only be reconciled if confidence as measured by weight is conditional on presumed knowledge. Thus, an investor in copper mining might exhibit a high degree of confidence if full knowledge of the determination of copper prices were *assumed* to be held.

Keynes's views on uncertainty, amplified by subsequent work, might be interpreted as follows: decision-makers gather all available information, given their underlying knowledge of the relevant processes, weigh up the absence of evidence relative to that knowledge, and weigh up their ignorance of the processes relative to their knowledge, weigh up their understanding of knowledge and ignorance of processes relative to lack of understanding, and so on. This is logically entailed in an epistemology applied to open systems (of the economy, of thought, of meta-thought, and so on).

Yet Keynes was not a purist (because he was not a dualist) in his epistemology or his economics. Thus, for example, he pointed out:

> It would be foolish, in forming our expectations, to attach great weight to matters which are very uncertain. It is reasonable, therefore, to be guided to a considerable degree by the facts about which we feel somewhat confident, even though they may be less decisively relevant to the issue than other facts about which our knowledge is vague and scanty. (Keynes, 1936, p. 148)

For some purposes it is convenient, and does not do too much violence to the facts, to treat a part of the economic process as a closed system, that is, to presume knowledge of structure. Then, for the purposes of that analysis, some measure can be made of weight, even w_2. In other words, we employ epistemic conventions to reduce uncertainty in theorising, just as decision-makers employ conventions to reduce uncertainty about actual processes. Given the openness of the actual economic system, the conventions will sometimes fail. Then there may be a crisis and higher order uncertainty must then be addressed. (The distinction is similar to that between normal science and extraordinary science in the Kuhnian framework.)

Further, different approaches to economics can be distinguished in terms of the order of uncertainty allowed: whether, for example, knowledge of general structure is assumed, and assumed to hold for the entire economic system rather than partially. Mainstream economics can be identified as presuming knowledge of the structure of economic relationships. The alternative open-system approach may be identified with political economy, which focuses on understanding underlying processes (see Dow, 1990b). Within this approach, the neo-Austrian approach allows for the greatest order of uncertainty, to the extent that the ignorance of economists plays a crucial part in limiting their perceived policy role.

It is being suggested therefore that, in Keynes, knowledge and ignorance do not constitute a dual; nor do knowledge, uncertainty and ignorance constitute a triple. Uncertainty further is as much a matter of psychology as of logic if perceptions may differ as to the appropriate domain of evidence. This is intrinsic to the role in Keynes's investment theory of animal spirits; this urge to act overcomes what would otherwise be a perpetual 'rational' refusal to act. Further, animal spirits may take a pessimistic or an optimistic turn. In the case of a collapse of confidence, there is a greater willingness to address the pervasiveness of ignorance. This changing admission of ignorance cannot be understood in objectivist terms. Further, in relation to the present topic, it can be suggested that there is a significant psychological propensity among those geared to action to ignore knowledge, including knowledge of ignorance. Thus, Earl's (1984) case studies of firms, for example, present evidence of managers choosing to ignore relevant evidence because it threatened well-established plans. It could even be said that economists choose to ignore relevant evidence because it threatens well-established representations of economic structure.

Conclusion

This discussion should provide some crumbs of comfort for the beleaguered academic. It is unkindly suggested that 'those who can, do, those who can't, teach'. Rather the argument presented here suggests that those who act only do so because they are prepared to ignore much of their ignorance; academics can then be regarded as people who know enough and are aware enough of their own ignorance to find it difficult to act. Both stances are valid in their own domains, which in turn can be said to be necessary to human existence.

As far as analysis of uncertainty is concerned, the discussion here suggests that the role of conventions is more complex than normally portrayed; not only do conventions supply knowledge to decision-makers, but they may provide a refuge from confronting ignorance. Further, this applies equally to economic theorists, where the conventions apply to the knowledge and ignorance of economists. Objective grounds for belief thus do not provide a complete account of probability and uncertainty; it is important also to take account of the willingness of different groups to ignore ignorance (and thus knowledge), and for the capability of this willingness to change for reasons which require recourse to psychology and sociology.

6
The Appeal of Mainstream Economics

A revealed preference criterion would suggest that the economics profession has already, over an extended period, decided on the best approach, identified here as the 'mainstream' approach. Even in the current unstable climate, however, there has been little explicit discussion of its merits relative to the alternatives. Keynes depicted the foundations of this approach as the special case of certainty or certainty-equivalence. His more general approach encompassed uncertainty, in which conventional knowledge plays a key role. The continuing appeal of the mainstream approach is analysed here as adherence to one such convention. But, being based on judgement, any convention is open to challenge.

Introduction

Part of our knowledge we obtain direct; and part by argument. The Theory of Probability is concerned with that part which we obtain by argument, and it treats of the different degrees in which the results so obtained are conclusive or inconclusive.

In most branches of academic logic...all the arguments aim at demonstrative certainty. They claim to be *conclusive*. But many other arguments are rational and claim some weight without pretending

The original version of this chapter was published under the title 'The appeal of neoclassical economics: some insights from Keynes's epistemology' in the *Cambridge Journal of Economics*, 19(6), 1995. It benefited from the helpful comments and suggestions of Anna Carabelli, Victoria Chick, Peter Earl, Frederic Lee, Brian Loasby, Andrea Salami, Tom Torrance and Roy Weintraub, members of the ESRC Post-Keynesian Study Group, and three anonymous referees.

to be certain. In metaphysics, in science, and in conduct, most of the arguments, upon which we habitually base our rational beliefs, are admitted to be inconclusive in a greater or less degree. (Keynes, 1921, p. 3, emphasis in original)

The publication of Keynes's *Collected Writings*, and in particular *A Treatise on Probability*, spawned a burgeoning literature on Keynes's thought which served to forge a new understanding of Keynes's (as opposed to Keynesian) economics. While interesting in its own right, this enquiry also holds considerable potential for application beyond the history of thought.

In the *Treatise*, Keynes developed a theory of knowledge (or epistemology) which was to lay the foundations for the methodology of his economics. While some (for example, Bateman, 1987) argue that there were significant discontinuities in Keynes's epistemology, Carabelli (1988) and O'Donnell (1989) demonstrate that there is an overriding consistency. In the process, they both set out a coherent and all encompassing epistemology with application to economics, which can be discussed in relation to modern economics and economic problems. This can be considered quite independently of any dispute as to what Keynes himself thought.

Lawson (1985) pointed out the relevance for modern economics of Keynes's theory of uncertainty, which was central to his epistemology. He proceeded to suggest ways in which economists could reduce the uncertainty associated with theorising. Hamouda and Smithin (1988) suggested that much may also be learned from Keynes's organicism. The purpose here is to broaden the discussion further by considering Keynes's theory of knowledge in its entirety (including the key elements of uncertainty and organicism). Not only will this be productive in terms of indicating fruitful avenues of enquiry for modern economists (thus extending Lawson's argument), but it will also provide insight into the prior question of why Keynes's methodology is not currently widely employed, or at least professed.[1]

The scope of the explanation to be developed below of the current state of economics[2] depends very much on the scope, in two senses, of

---

[1] Keynes's methodology is to be distinguished from the 'Keynesian' methodology of the neoclassical synthesis (see Kregel, 1976; Chick, 1983; Harcourt, 1987).

[2] 'Current' here refers to the 1990s, when the original paper was published. But the argument about the conventional nature of methodological approach

Keynes's epistemology. First, if we view economics in terms of Kuhnian paradigms (Kuhn, 1962), the problem of incommensurability limits the scope of any one paradigm's criteria of appraisal to that paradigm alone; there is no socially agreed set of extra-paradigmatic appraisal criteria. Thus, because Keynes was not a positivist, for example, it might seem that his epistemology would not shed much light on the practice within a positivist paradigm (other than to practitioners of the Keynesian paradigm). We draw here, however, on an important outcome of thinking on Keynes's epistemology as a system of logic, that is, a mode of reasoning. Carabelli (1988) demonstrated how apparently inconsistent aspects of Keynes's thought in fact derived from the consistent application of a logic which differs from formal logic; this logic is termed variously in the literature ordinary logic (Carabelli, 1988) and human logic (Winslow, 1986b, using Ramsey's, 1931, term).[3]

Keynes indeed introduced the *Treatise on Probability* by drawing the distinction between the certainty of the conclusions of demonstrative logic and the inconclusive nature of non-demonstrative logic on which most arguments are, in fact, based. Formal, demonstrative logic is contained within ordinary logic as a special case, with validity only under carefully specified conditions. Similarly, mainstream economics, which employs classical logic, is a special case within the overall Keynesian *schema*. Thus, Keynes's methodology and economics need not be seen in dualistic juxtaposition to mainstream methodology and economics, but rather as containing them (see Chick, 1995, and Gerrard, 1989).

The implications of Keynes's epistemology to be drawn here will focus on the appeal of demonstrative certainty on the one hand, and the question of the limitations on the scope for demonstrative argument in economics on the other. While the methodology of mainstream economics purports to limit itself to demonstrative logic, in practice, the limitations thereby imposed are judged too severe by many mainstream economists.

---

can also be considered as applying to modern mainstream economics; see further Chapter 13.

[3] The apparent consistency of Keynes's thought is to be understood, in turn, in terms of ordinary logic. Keynes's thought evolved over the years, in response to a range of influences; the essence of Keynes's epistemology, as will be developed below, is that knowledge is conditional on available evidence, where evidence encompasses a wide range of phenomena, including the ideas of others. Knowledge about epistemology, just like that of the economic process, is bound therefore to evolve; but if that knowledge is acquired according to consistent principles, the overall system of knowledge is consistent.

Keynes's epistemology provides guidance as to how to reduce the uncertainty associated with the undemonstrative, ordinary logic which many economists use in practice. This holds particular implications for the design of economics education. This argument is built up as follows. First, mainstream economics is defined and an account given of mainstream methodology both as it is professed and as it is practiced. An account is then presented of Keynes's epistemology, explaining in particular the role of conventions in relation to mainstream methodology. The third section develops the idea of conventions further in terms of rationalisation (in relation to rationality). Rationalisation is shown to be an important feature of rationality within intellectual (as all) communities. The notion of relevance, as an important factor in applied disciplines, is explored in the fourth section in relation to Keynes's theory of probability. These various threads of the argument are tied together in a discussion in the fifth section of systems of logic, particularly considering the implications of an open system of logic. Having returned thus to the question of the scope of Keynes's system of logic, the discussion is completed by drawing some conclusions as to fruitful directions which economics might now take, with particular reference to the education system.

The methodology of mainstream economics

Before discussing mainstream methodology in terms of Keynes's epistemology, some consideration is given in this section to a more general characterisation of mainstream methodology and the particular limitations which have caused concern with it, promoting a divergence between theory and practice. First, the question must be addressed of how to classify mainstream economics. It was argued in Dow (1985) that it is most helpful to categorise economics by methodology. Defined in these terms, mainstream economics encompasses a range of theories employing different methods. But they are included in the umbrella category of mainstream economics because they all profess to some key common methodological principles.[4] In particular, they all advocate mathematical formalism, in the sense that all scientific statements can and should be expressed mathematically. All also employ equilibrium as a central organising concept. All present mathematical models as closed systems, in the sense that it is a working hypothesis that all non-

---

[4] See further Chapters 1 and 2. This categorisation finds support in Hausman (1992).

random influences are accounted for, that is, all relevant variables are identified. Non-random influences not explicitly accounted for are represented as shocks to exogenous variables, that is, influences from outside the closed system. As these shocks become better understood, their determination may be incorporated within the closed system. Taking the assumptions as given and the logic as correct, the resulting arguments are demonstrably conclusive (within that system).

Differences in method within mainstream economics arise from the (not insubstantial) issues of the truth-value of assumptions and the theoretical relevance of observations. Pure general equilibrium theory derives propositions by application of mathematical logic to axioms which are regarded as self-evident truths; but direct application of propositions to facts is not generally regarded as admissible because there is no basis for assuming that observations correspond to equilibrium states (the axioms not being regarded as empirical truths). Neoclassical economics, on the other hand, accepts limitations on how far theory is derived explicitly from axioms, in order to test theory (expressed mathematically) against facts. New Classical economics purports to avoid both limitations by deriving propositions mathematically from axioms and testing them empirically; this requires, among other things, that observations refer to equilibrium situations. Game theory derives propositions from its own formal models, on the basis of axioms which may differ from those of pure general equilibrium theory. But these axioms require that behaviour be depicted deterministically, just as in general equilibrium theory, in order for demonstrative solutions to be derived. The representation of individual behaviour as deterministic, using predictable sets of information, is an important requirement of mainstream methodology, since in all cases the axioms are subjected to deductive mathematical logic. While randomness may be introduced to behaviour, this does not alter the basic principle that behaviour may be represented in this way.

While the above account represents the professed methodology of mainstream economics, there is considerable divergence between what is professed and what is practiced (see Blaug, 1980; McCloskey, 1986 and Hausman, 1992). This divergence stems from a variety of factors. First, the injunction not to apply general equilibrium theory empirically is hard to accept unless the interest in economics is purely aesthetic; even Hahn, who specified the reasons for this injunction most carefully,[5] did not abide by it (see, for example, Hahn, 1983). Second,

---

[5] See Hahn (1977, 1981, 1984); see Loasby (1989, ch. 8) for a commentary.

the scope for conclusive argument on the basis of empirical work is severely limited, not least by the Duhem-Quine problem of identifying what, if any, aspects of complex theories have been falsified by contrary facts. But even the notion of 'facts' itself is clouded by difficulties of quantification of theoretical concepts as well as the more practical problems of data-gathering. The third source of divergence is identified by McCloskey's (1986) study of the rhetoric which economists employ in their unofficial discourse (the official discourse reflecting the methodological principles outlined above). In practice, economists seem to find the official discourse too limiting in their efforts to persuade others of the worth of their arguments.

Divergence between theory and practice in mainstream economics is one way of attempting to escape the limitations imposed by methodological principles. But the result is a tension which manifests itself in concern both about the internal logic of theory, and about the policy relevance of economics. This latter concern has been expressed both by eminent economists who were subject to a set of early influences similar to those experienced by Keynes (see for example Robinson, 1990), and also by US graduate students:

> the interviews suggested a definite tension, frustration and cynicism that, in our view, went beyond the normal graduate school blues. There was a strong sense that economics was a game and that hard work in devising relevant models that demonstrated a deep understanding of institutions would have a lower payoff than devising models that were analytically neat; the facade, not the depth of knowledge, was important. This cynicism is not limited to the graduate school experience but is applied also to the state of the art as they perceive it. (Colander and Klamer, 1987, p. 100)

Meanwhile, some leading economists, in considering future developments in economics, expressed their doubts that the current domination of the discipline by axiomatic formalism will be sustainable (see Baumol, 1991; Hahn, 1991; Morishima, 1991; and Pencavel, 1991).[6] Discomfort with the methodological problems emerging within mainstream economics led some to view the discipline as being in a state of significant evolution, or even of crisis (see Hicks, 1974; Bell and Kristol, 1981).

But many economists would view this suggestion with amazement. Many are content to operate within the limits imposed by neo-Walrasian

---

[6] More recently see Blaug (1999).

general equilibrium theory, or have embraced alternative formal systems with an equilibrium focus. Others choose to ignore what they probably regard as esoteric questions of methodology, including Hahn's warnings about trying to apply general equilibrium theory beyond its limits. The majority of economists still employ and teach theory which accords with the methodological principles outlined above. The premise of Kirman's (1989) discussion of the limitations of general equilibrium theory was that 'This theory still furnishes the basic foundations of what many are pleased to call mainstream economics. Indeed such theory as is used by practical men to justify their economic recommendations is derived from this framework, albeit with unwarranted appendages' (Kirman, 1989, p. 126). Mainstream theory is not the only option facing economists. So '[w]hy are there, in the United States at least 98% Mainstream and 2% of all other kinds of economists?' (Weintraub, 1985c, p. 1117). This question was posed with respect to an account (Dow, 1985) of a range of schools of thought which attempted to demonstrate that each was legitimate in terms of its own methodological, and ultimately epistemological, criteria. Why then does such a large majority of economists choose to adopt the methodological and epistemological criteria of mainstream economics? We turn now to Keynes's epistemology for a possible answer.

Keynes's epistemology and the convention of mathematical formalism

Keynes's *Treatise on Probability* was addressed to the question of how knowledge, as a basis for action, is established. The argument has general application and accordingly can illuminate the acquisition of knowledge equally by consumers, economists and philosophers. Knowledge, he argued, is of two forms: direct knowledge and indirect knowledge. Direct knowledge is knowledge about propositions concerning objects of direct acquaintance, in which the propositions derive from experience, perception or understanding (as in understanding of the rules of formal logic); these are termed primary propositions. Indirect knowledge consists of secondary propositions which are the outcome of argument concerning primary propositions. Theorising is a matter of generating indirect knowledge.

Keynes represented the degree of belief in a proposition by its probability, a logical relation between the evidence (direct knowledge possibly in combination with other indirect knowledge) and the proposition. Certainty attaches only to those propositions when the evidence is known (with certainty) and the logical connection between evidence and propositions is a necessary one. The general case, however, is one of uncertainty, in which rational belief is only probabilistic. It was to this general case that Keynes's epistemology was addressed.

Keynes's notion of probability included quantifiable mathematical probability as a special case. Quantifiable probability on the basis of statistical inference similarly is only feasible in particular circumstances: the events to be observed must be replicable, which requires that the system of which they are a part has limited independent variety, that is, it is atomic rather than organic (see Carabelli, 1988, pp. 104–8, and Hamouda and Smithin, 1988). An ordinal probability estimate may be arrived at when this condition is not met, but that estimate may be held with varying degrees of uncertainty (depending on how much relevant evidence is brought to bear, that is, depending on the weight of the argument). Uncertainly held probabilities may or may not be comparable, depending on the degree of heterogeneity of the propositions to which the probabilities are attached; the possible outcomes of a war, for example, are at the time so heterogeneous as to make probability estimates of the outcomes of investment projects non-comparable. When probabilities are numerical but uncertain (the weight of evidence is low), non-numerical and comparable, or are not comparable, formal demonstrative logic may not be applied (see Carabelli, 1991a). Reasoning, therefore, in general requires ordinary logic as a basis for rational belief. Ordinary logic, in turn, lacking the demonstrative capacity of formal mathematical logic, relies on alternative, non-demonstrative strategies, most notably conventions or mental habits.

Keynes maintained (1972a, p. 262; 1973b, p. 286) that the social structures of which we have direct experience are predominantly organic rather than atomic, and that this in practice precludes sole reliance on statistical inference and demonstrative logic. Further, the complexity of the economic system limits the scope of any one individual's direct knowledge. Much of our theoretical knowledge about the economic process is therefore held with uncertainty. It follows that economists employ conventions when faced with uncertainty in their theorising. In a sense, the field of methodology consists of the study of conventions.[7]

---

[7] This is to be distinguished from the particular set of conventions entailed in what is commonly termed 'conventionalism'; see Katouzian (1980); Boland (1982, pp. 142–3). See Dais (1994) and Runde and Mizuhara, eds (2003) for further analysis of the origins and meaning of Keynes's analysis of conventions.

Keynes's most explicit discussion of conventions can be found in his analysis of the determination of long-term expectations by entrepreneurs and of asset valuations in financial markets. In the course of this analysis, Keynes (1936, p. 148) constructs a logical argument in favour of entrepreneurs employing the convention of relying on more certain rather than less certain 'facts', that is, it is not unreasonable (under uncertainty) to rank confidence in judgment over relevance. In financial markets, the logic supports the corresponding convention, in the absence of demonstrably correct valuations, of assuming the present to be a more reasonable guide to the future than experience would warrant and that current conventional opinion is a good guide for individual reasoning (Keynes, 1937, p. 114).

Considering this injunction in terms of economic theorising, the adoption of strategies to reduce the element of uncertainty is prevalent. The certainty attached to the methodology of general equilibrium theorising is frequently stressed; hence Hahn's (1983, p. ix) stress on the preference for 'clinching' as opposed to 'plausible' arguments. This certainty is closely associated with the concept of precision (a precision, which Coddington, 1975, noted applied to the theory itself, not its application). Certainty, in this case, derives from the application of formal logic to axioms which are held to be true, on the basis of direct knowledge.

Classical logic has the appeal of absolute certainty – certainty with respect to the rules of logic. Hahn thus occupied the high ground of requiring absolute certainty when he defined 'what can be said' in terms of a closed system of classical logic.[8] Any applied work, accordingly, inevitably ventures into the uncomfortable realms of uncertainty, and what cannot, necessarily, be said. Although empirical falsification might appear to lend applied work an element of certainty, the Duhem-Quine problem (of identifying what exactly has been falsified) severely limits the scope for definitive falsification. Unfalsified propositions, in turn, cannot be held with any certainty, since they may at any time be falsified. Indeed, Popper's work can be seen as setting out appropriate conventions to cope with the ensuing uncertainty (see Loasby, 1991).

For Keynes, the ultimate object of theorising was to attain knowledge which was as reliable[9] as possible given the available evidence.[10]

---

[8] See Hahn (1989) and Backhouse (1988) for further uses of the notion of 'what can or cannot be said' as a demarcation criterion.

[9] This term has been used to greatest effect by Ziman (1978).

[10] Keynes's views as to the possibilities, particularly as to the acquisition of certain knowledge, evolved over his intellectual career.

Reliability, in turn, was a concept founded on conventional judgement. Keynes's argument that conventions are employed when certain knowledge is lacking is a logical one (belying the charges of psychologism, as levelled for example by Boland, 1982, pp. 93–4 and Hodgson, 1988, ch. 10). Conventions can thus be appraised in terms of logic, as a means of reducing uncertainty. But elsewhere in the literature can be found discussions of the conventions of theorising also in terms of aesthetics, psychology and social organisation, which explain them as a means of reducing the discomfort associated with uncertainty; a consequence may be that uncertainty itself is reduced.

The first modern (as opposed to ancient) discussions of epistemology in terms of aesthetics and psychology in general, can be found in Smith's (1795) 'History of Astronomy', which in turn shows Hume's influence (see Skinner, 1979). Here Smith discussed 'wonder' as the motivating force behind theorising, which takes the form of imposing a causal pattern on observation. Unexplained events, in turn, cause a sense of wonder, which causes the discomfort of uncertainty; new theories are developed in order to remove that discomfort. More modern psychological theory uses the term cognitive dissonance[11] in the same way as Smith discussed wonder. Cognitive dissonance is created by a situation of choice under uncertainty; it motivates the formation of strategies designed to reduce the associated discomfort. While cognitive dissonance is conventionally employed with respect to the behaviour of individual agents (see Earl, 1990, pp. 735–6), it can also be applied directly to theorising, in the same way as Smith's concept of wonder (see Earl, 1991). The conventions of theorising can thus be understood in terms of strategies to reduce the discomfort associated with uncertainty. The degree to which cognitive dissonance is experienced may differ depending on what Shackle (1983-84) would identify as cultural differences (as between those classically or romantically inclined).

Theoretical conventions are not fully explained by the goal of reducing uncertainty and the discomfort associated with it. Earl (1983a) notes psychological goals which can be classified as having a sociological or ideological basis. (The goal of self-interest in the form of promotion seeking and so on can be subsumed in these two categories.) Mental habits need not be sociologically generated; creativity is a key element in theorising whether in pure mathematics (see Weintraub, 1985a, pp. 176–9) or among entrepreneurs (see Shackle, 1979). But there

---

[11] See Festinger (1957), and for its first application to economics, Akerlof and Dickens (1982).

is also a strong element of social convention in habit formation, mental or other.[12] Thus, for example, the esteem in which mathematical formalism is held in economics can be understood partly in sociological terms. Ideology too is frequently noted as a source of methodological and theoretical differences. Hausman (1992), for example, classifies mainstream economics in terms of 'vision'. Keynes himself recognised the importance of ideology in choice of methodology (see for example Keynes, 1936, pp. 32–3) as did Myrdal (1953).[13]

In terms of social organisation (whether referring to firms or academic communities), conventions perform the constructive function of providing social cohesion. Social conventions were an integral element in Smith's theory of the invisible hand which is often ignored by its modem exponents. In economic terms, conventions in the form of contracts lead to stability in decision-making (see Richardson, 1953, 1960). Similarly, within scientific communities, shared conventions create the kind of stable environment necessary for the conduct of normal science (see Kuhn, 1962). Thus, in addition to conventions themselves being designed to reduce the discomfort associated with uncertainty, the adoption of conventions itself may reduce uncertainty, and/or its associated discomfort in relations within a scientific community.

Conventions reduce uncertainty by limiting the range of possible actions or, in epistemological terms, the range of possible arguments. Although Keynes's epistemology consisted of a logical system, theorising for Keynes was a matter of belief, given the pervasive presence of uncertainty. Spreading belief is then less a matter of demonstrative proof than of persuasion. Persuasion in turn has social and psychological elements in the expression of ordinary logic. The conventions of ordinary logic thus have rhetorical content, a fact of which Keynes was keenly aware in his attempt 'to revolutionise the way the world thinks about economic problems' (Keynes, 1973a, p. 492; see further Dow, 1988).

The modem literature on the rhetoric of economics, of which the leading figure is McCloskey (1986), uses literary criticism as a technique for understanding the mechanisms by which economists persuade. At the methodological level, McCloskey's work is disturbing in implying that what persuades is best. But at the theoretical level, the appeal of neoclassical economics is seen to lie in the fact that it has been persuasive

---

[12] See Hodgson (1988, ch. 6) for an account of the interplay between individualistic and conventional behaviour.

[13] See more recently Backhouse (2010).

in the past. Cognitive dissonance can be avoided by accepting the dominant paradigm, whatever it is.

Let us consider further McCloskey's argument that mathematically formalistic arguments are most persuasive. An important element in that persuasion is the argument that science is coterminous with mathematical formalism (see Woo, 1986). Weintraub (1985, ch. 11) argues that mathematical thinking is inextricably linked to the process of growth of knowledge. Mathematical concepts, he suggests, are innate, so that '[i]f all knowledge is structurally organised, is developed out of some basic and unchanging mental structures, the connection between mathematics and the growth of knowledge is not accidental ... [E]conomic analysis or economic problem solving is a mathematical activity, and surprise at the success of mathematics is unwarranted' (Weintraub, 1985a, p. 179). While McCloskey urged economists to recognise the rhetorical nature of their arguments, Weintraub in effect urged economists to recognise the mathematical nature of their thought processes.

Weintraub's advocacy of mathematical formalism was novel in its explicit subjectivism. He avoided the traditional fact-theory dual of positivism by arguing that all 'facts' are theory-laden: they are mental constructs which accord with our mental structures. Since these structures are mathematical, Weintraub conflated (subjectively understood) reality with the mathematical models of mainstream theory. Theory then progresses by a process of conjecture and refutation, so to that extent knowledge is held with uncertainty. But the limits of knowledge are coterminous with the limits of mathematical formalism.

But mathematical formalism is simply one convention among many.[14] Mathematical formalism as a convention represents the view that only arguments which yield demonstrably certain conclusions are admissible. But it is not clear that the aim of increasing knowledge requires that uncertain knowledge be avoided in this way. Nor is it clear that devoting resources to extending the scope of mathematical formalism is a better way of increasing knowledge than efforts to reduce in other ways the uncertainty associated with knowledge which lies outside that scope.

Keynes has often been dismissed because the non-formal character of much of his theorising makes it 'non-operational' (see Lucas, 1980). Yet Keynes's views on mathematics have been shown (see Carabelli, 1988; O'Donnell, 1990) to be coherent in terms of his overall system of logic,

---

[14] Hahn (1984, p. 7) seems to have been coming round to such a view.

which he regarded as prior to mathematics. These views address and encompass the role of mathematical and non-mathematical conventions with respect to theorising, testing and persuasion. For Keynes, it is ordinary logic (rather than simply mathematics) which structures our thought. Indeed, this view arose from the argument being developed simultaneously in the epistemology of mathematics that mathematics is internally ungrounded; ordinary language may then be required to give it foundation (see Carabelli, 1988, p. 133.) As O'Donnell put it:

> Constitutive of Keynes's philosophy is a crucial principle that flows unabated through all his writings. It is the proposition that qualitative logical analysis (i) *precedes* quantitative or mathematical analysis, and (ii) *determines the scope* of its application. Translated into a slogan, it becomes 'first logic, then mathematics if appropriate.' And logic in Keynes's philosophy ultimately rests on the use of direct judgement or intuition. (O'Donnell, 1990, p. 35, emphasis in original)

Thus, increased knowledge and reduced uncertainty can be achieved by economists improving their capacity to judge when mathematical formalism is appropriate, and to conduct qualitative analysis when it is not. Keynes's criteria for quantitative analysis to be appropriate are now well known (see O'Donnell, 1989, pp. 191–5; 1990):

  (i) that the assumption of constant structure be reasonable for the subject at hand;[15]
 (ii) that the object of theorising not include significant non-quantifiable elements;[16]
(iii) that variables are commensurable;[17] otherwise there is quantitative indeterminacy.

Keynes recognised the role of mathematics as an aid to thought, independent of quantification, when appropriate. For it to be appropriate, first, it is important that the structure being analysed can reasonably be represented as constant, such that the variables can be represented as independent, or, if not constant, that interdependence can be expressed

---

[15] Keynes (1921, pp. 285–6) questioned in particular the general validity of the assumption of constant structure underpinning Tinbergen's multiple correlation analysis.

[16] See Keynes (1921, pp. 2, 287).

[17] See the consideration of measures of purchasing power in Keynes (1930, pp. 87–8).

deterministically. A case in point might be the interdependence between the private and public sectors; is it appropriate to represent this in terms of either perfect or zero anticipation by the private sector of policy action, or by either policy rules or randomness in the public sector, as required by conventional mathematical formulation?

A second requirement is that all relevant factors can in practice be expressed formally. The danger with giving priority to mathematisation is that the range of relevance is limited to those factors which can, given current capabilities, be expressed formally. Thus, for example, the determinants of confidence in the banking system may be difficult to formalise, and yet may be crucial in time of banking crisis. Formal models might therefore treat the onset of a banking crisis as an exogenous shock; but to limit economic inquiry to the formal model, rather than the emergence of the shock, is unnecessarily to increase theoretical uncertainty. Even more, an absence of analysis of confidence and trust makes it difficult to design policy to restore them.

A third requirement is that the internal logic of the mathematical model is sufficient for persuasion. McCloskey's (1986) work demonstrates that other modes of persuasion are in practice used to supplement mathematical logic. Indeed, mathematical logic cannot be separated from other modes of persuasion; the words employed in presenting mathematical argument ('rational' is the clearest example) themselves carry moral authority. The fact that even those economists who subscribe to mathematical formalism employ ordinary logic in persuasion confirms (even if it does not prove) Keynes's arguments about the limited role for classical logic in economics. Further, theorising would be more effective if explicit recognition were to be given to non-demonstrative elements of argument and resources devoted to making these elements more robust (by acquiring factual knowledge about the context of application of theory, for example).

Keynes's analysis therefore suggests that strict adherence to the principle of mathematical formalism could unduly limit the scope of economic knowledge to the extent that mathematisation at any time faces practical limitations. Further, and perhaps more important, mathematical formalism could unduly limit our capacity to make judgements about the scope of formal economic knowledge. The qualitative nature of the discovery of knowledge and of the methods of persuasion which is a necessary part of mainstream economics appears to be logically inconsistent with the formal nature of its official discourse. But perhaps the latter can be understood as a rationalisation of the former. We consider this possibility in the next section.

Economic theorising: rationality or rationalisation

Closely associated with the mathematical formalisation of economic theory is the underlying notion of rationality. In order to avoid semantic confusion, we shall proceed by using the term 'rationality' to refer to its narrow, mainstream sense;[18] the corresponding term in ordinary logic would then be 'reasonable'. When attempting, as here, to understand the process and presentation of theorising, the issue arises as to whether or not it is a rational process. One possibility to be considered is that the expression of theorising contains an element of rationalisation, that is, reformulation according to rational principles after a process of theorising which accorded with other principles. In Keynes's terms, reasoning based on ordinary logic is being rationalised in terms of formal mathematical logic. McCloskey (1986) suggested that the 'official' economics is a rationalisation of the rhetorical non-rational process of 'unofficial' economics. In the process of rationalisation, much that might have been persuasive is lost, but the persuasiveness of the rationalisation itself, according to the formalist convention, is overriding. Weintraub (1985a), like Popper (1959, p. 31), accepted that formal reasoning is not strictly rational in that it starts with conjecture; nevertheless, the formal expression of the outcome of conjecture represents the full structure of arguments. In this section, we consider whether this is the case. In other words, can the rationalisation of non-demonstrative logic by means of demonstrative logic be complete? Put more strongly, are the logical limitations imposed by mathematical formalism so severe that the principle itself needs to be questioned on epistemological grounds?

The theory of investment provides a useful case study of rationalisation. Long-term expectations of entrepreneurs are subject to discrete shifts when rationalisations are subject to shocks in the form of contradictory evidence (see Earl, 1984, pp. 85–7); firms do not have the option of eliminating uncertain knowledge from decision-making. Carabelli (1988) put forward an intriguing interpretation of Keynes's theory of investment in terms of firms' rationalising behaviour. In chapter 11 of *The General Theory*, Keynes posed the investment decision in terms of a comparison between the rate of interest and the marginal efficiency of capital. The latter is an expectational variable, but the implication is that it is quantifiable; entrepreneurs are portrayed 'as if' numerical probabilities required for the marginal comparison with the rate of

---

[18] The mainstream usage refers to optimisation with respect to the axioms of completeness, independence, reflexivity and transitivity of preferences.

interest existed. This practice was portrayed as a convention by which entrepreneurs express their investment decision-making process. This is a useful procedure 'which saves our faces as rational economic men' (Keynes, 1973b, p. 114). In chapter 12, however, Keynes pointed out the non-quantifiable nature of long-term expectations. Carabelli (1988, pp. 225–6) explained the apparent inconsistency in terms of the *onus* on managers to rationalise their investment decisions. The actual reasoning is the subject matter of chapter 12, in which animal spirits (the spontaneous urge to action) play such a pivotal role. Once the decision to invest is in effect taken, the marginal efficiency of capital can be assigned a magnitude for (favourable) comparison with the rate of interest. The comparison of two magnitudes lends an element of certainty to what is fundamentally an uncertain exercise.

The key to Keynes's analysis of investment is that, without animal spirits, no rational entrepreneur would invest. In other words, the rational reconstruction misses the decisive element which explains the investment decision. The implications for mainstream economics of this argument are wide sweeping. If economists were to be strict mathematical formalists, the limitations thereby imposed would make theory virtually sterile (see Dow, 1991).

But in practice, strict adherence to mathematical formalism is rare. Case studies of the great debates demonstrate the importance of criteria external to the mathematical systems in question. Thus, for example, Salanti (1989) argued that the capital theory debate was conducted using criteria external to the formal re-switching argument, on both sides of the debate. (The conventional wisdom is that external criteria were only employed by the non-formalist approach of Robinson.) In fact, in parallel to the argument that mathematics is externally grounded, Salanti argued that mathematical economics is externally grounded.

Thus, while the professed mathematical formalist convention of mainstream theory appealed to the desire of economists to aim for certain knowledge, so much of mainstream economics operates beyond the boundaries of mathematical formalism, that is, in the realms of uncertainty, that its methodological foundations arguably lack coherence.[19] In order to discuss how best to proceed or assess procedures, given this uncertainty, we return now to Keynes's argument for relying on 'facts of which we are more certain' for more insight into what that might entail. In particular, in the next section, we will explore Keynes's use of the terms 'relevance' and 'weight' in his system of logic.

---

[19] This conclusion finds support in Hausman (1992).

Relevance

Keynes advocated that more weight be given to facts of which we are more certain, than to facts of which we are very uncertain even if they are more relevant to the argument. Keynes firmly distinguished weight from probability.[20] Probability measures (numerically or otherwise) the degree to which given evidence supports a proposition; weight measures (numerically or otherwise) the amount of relevant evidence. Weight itself can be subject to uncertainty just as much as probability and the evidence on which probability is based (see Chapter 5). Weight can be low if the available relevant evidence is known only with considerable uncertainty; weight can be uncertain if it is unclear what evidence is relevant. Evidence is relevant if knowledge of it alters the probability estimate (see Keynes, 1921, pp. 59–60). But this can only be known *ex post*; it may be difficult to identify *ex ante* the universe of relevance. Indeed, Runde (1990) argued that new relevant evidence may show the extent of relevant ignorance to be greater than previously believed, thus *reducing* weight.

A clue to the issue of relevance may be found in Keynes's use of analogy (in particular, negative analogy) as a means of getting round the problem of induction (see Keynes, 1921, ch. 19; Carabelli, 1988, ch. 5). Statistical inference involves repeated experiments under constant (atomic) conditions, but the problem of induction prevents the resulting probability estimate from being applied with certainty. Keynes argued rather in favour of observations in which only one element was held constant. The commonality of that element ensures the similarity between the observations, that is, the analogy between them, and the difference between other elements of the negative analogy. Thus, for example, the logical argument in favour of the absolute income hypothesis, or the quantity theory of money, was stronger if it held under a wide range of circumstances. In these terms, evidence is relevant if it provides additional instances of negative analogy (price and money supply data under a new regime of monetary control, for example).

But relevance has broader application than empirical evidence. Direct knowledge is based on a wide range of experiences, understandings and meanings which extend well beyond quantifiable economic data (see Keynes, 1921, p. 12). Further, indirect knowledge can draw not only on direct knowledge, but also on other indirect knowledge; as we have

---

[20] See Keynes (1921, ch. 6); Carabelli (1988, pp. 55–9); O'Donnell (1989, ch. 4).

seen, this latter includes non-demonstrative as well as demonstrative arguments. What is relevant is, for Keynes, a matter of logic rather than material conditions. Relevance is thus conditional on the theoretical specification involved. Thus, theories specified in terms of formal mathematical logic can only admit evidence expressed in terms of classical logic. If deduction from the rationality axioms shows that in equilibrium there can be no involuntary unemployment, and if observations have to be defined as reflecting equilibrium states to allow the formalist analysis to proceed, then evidence of involuntary unemployment is inadmissible.

But Keynes's epistemology suggests that the adoption of mathematical formalism is itself a convention, that is, it involves judgement. Then evidence relating to that judgement (such as the palpable existence of involuntary unemployment) is indeed relevant. Following on Runde's (1990) argument, weight of argument may decrease if increasing evidence reveals increasing degrees of relevant ignorance.

Nevertheless, Keynes did argue in favour of more certain evidence, even at the expense of relevance. The type of evidence of which economists are more certain is not given, however; it reflects past choices as to admissible evidence. Thus, for example, it is commonly pointed out that the International Monetary Fund's early introduction of monetarist principles (see Polak, 1957) was strongly influenced by data availability. GNP, money supply and general price level data were the most certain information on member countries' economic conditions. It was also the information most readily assimilable within a formalistic model for universal application.

Lawson (1985) made the case, also on the basis of Keynes's epistemology, for economists to assimilate more direct knowledge. But the argument can be extended also to more indirect knowledge. Thus, for example, to construct and make sense of negative analogy, it is helpful to have knowledge of the institutional structure of and history behind each circumstance in which the common element is being observed. There is no need for economists' knowledge of institutions and economic history to be 'vague and scanty'. The allocation of resources to acquiring knowledge involves trade-offs. But there is no *a priori* reason why devotion of resources to formal mathematical models, with limited application but certainty of conclusions, generates more knowledge than devoting resources to the wider realm of ordinary logic and reducing the uncertainty attached to the wider realms of evidence which are accordingly admitted.

Open and closed theoretical systems

Keynes's system of ordinary logic is necessary for application to open theoretical systems, in contrast to the closed theoretical system to which formal logic may be applied. In an open theoretical system, the starting point is that it is not known what the full range of relevant variables is and that the full range is in practice unknowable. The implications are wide ranging. First, uncertainty cannot in general be represented stochastically, since there can be no presumption that omitted influences are purely random. Second, variables cannot in general be dichotomised in terms of endogeneity and exogeneity except with respect to partial systems. These systems may be treated as if closed in order to allow formal analysis to proceed. But the burden is on the theorist to argue the case that the major influences can be identified. The case has to be made for each piece of analysis because structural relationships may differ from one context to another. Finally, if the scope of mathematical formalism is in practice limited, formal analysis in terms of partial systems needs to start with qualitative analysis in order to be justified, and combined with qualitative analysis in order to be applied.

Ordinary logic thus contains formal mathematical logic as a special case. Keynes praised the virtues of mathematical expression in those circumstances which met the conditions he specified, and himself used formal argument in both philosophy and economics. Whether or not those conditions are met in a particular instance is a matter of judgement, taking account of the availability of relevant formal techniques. It was Keynes's judgement that some parts of the economic system approximate sufficiently to atomic systems to admit mathematical formalism; further, mathematical techniques may be applied to those parts of organic systems whose interdependence can be represented deterministically. For Keynes, organicism did not preclude formal partial analysis.

Similarly, the argument has been put forward that econometrics in general lacks logical validity (see Lawson, 1989a). Darnell and Evans (1990, ch. 1) have made the counterargument that relationships can be modelled and tested econometrically as if they were Bayesian (that is, as if the underlying system were atomic). For all his criticisms of econometrics (Keynes, 1921, pp. 306–19), Keynes would entertain this argument as providing a good logical justification of econometric practice. But this justification would only be admissible if each case were open to questioning whether the 'as if' argument were reasonable; it would not be logically acceptable as a blanket justification. Given the logistical problems with justifying each case separately, conventional judgements about types of cases would be acceptable, but conventions could always be queried in a particular case. The *onus* should be on the econometrician to demonstrate the amenability of the data to econometric analysis.

While involving uncertainty, open theoretical systems are nevertheless systems. A good example is Smith's system (see Skinner, 1979). Smith (1795) quite explicitly recognised the appeal of understanding the economy in terms of a system, in the same way as Newton understood the solar system. Yet, by the criteria noted above, it is not at all clear that his social system is amenable to formal mathematical expression. The attempt to formalise this system in the Arrow-Debreu model illustrates the practical limitations of formalism: one example is that the Arrow-Debreu model does not (and arguably cannot satisfactorily) incorporate Smith's notion of sympathy which is inextricably bound up with his theory of self-interest (Smith, 1759) or his theory of tendency towards industrial concentration (Smith, 1776). For example, an implication of Smith's use of sympathy is that supply and demand schedules are fundamentally interdependent, since each is constructed on the basis of sympathy with the other's notion of what would be a reasonable price. The difficulties posed by oligopoly for formalising pricing behaviour do not bode well for the prospects for formalising this more complex form of interdependence.

A source of unease with open theoretical systems is that, outside the comforting certainties of formal mathematical logic, judgements appear *ad hoc*. This was the import, for example, of Coddington's (1982) criticism of Keynes's theory of expectations. Since Keynes emphasised the uncertainty facing entrepreneurs, but not that facing consumers, Coddington concluded that Keynes lacked a consistent theory of rational behaviour. Coddington then employed the typically dualistic judgements of formal logic to classify Keynes's theory as nihilistic (see Dow, 1990/Chapter 4). But in fact, as Runde (1991) pointed out, Keynes did employ a consistent logic in his theory of expectations. Keynes's epistemology suggests that degrees of uncertainty will differ as between different types of judgement, given different types of evidence. Thus, it should not be surprising that entrepreneurs and consumers should face differing degrees of uncertainty. Keynes's judgement was that it was a reasonable approximation when modelling the British economy in the 1930s to assume that entrepreneurs faced a high degree of uncertainty, while consumers did not. This does not preclude the possibility that for the British (or any other) economy in another era the situation might be different, requiring a different set of assumptions.

In general, Keynes's epistemology implies that all theorising be preceded by consideration of the applicability of particular arguments (assumptions, theories or techniques) to the circumstances under consideration. Popper (1970) took this argument too far by advocating such radical contemplation that science could not feasibly proceed at all (in Kuhnian terms he advocated that all science be extraordinary science). There is a positive role for conventions in theorising, as Keynes himself pointed out. Thus, judgements may become shared, and become almost automatically employed. But Keynes's epistemology also points out the dangers of entrenched conventions; in economics, a relevant analogy is the cyclical instability that attends discrete shifts in conventions (see Lawson, 1985b). Hicks (1939) pointed out that the theory of imperfect competition was not fully incorporated into mainstream theory because the cost in terms of knowledge which would then have to be abandoned was too great. While Keynes would accept that choosing between different sources of certainty is a matter of judgement, there is a strong argument that the appeal of formal certainty has been given too much weight relative to certainty in the form of knowledge about the economy.

If formal mathematical analysis is to be preceded by qualitative judgement, however, there are strong implications for economics as a discipline. Given the prevailing trends in economics education, the conventional view that formal mathematical economics is the most scientific and the various incentives within the academic system, our knowledge base for qualitative judgement is becoming ever more 'vague and scanty'.[21] If formal mathematical economics is to play its role to fullest effect, it needs to be backed up by less uncertain knowledge of its field of application. Such knowledge could well be relevant in Keynes's sense of altering probability judgements; in particular, it could well change conventional judgements as to the scope of formalist theory.

Conclusion

Keynes's epistemology is addressed to the issue of generating knowledge on the basis of uncertain knowledge; the issue of generating knowledge under conditions of certainty was too straightforward to warrant

---

[21] This argument has been put in different form by Simpson (1988) and Rothschild (1989).

much philosophical attention. Keynes was concerned with logical strategies to cope with uncertainty; in its purest form, general equilibrium theory has adopted the strategy of attempting to eliminate uncertainty altogether.

Because the formalism of general equilibrium theory accords with economists' perceptions of good scientific practice, the result has been a tension within mainstream economics. On the one hand, general equilibrium theory generates certain knowledge (given the axioms); on the other hand, that knowledge is not directly applicable to the policy questions most economists wish to address. Mainstream economics thus on the one hand includes pure theory with a solid foundation in formal logic but no mechanism for justifying application; on the other hand, it includes applications of general equilibrium theory without adequate logical justification. Keynes's ordinary logic provides a justification for the application of mainstream theory under particular carefully specified circumstances. But it also justifies other types of theory which are not tied to the reductionist, axiomatic structure of general equilibrium theory. Intrinsic to the logical justification of all theory, formalist or non-formalist, is qualitative judgement.

Keynes's epistemology thus suggests that uncertainty in theorising will be better approached by explicitly incorporating a range of lines of argument, reflecting the range of methods employed in ordinary logic. These methods do not in general yield certain knowledge, but they do reduce the uncertainty attached to indirect knowledge. This in turn requires support from a wider range of indirect, as well as direct, knowledge than is currently encouraged within the profession. The appeal of mathematical formalism is understandable. But the case has not been satisfactorily made that it is better to attempt to reduce uncertainty by extending the scope of mathematical formalism than by devoting resources to other sources of knowledge. Nevertheless, the economics education system, in its increasing emphasis on technical skills, is diverting attention from the acquisition of knowledge of economic history, economic institutions and economic policy, which is necessary before judgements can be reached about which techniques to apply. At a time of rapid institutional (and indeed behavioural) change, the importance of such knowledge for effective theoretical judgement acquires a note of urgency.

7
Mainstream Economic Methodology

Most economics discussion proceeds without reference to methodology although, like prose, we use it all the time. Yet, even if there is no independent set of methodological rules we can call on, we do need some basis by which to make our practice coherent. Here, we explore how the field of methodology evolved in such a way, paradoxically, as to appear to legitimise an absence of discussion of methodology. Here again, we see the importance of a dualistic mode of thought for defining theory, this time in methodology. In the meantime, mainstream economics had been evolving in a way defined by its traditional deductivist mode of thought, but without explicit methodological appraisal. It is argued here that mainstream economics was thus risking incoherence. Methodological awareness is needed, not just to guide new economic thinking, but also to take stock of where we currently stand.

Introduction

What might reasonably be expected of a survey of mainstream economic methodology would be a statement as to the nature and role of methodology, and a discussion of how it impinged on economic practice. However, the mainstream understanding of the nature and role of methodology has been in a state of transition. Further, mainstream economics has evolved virtually independently of explicit methodological

The original version of this chapter was published in the *Cambridge Journal of Economics*, 21(1), 1997, 73–93. It benefited from the helpful comments and suggestions provided by two referees and at presentations at Strathclyde University, the University of Dundee and at Magdelene College, Cambridge.

analysis. Nevertheless, the outcome of current thinking among methodologists could well be the development of a closer bond between methodology and practice. Theorists too are contemplating potentially profound methodological changes. This is therefore a particularly good time to take stock and identify the direction of change and its implications for the future of mainstream economics.[1]

It must be emphasised that the focus here is on mainstream economics. Methodological discussion has always played an important and integral part in other approaches to economics. Thus, for example, Robinson (1979, section one) and Kaldor (1985, lecture I) explicitly used methodological arguments in explaining the foundations of their own theoretical approaches. Perhaps because these arguments were integrated with theory, they have not generally been recognised as contributions to the field of methodology. Thus, for example, Backhouse (1994, p. 2) acknowledged methodological writing among non-mainstream (or heterodox) economists, but concludes: 'Such writing, though clearly methodological, is very closely linked with the heterodox traditions out of which it arises'. Nevertheless, many of the explicit methodological statements of mainstream economists have been responses to the non-mainstream literature. We shall turn our attention briefly to those contributions to methodology later in the chapter. In fact, since one of the main developments in mainstream methodology has been to advocate an integration of methodological study with theoretical study, there should now be a greater openness to the non-mainstream literature which has always been integrated in this way.

The purpose here will be to attempt a fairly broad-brush account of the field in order to draw out the way in which thinking has been developing. Inevitably, any field becomes involved in an internal discourse which is relatively inaccessible to other economists. But if methodology is to impinge on practice, it is particularly important for communication with non-methodologists to be effective (see Gerrard, 1990). The aim, therefore, is to attempt an account which is generally accessible, while giving pointers to the relevant literature on detailed issues.[2] The field of methodology has expanded tremendously since the 1980s, developing a rich internal discourse; the literature is large and increasingly specialised. Fortunately, there are aids to literature search in

---

[1] The meaning of 'mainstream economics' is discussed in Chapter 1.

[2] Other surveys which should be consulted are Hausman (1989, and 1992, Appendix), Gerrard (1990, 1995) and Backhouse (1994, Introduction).

economic methodology, such as Redman's (1989) bibliography.[3] These sources date quickly, given the liveliness of ongoing debates; for a feel for the most current literature, the *Journal of Economic Methodology* is the best source.[4]

The survey starts with an account of ongoing developments in mainstream methodology. These developments can be summarised as shifting the balance, with respect to the role of methodology, from prescription towards description. The third section provides an account of the methodologies implicit in mainstream economics (drawing on the work of the rare mainstream economists who are explicit about methodology). This account suggests a greater degree of methodological disarray than that of the methodology field itself. Yet common influences can be detected in economic methodology and the methodology of economics. The fourth section discusses trends in other disciplines and in society at large which might account for these developments in economics. On this basis, and by reflecting on the changes within the methodology field which might impinge on mainstream economics, consideration is given to the future of this approach. Reference is made in the fifth section to developments in economic methodology outside the mainstream which offer a solution to the tensions identified as emerging in mainstream economics.

Developments in mainstream methodology

The traditional methodology of mainstream economics, as propounded most notably by Hutchison (1938) and Blaug (1980), and reflected in the methodological statements found in introductory textbooks (see Haas's 1993 historical survey), consists of rules for good scientific practice with a view to theory appraisal. These rules acted as a means of demarcating between science and non-science, as well as providing economists with the criteria on which to decide on the best theory. These rules required

---

[3] See also the collections edited by Hahn and Hollis (1979), Hausman (1984) and Caldwell (1984, 1993) and textbooks by Blaug (1980), Caldwell (1982), Pheby (1988), Glass and Johnson (1989), Gordon (1991) and Redman (1991). More recently, see Davis et al, eds (1998, 2004), Hands (2001), Dow (2002), Davis (2006) and Boumans and Davis (2010).

[4] Other relevant journals include *Economics and Philosophy, Research in the History of Economic Thought and Methodology*, the *Review of Philosophical Economics*, the *Erasmus Journal for Philosophy and Economics* and *Philosophy of the Social Sciences*. Other journals which frequently carry methodological material are the journals specialising in non-mainstream economics of various kinds.

that theories be tested against the facts; the traditional methodology literature consists of debate over the nature and role of the rules for testing. The main influences have come from the philosophy of science, reflecting the monist position that the rules for good science apply to all disciplines. Indeed physics has most commonly been held as the model which economics should emulate if it is to be regarded as a science (see Mirowski, 1989). Yet the peculiarities of economics as a social science have raised questions about the scope for empirical testing, given the relative absence of experimental evidence.[5] The result has been a long-standing tension between empiricists or positivists, for whom testability is the demarcation criterion and deductivists or *a priorists*, who reflect an increasing shift of attention to pure mathematics as the appropriate model, with axioms drawn from introspection. This tension persists to this day.

The philosophy of science on which traditional economic methodology is based is termed by Caldwell (1982) as 'logical empiricism' – an outgrowth in the 1950s of logical positivism. This philosophy does not necessarily entail any tension between empiricism and deductivism. It requires that all scientific statements be testable, even if they are the product of theories which have elements with no empirical counterparts. Thus, a deductivist theory may still be appraised with reference to the facts. This was the core of Friedman's (1953) argument that predictive success is the primary appraisal criterion, not the truth content of assumptions; this position is termed instrumentalism.[6] Methodology thus guided theory construction only insofar as that construction facilitated empirical testing. Free rein was thus given to deductivists to develop theory according to an internal agenda, with only token reference to empirical testing of the end results.[7] This internal agenda is termed conventionalism because of its lack of grounding in external methodological principles.[8]

Deductivism was fuelled by the limitations on empiricism in economics. Empiricism is limited not only by the limits to experimental evidence, but also by the problem of induction: no amount of confirmation of a theory can prove it to be true. The use of data to verify theories

---

[5] The reasons for this also raise issues for interpreting experimental evidence in economics: how far can experiments isolate subjects from other factors on the one hand, and do experiments isolate subjects too much on the other?

[6] See Caldwell (1984) for a flavour of the ensuing debate.

[7] See for example Hahn (1973) and Coddington's (1975) critique.

[8] It has been the object of much of Boland's (1982) critical analysis.

does not satisfy the requirement of demonstrating which theory is best. By advocating falsification as the appropriate testing procedure, Popper (1957, 1965) appeared to have provided a satisfactory logic which would produce true results (albeit in the negative form that a theory had been refuted). He proposed a strict procedure whereby conjectures should be expressed in such a way as to invite falsification. Popper was keenly aware of the practical difficulties involved in generating falsifiable statements. Nevertheless, he allowed for the possibility of axioms which would be immune from testing. Most notable for economics was the immunity granted to the rationality principle. Popper (1957, 1963a) saw this principle as being employed within situational analysis (analysing the implications of the rationality principle in given situations); he regarded this as the appropriate method for the social sciences. Popper's expectations of science were modest, given the fallibility of knowledge; he advocated, therefore, a critical rationalist position, whereby the role of the scientist should involve the perpetual subjection of theories to criticism (see Caldwell, 1991a).

The aspect of Popper's philosophy to be picked up most explicitly by economists was his falsificationism. Yet while many economists paid lip service to this, their practice conformed more to the earlier principle of verification, whereby theories could continue to be held as true as long as they were confirmed by the evidence, as amply demonstrated by Blaug (1980). Popper's idea of falsification has in fact proved impossible to put into practice. Quite apart from the socio-psychological drawbacks with a system which requires rejection rather than confirmation of theories, the Duhem-Quine problem made it impossible to decide on whether or not a theory was refuted. Theories are complex combinations of hypotheses, such that it is impossible in practice to identify which is refuted by contrary evidence. While the Duhem-Quine problem is general, Klant (1990) argues that it is more serious for economics than physics, explaining the coexistence of a range of economic theories.

More recently, the view has gained force in the economic methodology literature that Popper's distinction between theories or knowledge (which inhabit his 'world 3') and facts or the objects of knowledge (which inhabit his 'world 2') is unworkable – that is, facts are theory-laden. The notion of confronting a range of theories with a common set of independent facts, then, is misconceived. Moreover, the growing incidence of probabilistic expressions of theory (most notably with the increasing use of the Bayesian framework) has rendered impotent the notion that a contrary observation is sufficient to refute a theory; Bayesian theory accepts that evidence will fall within a frequency distribution. De Marchi's (1992) collection of papers on Popper reveals a majority view that Popper does not provide a satisfactory methodology for economics. Yet many methodologists still describe themselves as Popperian.

Two of the strongest advocates of falsificationism have been Hutchison (1938, 1977), who first introduced the principle to economics, and Blaug (1980). While aware of the limitations on implementing falsificationism, both nevertheless argued that the scope for its implementation has not been fully exploited and feared the degeneration of economics into dogma. Klant (1994) too stressed the importance of falsificationism, but went to much greater lengths to analyse its limitations within a social science; he developed the notion of plausibility as the more powerful basis for theory appraisal than absence of falsification. Like Klant, Boland (1989) distinguished between models (which are in practice severely tested) and theories (which are not, and which many would now argue cannot be tested by falsification). While falsificationism as such was on the wane, the overall Popperian framework of critical rationalism continued to attract support among methodologists.[9] The importance of unfalsifiable, metaphysical assumptions as part of the critical rationalist approach also was stressed by Agassi (1965, 1979) and by Boland (1989). In contrast, within mainstream economics itself (as opposed to methodology) the only aspect of Popper's work which was most influential in practice was the rationality principle, with its immunity from testing (see Hausman, 1992).

The critique of falsificationism on the grounds that facts are theory-laden gained force under the influence of Kuhn's (1962) argument that science operates within incommensurate paradigms; each paradigm is distinguished by its own disciplinary matrix, encompassing worldview, techniques and appraisal criteria. Kuhn's work was a direct challenge to the traditional philosophy of science which presumes that the best rules of good scientific practice can be identified by philosophers of science/methodologists independently of any theoretical perspective. Economic methodologists have in general been critical of Kuhn's argument because it denies the perceived prescriptive function of methodology (see for example, Blaug, 1980, p. 33). Yet they took on board Kuhn's account of actual scientific practice as differing significantly from the

---

[9] Thus Boland, for example, subjected mainstream theory to internal criticism, an approach espoused by de Marchi (1988, 1991, 1992) and Hands (1991), and more explicitly with respect to a wider range of schools of thought by Caldwell (1991a).

austere strictures of positivism; theories were not in practice appraised solely on the basis of evidence.

The appeal of Lakatos's (1970) methodology of scientific research programs was that he offered a less stringent set of rules than Popper did, allowing for the persistence of theories in the face of contrary evidence; these rules were offered as independent of any research programme, allowing the identification of the best research programme. Lakatos's approach depicted research programmes as having a hard core of unquestioned principles, with a protective belt of theories derived from the hard core. The protective belt evolves according to a positive heuristic (rules for good practice) and a negative heuristic (proscription of bad practice). Falsification need not require abandonment of a theory if it is part of a progressive research programme, that is, one which yields novel facts (or excess empirical content). A degenerating research programme in contrast makes *ad hoc* adjustments in order to accommodate novel facts. Thus, Lakatos attempted to address the Duhem-Quine problem by recognising that theoretical propositions form part of a body of theory.

However, Lakatos's criterion of scientific progress is, like Popper's, empirical and thus faces many of the same problems, notably the interdependence between observation and theory. Rosenberg (1986) pointed out that appraisal of research programmes is accordingly internal to the program. The Lakatosian framework faces the additional requirement of specifying the hard core, positive and negative heuristics and novel facts. The main focus of Lakatosian appraisal in economics was on identifying novel facts (see Hands, 1991); very little effort was put into specifying the hard core and heuristics.[10] Weintraub's (1985a, 1985b) careful efforts to fill this gap for neo-Walrasian economics simply served to reveal the difficulties involved, sparking off a long-running debate in *Economics and Philosophy* about whether or not the Lakatosian framework is prescriptive, with Weintraub moving further towards the view of the Lakatosian framework as descriptive.[11] Backhouse (1991) amended Weintraub's (1985a) specification of hard core and heuristics for describing mainstream macroeconomics, but still maintained that this allows empirical appraisal. But doubts about the capacity of the Lakatosian framework to allow appraisal predominated in de Marchi

---

[10] See Fulton (1984) for a critical account of early attempts at such specification.

[11] See Weintraub (1985b, 1987, 1993), Rosenberg (1986, 1987) and Salanti (1991, 1993a, 1993b). The Lakatosian framework has been used to classify descriptively a range of schools of thought in Mair and Miller (1991).

and Blaug's (1991) collection. In his introduction to the collection, de Marchi (1991, p. 18) offered a detailed critique of the Lakatosian framework, making the telling point that empirical appraisal had proceeded in general without a specification of hard core and heuristics.

The search for some independent standards for economic theorising continues, even though for some methodologists the possibility is accepted that there may not be one single set of standards for all of economics (see Boland, 1982, and Mayer, 1993). Blaug and de Marchi differed over how to identify any such standards: Blaug continued to seek them in the traditional philosophy of science, while de Marchi advocated that the search should take place within a study of actual economic practice (a position which found some support within philosophy of science itself; see Rosenberg, 1986). In so doing, de Marchi was reflecting a quite different development in economic methodology which brought into question the whole notion of the role of methodology; this development involved studying the conduct of economics in order to promote understanding rather than to decide on standards. This approach stemmed from Kuhn's account of the history of science, which demonstrated the disparity between 'official' methodology based on logical positivism and actual practice. In particular, contrary facts had not in general caused theory rejection; that would only result from a complete change in worldview. In economics, the impetus came on the one hand from Blaug (1980), who noted, but lamented, this inattention to contrary facts, and on the other, from Boland (1982), who lamented rather the nature of the official methodology and questioned as a result the whole notion of methodology as a standard-setting exercise.

Much of the work in methodology since the mid 1980s thus consisted of methodological analysis of what economists do and how they argue. The context of this work was formed by a pivotal article published by McCloskey in 1983. This article had as much impact as that of another Chicago economist published thirty years earlier, Friedman's (1953) argument for instrumentalism. The style of the two pieces was quite different. Friedman argued that theoretical content (including the realism of assumptions) was of no importance; only predictive success was a proper basis for deciding on the best theory. McCloskey analysed the rhetoric of mainstream economics, demonstrating how it departed from the official methodology, concluding that (prescriptive) methodology was unhelpful for economic discourse. Persuasiveness was then the criterion actually employed by economists for appraising theories; prescriptive methodology had no role. The import of the two articles was thus very similar: economists should not concern themselves on methodological grounds with the content of theories. But in addition, McCloskey ruled out concern among methodologists with appraisal. McCloskey's article caused a *furore* in methodological circles.[12] As we shall see in the next section, however, it struck a chord among practising mainstream economists.

McCloskey found inspiration in Rorty (1979), who on the one hand denied that philosophy (or by implication economics) has any direct connection with an objective reality, and on the other argued for a hermeneutic approach to science (whereby the relationship between scientist, text and context are seen as organic rather than atomistic; see Gerrard, 1991). The emphasis then is on tolerant understanding of a range of different approaches without the capacity to form judgements as to which is closer to the truth. Another major influence was Fish (1980) who spawned the use of literary criticism of economic texts. The result was a proliferation of rhetorical analyses, notably collections of papers by economic methodologists under the headings of rhetoric (see McCloskey, 1986, and Klamer, McCloskey and Solow, eds, 1988), discourse (see Samuels, ed, 1990), language (see Henderson et al, eds, 1993) and hermeneutics (see Lavoie, ed, 1990).

This line of thinking was in many cases compatible with another major development in economic methodology: the application of post-modernism (see for example Doherty et al, eds, 1992). In its strong form, postmodernism set itself up in dualistic opposition to rationalism: in the social sciences, this involved the rejection of the assumption of a sovereign independent actor, the rejection of a correspondence theory of truth and the rejection of the idea of progress (ibid, pp. 14–20).[13] Postmodernism thus denied a role for prescriptive methodology, and rejected the notion of general laws or theories; by implication, it also involved a denial of the basis for humanism or government intervention. Like neo-Austrian theory, postmodernism rejected both the feasibility and usefulness of macroeconomic analysis. But the centred self of methodological individualism was incompatible with postmodernism: even the self was seen as fragmented so there were multiple subjective perceptions of reality on the part of each individual (see Amariglio, 1988). And yet there has been an active postmodern discourse within Marxism.

---

[12] See, for example, Caldwell and Coats (1984), Mirowski (1987) and the Symposium in the April, 1988 issue of *Economics and Philosophy*.

[13] See Chapter 4 on dualism, and Chick (1995) on rejection.

Postmodernism is difficult to grasp within conventional categories, which is not surprising since it deliberately eschews conventional categories. Some postmodernists have embraced the term 'nihilism' (see Amariglio and Ruccio, 1995) but this terminology is problematic. While a dictionary definition of nihilism is 'complete scepticism', Samuels (1993) clearly saw it differently, allowing for theorising and prediction. Taking postmodernism literally, it is not clear on what grounds theorising and prediction can be justified; what is required for further elucidation is further attempts (as in Amariglio and Ruccio, 1995) to apply postmodern principles to particular economic questions. As far as methodology is concerned, the forces for scepticism which spawned postmodernism have been influential in encouraging the move away from prescriptive methodology in the direction of denying methodology any prescriptive role at all.

These recent developments caused much discomfort by their apparent rejection of foundations for economic theorising and its appraisal.[14] In fact, intrinsic to these alternative approaches are ontological foundations. Rhetoric entails a description of actual economic theorising (see Mäki, 1988), hermeneutics entails a hermeneutic interpretation of actual economic practice (see Berger, 1989) and, although it denies a correspondence theory of truth, nevertheless postmodernism does seem to entail a belief in the fragmented nature of reality. McCloskey (1994) responded to charges of anti-foundationalism by being more explicit in offering a pragmatist criterion of appraisal (see Hoover, 1994, for a useful account of pragmatism): a theory is to be preferred which is accepted by an academic community, that is, which has proved to be most persuasive. However, the role of rhetorical analysis is to describe modes of persuasion, not to appraise them.

It might be argued that there is scope for cohesion between the hermeneutic approach and the version of critical rationalism which allows coverage of a range of approaches. This latter approach was advocated by Caldwell (1982, 1988 and 1990) in putting the case for methodologists to be pluralist. Thus, the role of methodologists as he saw it is to analyse each methodology in its own terms. Logically, pluralism must follow from a pluralist ontology (the view that nature is fragmented) as with postmodernism, and/or from a pluralist epistemology (the view

---

[14] See Backhouse's (1992a) critical review of what he terms constructivism, that is, rhetoric/postmodernism, from the traditional prescriptivist-methodology perspective, and the subsequent exchange between Backhouse (1992c) and Weintraub (1992).

that understanding is fragmented) as with the rhetoric approach (see Dow, 1997/Chapter 8). But then there are no foundations within mainstream economics for the critical analysis of methodology Caldwell advocates. Since mainstream economics takes a unitary view of nature and/or knowledge, there is no rationale for pluralism (see Chapter 13). A modified pluralist position requires the type of foundations provided by non-mainstream approaches to methodology, as noted in the penultimate section below; it is such foundations which Caldwell (1997) appeared to be espousing.

The purist (non-critical) pluralist position leads to the type of untenable position occupied by McCloskey's denial of a role for prescriptive methodology in prescriptive methodological terms; why should methodologists' analysis of theory not be methodology-laden in the same way that economists' analysis of facts is theory-laden? Certainly, at the methodological level, awareness of the importance of perspective is higher than at the level of theorising, but the whole import of the constructivist position is that a truly independent stance on anything is impossible.

By the 1980s, the state of mainstream economic methodology in general therefore reflected a polarisation of positions on the role of methodology. The 'old guard' traditionalists continued to see methodology's role as being prescriptive of good scientific practice ('Methodology' with a capital 'm'). The 'new guard' denied that role and concentrated on using the methodological perspective as a means of describing the methodology implicit in economic theorising ('methodology' with a small 'm'). Yet neither position appeared ultimately to be tenable. The inadequacies of the range of prescriptions on offer are well rehearsed, while the descriptive pluralist approach was turning methodology into a version of history of thought (see Weintraub, 1989). The discomfort with this polarisation was evident in much of the subsequent literature. Caldwell (1989), like others, introduced extra-paradigmatic criteria by which to appraise methodologies within a framework of critical rationalism in Caldwell (1991a), as did Redman (1991); thus nihilism was avoided in methodological practice. Redman (1991, p. 173) defined critical rationalism as espousing 'tolerance, honesty, commitment to the advance of science above personal advance and to the freedom to exercise criticism, a willingness to listen and learn from others, and so on'. This definition captured all that is good and civilised in the constructivist approach. But at the same time, it did reintroduce the traditional notion of the advance of science. This brought thinking back to the old questions of how to promote that advance, and how to recognise it when it occurs, questions quite contrary to the perspective of constructivism.

In the past, methodology could be understood as an irresolvable debate between the two untenable methodological positions of deductivism and inductivism. By the 1980s, it was taken up with the irresolvable debate between the meta-methodological positions of prescription and description. Both stemmed from a dualistic mode of thought; the only possible escape lay in stepping outside this mode of thought. Much of the move to descriptivism was very constructive. It yielded a range of conclusions over which there was a broad consensus.[15] Yet it was becoming apparent that descriptivism could only be taken so far; it was indeed impossible to sustain without the introduction of some prescriptive element.

Clearly, there was much scope for further descriptive work (as the next section's attempt at describing mainstream methodology illustrates). Boland (1989), Gerrard (1990) and de Marchi (1991) saw prescription as coming out of detailed study of actual economic practice. Mäki (1990) saw a role for prescriptive methodology but elsewhere in his work implied that the move to prescription was not currently on the horizon. Nor did critical rationalism in itself map out the path to such progress. Indeed, as long as the discussion of standards used the same framework as traditional methodology, methodology would be in an *impasse*. The solution offered by critical rationalism required a perspective other than that of logical empiricism on the key related concepts of rationality and epistemology (the advance of science). Elements of prescription gradually resurfaced in the methodology literature, given the limitations of the descriptive approach (see further Chapters 8, 10). In the meantime, developments in methodology outside the mainstream offered constructive possibilities which we will explore in the penultimate section. These possibilities could satisfy the need evident from much of current methodological writing for a discussion of standards which recognises that facts are theory-laden, and that theories are paradigm-laden, yet still requires theorists to persist in a search for some form of (unattainable) truth.

First, however, we turn to consider methodological practice in mainstream economics, and how it accords with developments in methodological thinking. In the process, we will explore some of the major issues: the relationship between theory and empirical work, the axioms of rational individual behaviour and developments in econometrics.

---

[15] See for example Hands's (1990) listing of 13 descriptive points of agreement.

We shall see that economic theory was also infected by discomfort with an untenable dualism.

Methodology implicit in mainstream economics

Identifying mainstream methodology used in practice is made rather difficult by the belief (usually implicit) that methodological discussion is inadmissible. One of the most explicit statements comes from Hahn (1992), in which he argued that economists are not equipped for discussing methodology, that it makes little difference to economic practice and any effect it does have is unhelpful. Of course, as Backhouse (1992b) points out, this in itself constitutes a methodological statement; indeed, Lawson (1992) points out that Hahn's economics represents a methodological position whether he acknowledges it or not.

This marked reluctance to discuss methodology mirrored the anti-Methodology position of the 'new guard' methodologists. However, if reference was ever made by practising economists to this position, it was a matter of *ex post* justification rather than *ex ante* influence. In other words, given the lack of attention to methodological discussion, the anti-methodology position among practising economists must have another explanation. Lawson (1994a) argued that this position is intrinsic to the methodology implicit in mainstream economics. He argued that mainstream economics was still dominated by a positivism which appraises theories by predictive success. Because positivism entails a belief that empirical success is sufficient to establish closeness to the truth, there is no need for methodological discussion. Boland (1991) made a similar point when he argued that mainstream economics had not, unlike the philosophy of science, gone beyond positivism; rather it had accepted so wholeheartedly Samuelson's conventionalist version of positivism that there was no perceived need to discuss the matter further.

But while Boland and Lawson identified the dominant methodology of mainstream economics as being positivist, Blaug (1980) and McCloskey (1983) argued that actual practice departed from the positivist rhetoric. There was certainly a shift (noted for example, by Boland, 1991, and Mayer, 1993) in the priority given to deductivism over empirical testing: by the 1990s, the emphasis within logical empiricism was more on the 'logical' than on the 'empiricism'. But this shift took the form of a shift in the relative power exercised in the profession by pure theorists relative to empiricists, with a growing gulf emerging between the two groups. The existence of such a gulf can be understood as an outgrowth of logical empiricism driven by a search for certainty (which mirrors the appeal to methodological certainty of Popper's falsificationism). Because empirical work lacked a watertight logic (given the impracticalities of falsificationism), the search for truth seemed to be more satisfactorily addressed within closed deductive mathematical systems. Thus, the internally generated principles of mainstream theory construction flowered in the vacuum left by traditional methodology, which was caught up with the difficulties of empirical theory appraisal. 'In principle' pure theory was perceived to be testable, but theory was not constructed with testing in mind. The few attempts explicitly to refer to positivist methodological principles accordingly appeared tortuous (see Stiglitz, 1991, p. 136).

The special centenary issue of the *Economic Journal* was particularly welcome because it provided an array of methodological statements from leading mainstream economics. Some reveal parallels with 'new guard' methodology. Reflecting postmodernist discussion, several contributors identify a fragmentation in mainstream economics. Hahn (1991) and Malinvaud (1991) saw the fragmentation as arising from a discrediting of the notions both of the natural order of markets and of beneficial public action. According to them, mainstream analysis needed to become more context-specific; in other words, the trend towards fragmentation was to be welcomed. The consequent injunction (from Hahn, 1991, and Fishburn, 1991) was to retreat from axiomatisation.

Pencavel (1991) saw a fragmentation in the polarisation in practice between pure theory and empirical work. While pure theory was deductivist, based on the axioms of deterministic rational economic behaviour, empirical work was increasingly inductivist, as what Johnston (1991) calls the Minnesota Agnostics employed econometric techniques deliberately designed to be atheoretical. This theoretical agnosticism paralleled developments in the methodology field which shed doubt on the scope of general theories. Classical econometrics, after all, was designed to seek confirmation of stable equilibrium relationships (see Johnston, 1991; Morgan, 1988) whose relevance was now open to question according to several contributors to the *Economic Journal* volume. Mayer (1993) argued that empirical science theory, as he called applied theory, should be subject to different methodological criteria from pure theory; the balance had shifted too far in favour of formalism because it was, he argued, formalist criteria which have been universally applied. In particular, empirical science theory should be more client-oriented, a suggestion which would tend to increase the polarisation between theory and empirical work which Pencavel lamented. Thus, not only was the field of econometrics itself fragmented (see Pagan's, 1987 survey), but also there was a fragmentation between theory and empirical work which some were happy to welcome.

Gerrard (1995) argued that Hendry's approach to econometrics represented the best available attempt at empirical testing of theory, that is, of bridging the gulf between theory and empirical work. While Hendry's approach to econometrics, like that of the Minnesota Agnostics, was one of 'letting the data speak for themselves', in the sense of avoiding as far as possible theoretical priors when approaching data (see Hendry and Doornik, 1994), the aim of empirical work was nevertheless seen as theory specification. This approach represented an attempt to recapture the coordination between theory and empirical work which broke down in the 1940s (see Morgan, 1990). To the extent that mainstream economics had a unitary ontology and epistemology (such that 'data' offered an objective foundation for theory), the approach was probably the best alternative to falsificationism available. Yet since there was no necessary requirement for the data to throw up theories which could then be explained in terms of the rationality axioms, the potential for significant fragmentation remained between empirical work and the theorising in which most mainstream economists were engaged.

Others did not share this fragmentist interpretation, seeing rather an underlying unity in mainstream economics. Pencavel (1991) and Turnovsky (1991) identified a fragmentation arising from increased specialisation; they did, however, perceive an underlying unity stemming from shared methodological principles *which they did not specify*. Others identified a (unifying) trend of an overextension of mathematical formalism (see for example Baumol, 1991, and Friedman, 1991). Wren-Lewis (1992) argued that axiomatisation had been increasing its hold (notably on an area which had long resisted it: macroeconomic modelling). This had been facilitated by an increased recourse to simulation exercises, rather than testing with actual data. Contrary to Mayer's client-driven criteria for applied work, Wren-Lewis lamented that it had been the short-term requirements of clients for forecasting that had made macro modelling still fall short on formalist criteria. Meanwhile, the new descriptive methodology had yielded arguments in favour of the unified-mainstream-economics view. Lakatosians like Weintraub (1985a) saw an overriding unity between pure theory, which focused on the hard core of mainstream economics, and applied theory, which accounted for the evolution of the protective belt. Hausman (1992) too saw the requirements of equilibrium theorising as a unifying (if limiting) force; but he was careful to emphasise 'equilibrium' as the unifying force, not 'general equilibrium'. Similarly, Backhouse (1993) saw unity in a neo-Walrasian research programme, with general equilibrium only part of the protective belt. The nature and foundations of the unity were accordingly being thrown into increasing doubt.

Central to the question of formalisation is the role of the rationality axioms. The internal goal, derived from a particular form of mathematics, of developing a closed axiomatic mathematically expressed theoretical system which yielded equilibrium solutions required reductionist axioms of deterministic individual behaviour. The notion of optimising atomistic agents with full knowledge, rational according to a particular definition (as specified in Weintraub's, 1985a, depiction of the hard core of neoclassical economics) had been the subject of much debate, not least on the grounds of it being unrealistic (see for example, Hargraves-Heap, 1989). But the alternatives sought within mainstream theory were forced into determinism and quantifiable probabilistic knowledge in order to generate equilibrium solutions (see for example Hey, 1993). Thus, while game theory did not replicate the axioms of more traditional theory, it entailed the same essential features: the presumption of rationality (in the narrow sense employed elsewhere in mainstream economics), prior beliefs taken as given, no attention to the equilibrating process and a lack of attention to non-formalisable elements (see Binmore, 1987). The fact that the internalist criteria entailed in a closed axiomatic system are only rarely made explicit did not in any way limit their power.

The challenge to the rationality axioms came most forcefully from the contrary empirical evidence arising from the decision-making-under-uncertainty project, which used experimental techniques. Several of the contributors to the *Economic Journal* issue saw this work as defining the future of mainstream microeconomics.[16] Support for this approach was also evident in Gerrard, ed. (1993) and Hausman (1992). Implicit in this view was the hope that the project would yield more sophisticated rationality axioms which would therefore provide a more realistic foundation for mainstream theory. However, also implicit was the notion that experiments could replicate the essentials of real situations, a notion which had traditionally been denied when economists have compared economics with the physical sciences. This fundamental reversal had not been addressed head-on; the observer was left with the impression that empirical testing of theoretical propositions, following

---

[16] See for example Buchanan (1991), Fishburn (1991), Hahn (1991), Roth (1991), Schmalansee (1991) and Stiglitz (1991).

physics, had been found wanting, but that mathematics had not ful-filled its promise as an alternative, so the only course left open for those wishing to model economics on other more 'scientific' fields was to try experiments.[17]

But, as Hausman (1992) argued, economists could not hope to model individual behaviour adequately without opening analysis up to other disciplines; mainstream economics had created difficulties for itself by insisting on its separateness. Indeed, the need for openness to other disci-plines was noted by some contributors to the centenary *Economic Journal* volume (see for example, Malinvaud, 1991, and Stiglitz, 1991); Baumol (1991) added a plea for greater attention to economic history and institu-tions. Similarly, Morishima (1992, p. 203) advocated 'a multi-disciplinary systems analysis in which ... economic theory ..., history, sociology, psy-chology .... are ... used [to construct] a satisfactory empirical model of the system.' At the same time, Baumol (1991) argued for eclecticism (or pluralism of method, without any apparent methodological underpin-nings), while Hahn (1991) and Malinvaud (1991) argued for a retreat from axiomatisation into context-specific analysis. Putting these arguments together, we see a denial of the fundamental principles of mainstream theory construction, that is, the principles of axiomatic, closed-system, mathematically expressed theory which yields equilibrium solutions. Yet it was this fundamental commitment to equilibrium theorising which Hausman (1992) identified as the core of the coherence of mainstream theory. The range of developments which had been advocated would rep-resent a radical departure from this core, with no alternative methodo-logical foundation specified. Either that, or the intention was innocuous, to seek ever-more-sophisticated mathematical systems which enveloped other disciplines, history, institutions and different contexts along the same lines as existing mainstream theory. But no justification was pro-vided for believing that such a project was feasible.

Tensions had thus been identified in both the logical and the empiri-cist ends of logical empiricism, and not least between them. No satis-factory analysis seemed to have been offered to explain how empirical results were to be incorporated in pure theory, or how agnosticism in empirical work might assist this process. The experimental work on decision-making was an exception as it was directed at the truth value of the rationality axioms, but much of its value was dependent on the

---

[17] The increasing importance of experimental economics has encouraged methodological analysis, as in the June 2005 issue of the *Journal of Economic Methodology*.

(contested) preconception that rational behaviour under uncertainty could be formalised. Meanwhile, axiomatisation was increasing its grip just as pure theorists had been realising the limitations of a universally applied set of axioms referring exclusively to deterministic economic behaviour. Perhaps Hahn (1991, p. 49) provided the answer when he wrote: 'one often encounters increased orthodoxy amongst some just when religion is on the decline'.

The picture that emerged was thus one of serious methodological fragmentation in mainstream economics. Theorists, experimentalists and empiricists were all pulling in different directions, while hopes were expressed for developments which would fundamentally alter the methodological foundation of mainstream economics. What is more, this situation arose in a vacuum as far as methodological discussion was concerned. Methodological pronouncements seemed to be reserved for (negative) appraisal of non-mainstream theory, something which could perhaps best be analysed in terms of the sociological approach to methodology (see Backhouse, 1994, pp. 11–2).

By the 1980s, it was conventional to think of mainstream economics as being in a state of crisis. By the 1990s, such talk was rejected. Bleaney (1991, p. 145), for example, started an overview of emerging theory as follows: 'One of the characteristics – perhaps in retrospect it will be viewed as the chief characteristic – of theoretical economics over the past decade has been the cooling of controversy and a gradual re-establishment of some form of consensus in the profession for the first time since the mid-1960s'. This alarming lack of concern with the tensions identified above must have stemmed at least in part from the same thinking which spawned the rhetoric/postmodernism literature; once postmodernism legitimised fragmentation and paradox, the whole notion of crisis lost its meaning.

In order to form a view as to whether such a position was sustainable, we take an excursion in the next section into the broad cultural/intellectual environment in which both methodology and economics itself have evolved.

Methodology and the spirit of the age

We have now seen broad developments of thinking in economic methodology and in mainstream economics which had much in common, although mainstream economists made scant reference to methodology. It is reasonable to conjecture that both theory and methodology reflected trends in the thought of society in general.

Just as the Enlightenment of the eighteenth century involved a challenge to the authority of religious dogma, and the 1920s saw a challenge to authority born out of the disillusioning experience of the First World War, so the 1960s was a period of challenge to authority in its various forms. All three were periods of significant change in perception of the nature and role of scientific knowledge. The work first of Popper, then of Kuhn and Feyerabend challenged the capacity of science to identify truth, and appealed to the growing popular sentiment in the 1960s that different sociological, political or racial groups legitimately held different perceptions of the truth. The work of Kuhn and Feyerabend further challenged the role of methodology as setting universal rules for good scientific practice.

These challenges met with resistance, and we can see much of the controversy in economic methodology in terms of such a conflict. Yet the conflict took on a particular character from a key feature of the old orthodoxy: dualism, the practice of thinking in terms of mutually exclusive, all embracing categories with fixed meanings (see Chapter 4). Out of the original 1960s perception of different understandings of the truth (but an attendant eagerness to discover and proclaim one's version of the truth) arose the dual of one-truth/no-truth. As with all dualistic categorisations, this position involves a paradox which ultimately makes it untenable as a general (rather than partial) principle. The cultural manifestation of the 'no truth' position arose out of the perception of cultural pluralism: the notion of 'political correctness' which outlaws commentary on any sociological, political, racial or gender group other than one's own. It is an intolerant imposition of the principle of tolerance. The same trend may be found in the philosophy of science. Influenced by Rorty's challenge to the notion that philosophy mirrors nature, the study of rhetoric had set itself up as an alternative to methodology, as a study of how scientists persuade rather than as an appraiser of science. Further, influenced by Derrida's and Lyotard's challenge to modernism, postmodernism denied the validity of theory and thus of knowledge. Both approaches denied the possibility of identifying truth of any kind, and they were adamant in their attempts to persuade that this is correct. There was a shift to the view that the nature of the world and of knowledge is such that it is impossible to identify absolute truth categorically; we can only understand the world as an open system. However, this epistemological shift was addressed with the tools of the old dualistic epistemology which was designed for a closed-system understanding of reality (see further Chapter 11).

The untenability of this position was beginning to make itself felt in attempts to generate knowledge in new ways more apt for open systems; such attempts required a presumption that knowledge of some sort was attainable. There was a growing literature in the physical sciences and mathematics which developed non-dualistic notions of scientific knowledge. An example is Prigogine and Stenger's (1984) notion of open, self-organising systems. Out of what would traditionally be regarded as the dualistic categories of chaos and order, Prigogine and Stenger showed not only that chaos may come out of order, but also that order may come out of chaos; it is the interconnecting processes, not dualistic states, which are the appropriate focus of attention. From this, Chick identified a change in the epistemology of science, suggesting 'that man is undergoing a rapid phase of evolution of his/her *consciousness* and that the manifestation of conflict between schools of thought is actually a clash between different forms of psychic organization, coexisting in a transition' (Chick, 1995, p. 35, emphasis in original). In mathematics, it was evident in the growing interest in the notion of fuzzy sets as a way of grounding knowledge within open systems on a different logic from classical logic.[18]

These developments in ways of thinking can perhaps be understood as a dialectical process.[19] In these terms, the thesis of modernism, with its claims to absolute truth, was challenged by the antithesis of rhetoric and postmodernism with their denial of any truth. In the 1990s, we were potentially in transition to a synthesis consisting of new ways of generating knowledge which aim to identify a version of the truth, while admitting the impossibility of identifying absolute truth on the one hand but asserting the feasibility of different versions of the truth on the other.

The continuing inattention to methodology in mainstream economics indicated a total lack of preparedness for this way of thinking; thoughtful mainstream economists had perceived its necessity, but impeded its development by discouraging methodological discussion. There are, however, methodological positions which represent an attempt to provide guidance in the search for truth, while recognising the limitations on knowledge, and which have been applied extensively to economic issues. An important example is based on Keynes's philosophical work,

---

[18] See Dubois and Prade (1980) for an early survey of the mathematical literature. See Dow and Ghosh (2009) for an application to economics.

[19] Klamer (1988, p. 37) uses the expression 'dialectical moment' to characterise the focus on rhetoric.

subsequently applied to economics. Similarly, various forms of political economy are identified by their realist methodology: critical realism represents one important attempt to develop an open-system philosophy of science. In the next section, we explore some of these possibilities briefly; the intention is not to provide a complete account of non-mainstream methodological approaches, but rather to demonstrate that the tensions so far identified on the methodology of mainstream economics are amenable to solutions.

Alternative methodologies

The coverage of methodological thinking above is partial; it refers only to what may be termed mainstream methodology. Yet in addition, there has been a rich literature in methodology outside the mainstream. This literature is distinguished by its integration with theory. Indeed, methodological awareness has been a distinguishing feature of non-mainstream economics because it is most clearly on methodological grounds that these approaches differ from the mainstream. Thus, methodological analysis was integral to the work of key non-mainstream figures like Hayek, Keynes, Robinson and Kaldor. Indeed, Robinson's first publication, in 1932, which she returned to in later years (see Robinson, 1979, p. 110), dealt with methodological issues. In this piece, she warned against the dangers of being 'too rude' (asserting truth along the lines of the 'old guard' methodology) and being 'too polite' (along the lines of the 'new guard'); with neither approach could argument proceed. Further, the view of these key figures did not entail the same dichotomisation between descriptivism and prescriptivism as mainstream methodology. Their methodological perspective entailed description of differences from mainstream methodology on the one hand, as a basis for prescribing their alternative methodologies on the other. Thus the prescription of standards was offered in the recognition that these standards could not be claimed to apply with absolute authority; other schools of thought have their own sets of standards.

If any modern search for standards is not to revert to traditional methodology with all its problems, then a new logic is required which can deal with open theoretical systems. (Closed theoretical systems inevitably generate absolute standards.) Such a system is provided by Keynes's philosophy; analysis of this system and its implications for modern economics constitute one of the major developments in non-mainstream methodology. Another major development is the critical realist approach which fits well with Keynes's philosophy, but which puts the arguments in a rather different way. In this section, we will briefly explore both of these areas as examples of how economics could escape from its dualistic approach to methodology. At the same time, this alternative methodology would provide a solution to much of the tensions of mainstream economics, but at the expense of some of the elements which have unified it in the past.

Keynes's (1921) philosophy was designed to address the problem of induction: given the limited scope for empirical proof of propositions, what can (and does) provide rational grounds for belief, as a basis for action? Certain knowledge is either tautological (that is, based on internal logic) or it is based on observation of replicable events. But most knowledge of social systems is uncertain, because they can only be understood as open systems. Logical certainty is limited because in open systems the full range of relevant variables is not known; empirical certainty is limited because in open systems evolutionary processes and discontinuities limit the incidence of replicable events. Belief under uncertainty is grounded in such evidence as is available and recognised as relevant given theoretical understanding; beyond that, recourse is made to conventional knowledge. This understanding applies to economic agents, but also to theorists. Thus, while economic and theoretical knowledge is inevitably generally uncertain, it is open to reasoned justification, and also to amendment as new evidence and new circumstances emerge. Open system logic thus provides the grounding for critical rationalism which avoids the danger of prescriptivism on the one hand, and of descriptivism on the other. It provides the basis for a range of types of theorising, since none can possibly be complete, but also the basis for argument as to which are the preferred types. Further, it provides the basis for an understanding of an economy as basically stable but with inbuilt potential for instability. The nature and implications for economics of Keynes's 'ordinary logic' are the subject matter of substantial literature.[20]

The critical realist literature too provides foundations for a version of critical rationalism founded on a different logic from the classical logic of closed-system analysis.[21] Just as Keynes's starting point was an ontological position which determined his epistemology, methodology and

---

[20] See Lawson and Pesaran, eds (1985), Carabelli (1988), Fitzgibbons (1988), O'Donnell (1989 and ed., 1991), Bateman and Davis, eds (1991), Gerrard and Hillard, eds (1992) and Dow and Hillard, eds (1995). See more recently, Runde and Mizuhara, eds (2003).

[21] The connections with Keynes have been explicitly drawn by Lawson (1995b).

theory – that social systems are organic rather than atomistic – so critical realism stresses the requirement to ground all epistemology, methodology and theory in an ontology. Specifically, it is argued that observed reality is generated by underlying structures and processes and that it should be the purpose of science to identify these structures and processes. However, because these structures and processes are organic, our knowledge of them is inevitably incomplete; reality can only be understood as an open system, so there is scope for a range of understandings. But each understanding can be discussed rationally in relation to perceptions of the underlying structures and processes. The logic is thus fundamentally different from that of mainstream economics, which is geared to identifying empirically, or formalising mathematically, event regularities along logical positivist lines. Like the Keynes philosophy literature, the critical realist literature is substantial.[22]

According both to Keynes's approach and to the critical realist approach, methodological awareness is crucial, but it does not go far enough – even more crucial is ontological and epistemological awareness. Thus, the trend in mainstream methodology in the 1990s towards studying economic practice in the hope that some prescriptive possibilities would emerge was inadequate and a more balanced approach to methodology was accordingly emerging. Open-mindedness on theoretical possibilities needed to be accompanied by alertness to evidence of particular ontological and epistemological positions. Methodologists cannot escape their own ontological and epistemological positions. But just as mainstream economists may ignore theoretical possibilities through lack of methodological awareness, so methodologists may unwittingly ignore methodological possibilities through lack of ontological and epistemological awareness.

Conclusion

The mainstream field of methodology was by the 1990s at a crucial stage, having veered from one untenable position of prescribing positivism to the equally untenable position of denying any prescriptive role whatsoever. This was mirrored by the tensions in the practice of mainstream economics. Mirroring the prescriptive methodology approach was the ever-present grip of axiomatisation. Mirroring the descriptive approach was an apparent fragmentation of theory away from the unified-system approach and the development of theory-less empiricism.

---

[22] See for example, Lawson (1994b, 1995a, 1995b) and Pratten (1993).

This disarray was united by lip service to logical empiricism and a denial of the value of methodological discussion. It was this last which threatened to impede the evolution of a synthesis which transcended the dualisms of mainstream methodology. Without such a synthesis, the future of mainstream economics was vulnerable; only if the more general move away from postmodernism in science and society permeated mainstream economics in time would the potential for crisis even be perceived.[23]

The dearth of methodological discussion in mainstream economics allowed a gulf to emerge between professed methodology and practised methodology. Thus, analysis of the actual practice of many mainstream economists revealed in many cases recourse to knowledge outside the strict bounds of the formal theoretical system. This has been a particular contribution of McCloskey's (1986) work. Economists live in a world which we can only understand as an open system and so habits of thought have evolved in order to deal with open systems. Yet progress cannot be made until the relevant methodological issues are addressed directly.

This brings us back to the initial question of the role of the field of methodology. The first role of methodology in the present context is to increase methodological awareness; this was a task well addressed by the descriptive methodology in vogue since the 1990s. But methodologists cannot be persuasive that methodological awareness is useful unless some explicit prescriptive element enters into the discussion. This inevitably raises further questions. Gordon (1991), for example, argued for logical coherence, and good standards in gathering facts, both on the face of them laudable goals. But then, which type of logic did he mean, and how do we deal with the theory-ladenness of facts? Gordon's standards, or Redman's standards of critical rationalism noted above, are no more absolute than anyone else's. But progress can be made by discourse over the questions such expressions of standards raise. Worldview cannot be eradicated, no matter how high the level of discourse; but that does not rule out discussion and communication, just as social/racial/gender difference does not rule out discussion and communication. The problem for mainstream economics is if such discourse is ruled out in mainstream circles.

---

[23] Recent experience has shown that reality also has the potential to break through to challenge economic theory. Just as there is an impetus to change theory in the light of the crisis, so methodologists are more forthcoming with arguments in favour of methodological change; see the 'Financial Crisis symposium' in the December 2010 issue of the *Journal of Economic Methodology*, for example.

8
Methodological Pluralism and Pluralism of Method

> *There has been increasing support in various quarters for pluralism of some sort and indeed this volume contains an argument particularly for methodological pluralism. But the meaning of pluralism differs partly due to difference in underlying framework and partly in terms of the level to which it refers. This chapter aims to unravel some of the resulting confusion. In particular, while an economist may adopt a pluralist methodology (using a particular variety of methods), it would be incoherent to think in terms of adopting a variety of methodologies simultaneously. Methodological pluralism is instead recognition and understanding of other methodologies than one's own preferred methodology. Different approaches to economics are categorised here according to their attitudes to pluralism at different levels.*

Introduction

Pluralism is the philosophical position that the ultimate reality of the universe consists of a plurality of entities; it is an ontological position. But the concept of pluralism can be applied at a variety of levels: to the (epistemological) understanding of reality (whether its ultimate nature is a plurality or not), to the methods employed to theorise about that understanding of reality, to the methodology which sets the criteria for theory choice and to the study of methodologies themselves. Pluralism has been advocated at all of these levels in economics discourse. Yet

The original version of this chapter was published in A. Salanti and E. Screpanti (eds), *Pluralism in Economics: Theory, History and Methodology* (Cheltenham: Edward Elgar), 1997, pp. 89–99.

an understanding of what is entailed by methodological pluralism and pluralism of method has been hampered by lack of reference to epistemological and ontological foundations. In particular, pluralism takes on a different meaning in a closed-system mode of thought (as in mainstream economics) from its meaning in an open-system mode of thought (as in Post-Keynesian economics or institutional/evolutionary economics). The former can be thought of as 'pure pluralism', as the dual of a monist position, while the latter involves a more limited, although crucial, pluralism.

It is the purpose of this chapter to attempt to distinguish pluralism at the different levels and according to different ontological and epistemological positions, and to assess whether the validity of the pluralist position differs as between these different levels. It is concluded that a pure pluralist position is untenable at any level, but that a modified methodological pluralism is to be welcomed if grounded in a corresponding ontological and epistemic position, that is, that reality and knowledge of it are understood as open systems.

Open and closed systems

Much of the following argument rests on the distinction between open and closed systems. Therefore, before considering pluralism as such, we consider first the nature of that distinction (see further Chapter 11). An open system is one whose boundaries are not predetermined. Further, the nature and range of its constituent variables and the structure of their interrelationships are not predetermined. This is not a matter of stochastic variation. In contrast, the boundaries of a closed system are predetermined, as are the full range of constituent variables and the structure of their interrelationships. This does not preclude the possibility of stochastic variation. While closed systems are the province of classical logic, open systems are the province of a broader system of logic – ordinary logic, or human logic, as exemplified by Keynes (1921). While including classical logic as a special case for application under conditions of certainty, ordinary logic can also be applied to conditions of uncertainty, as they pertain in open systems.

At the ontological level, the system is one of real processes and phenomena. An understanding of reality as conforming to an open system may involve notions of human creativity and freedom of choice, for example. A closed-system understanding of reality may involve the notion of a grand plan on the part of the deity and the absence of free will. Knowledge systems applied to this reality may be open or closed in either case. On the face of it, it might seem that an open-system ontology would entail an open-system epistemology, and similarly for a closed-system ontology. However, even if reality is an open system, it can be argued that knowledge can only be acquired by proceeding as if reality were a closed system.[1] Alternatively, even if reality is a closed system, it can be argued that human knowledge inevitably cannot encompass the full system, so that it must itself conform to an open system.

General equilibrium theorising is a fine example of a closed-system theoretical structure. Variables are clearly defined with fixed meaning, and the boundaries of the system are well defined according to which variables are endogenous and which are exogenous. The aim is to reach agreement on the best representation of the structural relationships between variables, for universal application. This entails conformity of representation through formalism. The appraisal criterion of conformity to the principles of classical logic reflects a closed-system epistemology. Where the additional criterion is applied of goodness of fit in econometric testing, a closed-system ontology is evident.

If reality is an open system, then any closed theoretical system can only have partial application. Formal systems are necessarily closed, since it is necessary to give variables fixed meaning, and to specify structural relationships and the exogenous variables. Other methods, however, can themselves be open; verbal analysis in particular allows for shades of meaning.

Once we move away from a closed-system ontology and/or a closed-system epistemology, the question of pluralism – its meaning and role – becomes interesting. If reality is an open system, how do we specify open systems of knowledge and what role can closed subsystems of knowledge play? If knowledge is open (even if reality is closed), how do we choose the forms of (inevitably partial) knowledge to aim for? In what follows, we attempt to unravel the different possible senses of pluralism and how they relate to different ontological and epistemological positions.

In order to assist the process of clarification, Table 8.1 offers a highly simplified account of three positions: a monist closed-system ontology as the basis for a monist closed-system epistemology, pure pluralism and a modified pluralist open-system ontology as the basis for a modified pluralist open-system epistemology. The corresponding positions of each at the levels of methodology and method are also shown. These various positions will be explained below.

---

[1] However, Lawson (1997a) develops the argument that this is an incoherent approach.

Table 8.1   Pluralism in economics

Level	Pure monism	Pure pluralism	Modified pluralism
Ontology *(vision of reality)*	Unifying forces in nature; reality a closed system.	Nature is fragmented: open but not systemic. Or deny ontology altogether.	Range of understandings of reality as an open system, corresponding to schools of thought.
Epistemology *(theory of knowledge)*	Identify laws using objective facts and fixed meanings of terms	No means of comparing understandings; no regularities so no schools of thought.	Open system of knowledge Aim is to identify causal mechanisms rather than laws.
Methodology *(role of the methodologist)*	Prescriptive: identify best way of gathering knowledge.	Descriptive or no role	Critically analyse a limited range of methodologies, associated with different schools of thought.
Method/practice *(actual methodology employed)*	Deductivist: formal math. + empirical testing	Nothing to say since no methodological discussion	Range of methods corresponding to particular ontology

Ontological pluralism

Pluralism at the ontological level involves the belief that reality constitutes a plurality of entities. If this position is to be non-trivial, it involves a rejection of the notion of the unity of nature. In its pure form, ontological pluralism denies the existence of unifying forces in nature; if nature is pluralistic, then there is no scope for general theorising. In economics, this position is most closely associated with postmodernism; postmodernism emphasises fragmentation, even of the self (see Amariglio, 1988). Ontological pluralism entails epistemic pluralism (understanding is fragmented). Together these pluralisms deny any scope for theory (see Amariglio, 1990); indeed some postmodernists have embraced the term 'nihilism' (see Amariglio and Ruccio, 1995), the term with which Gordon (1991) chose to characterise pluralism. Similarly, they have denied any role for methodology.

Yet the content of postmodernism belies these implications; general statements are made about reality, theories are put forward and methodological statements are made. In other words, pure ontological pluralism and its implications are untenable; any theoretical statement requires the belief in some regularity in understanding and/or in nature. The only possibilities then, if discourse is to occur at all, is a modified pluralism (partial regularities), or the belief in universal regularities. Many non-mainstream economists, other than postmodernists, hold a modified pluralist position, based on an organicist ontology.[2] This position holds that there are regularities in nature which science should aim to identify, but that these regularities are of process rather than events (see Lawson, 1989b, 1995b); they cannot be isolated from evolutionary or other irregularities. The economy, like knowledge, is therefore best understood as an open system.

Mainstream economics, on the other hand, has traditionally seen its scope as being defined by universal regularities which can be separated dualistically from irregularities and which are best understood within a closed theoretical system. Most mainstream economists, notably deductivists, are not explicit about their ontological position. But Lawson (1994a) demonstrated that the view of science on which deductivism is based entails what he refers to as a 'Humean' ontology[3] in terms of event regularities.

How far regularities can be perceived, if they exist, is an epistemic issue. We shall see in the next section that epistemic pluralism is not the sole preserve of ontological pluralists.

Epistemic pluralism

Epistemic pluralism entails a plurality of understandings of reality; there is no known way of establishing what constitutes true knowledge. Logical positivism requires that theory be appraised with reference to an independent set of facts, implying that there is only one way in which (correctly) to know facts. Logical positivism came under serious threat in the 1960s, a period in which the notion that authority had sole access to the truth was fundamentally questioned. In the philosophy of science, Popper's (1959) fallibilism had laid the groundwork, but it was Kuhn (1962) who captured the imagination with his argument that understanding is paradigm-specific; what appears to be contrary evidence may not be perceived as such if it threatens the power of the dominant paradigm.

---

[2] See, for example, Carabelli's (1995) account of Keynes's organicism.
[3] Dow (1992) challenged this interpretation of Hume.

Out of this change developed a distinctive perspective on understanding; this perspective is evident both in the rhetoric/hermeneutic approach as well as in postmodernism. Both take a pluralist position on understanding. The postmodernist epistemic pluralism follows directly from the postmodern pluralist ontology; even the individual has the potential for a plurality of understanding. The rhetoric/hermeneutic approach was inspired by Rorty's (1979) view that philosophy cannot mirror nature; no position is taken on whether ultimate reality is a plurality or not.[4] Rather, understanding of reality is expressed by means of a plurality of narratives. Thus, not only is reality discussed by means of a plurality of narratives, but also reality itself is to be read as a plurality of narratives (see Lavoie, 1990, Introduction, and Brown, 1994). There is no basis for choosing one narrative over another.

The logical positivist belief in a unitary objective understanding of facts nevertheless has persisted in much of economics (see Boland, 1991 and Lawson, 1994a). The difficulty of devising definitive empirical tests threw increasing doubt on the truth-value of theory (see Boland, 1989, p. 88), but in general the truth-value of the facts themselves was not questioned among mainstream economists. For the increasingly dominant deductivists, questions over the truth value of facts was seen as having relevance only regarding axioms and these are asserted to be self-evidently true. A significant exception was the explicitly pluralist epistemic position taken by Weintraub (1989); his position has shifted from being Lakatosian (which as a basis for theory appraisal requires a unitary set of facts) to denying the scope for theory appraisal on the grounds that facts are theory-laden, that is, there is a plurality of understanding of reality.

Epistemologically, there should be a direct parallel between a pluralist understanding (possibly of a pluralist reality) among economic agents and economists alike. This is the case for postmodernists and the rhetoric approach; there is no basis for choosing between understandings among agents or among economists. In contrast, the logical positivist position entails a unitary understanding of facts by agents and a corresponding unitary understanding by economists (though both may be expressed probabilistically). Curiously, no such parallel is evident in Weintraub's work; if facts are theory-laden for economists, surely they must also be theory-laden for agents. An acceptance of this point would have profound implications for mainstream theorising. It

---

[4] See the exchange between Mäki's (1988) attempt to tease out an ontology of rhetoric, and McCloskey's (1988) reply.

is the plurality of understanding (or framing) by economic agents, in the postmodern view, which undermines theorising in general. Non-mainstream economists other than employers of postmodernism and the rhetoric approach (Post-Keynesians, or institutionalist/ evolutionary economists, for example) employ an open-system epistemology which allows for a range of understandings but also for theorising. Following directly from an organicist ontology, or from the view that human understanding of reality (whether ultimately organicist or not) is necessarily limited, it is argued that we can only understand reality as an open, organic system. Keynes's (1921) philosophy provides an epistemology for open organic systems; since knowledge in general is based on imperfect knowledge, it is inevitable that there will be a range of understandings of reality, among agents as well as economists. However, this epistemology differs from pure pluralism in that there are regularities in the knowledge-generation process of agents and economists which limit the range of rational beliefs; the choice of belief (among agents and economists) is a matter for rational debate.

We now see how these different epistemologies feed through into positions on method, and then on methodology.

Pluralism of method

Pluralism of method is the methodological position that there are no decisive criteria for selecting one best method of analysis (for example the deductivist method, or the experimental method). Economists should therefore employ a plurality of methods. The major influence is Popper (1959), who saw a role for situational logic in the social sciences, given the difficulties with falsificationism; the choice of method should then be problem-dependent (see Caldwell, 1991a). This version of pluralism (also known as eclecticism) has been advocated by Hutchison (1988), Boland (1982) and Solow (1988) without any hint of pluralism at the epistemic or ontological levels; all three subscribe to a unitary, or monist, epistemology and ontology. But if there is unitary understanding of such regularities as can be perceived (that is, the epistemology and ontology conform to those of logical positivism), then pluralism of method can only be explained in terms of the failure of traditional methodology to produce satisfactory criteria for choosing methods. Practising economists must choose methods by some criteria; on what grounds are these criteria to be selected? In principle, it should be possible to construct a taxonomy of problem types and advocate methods accordingly, given the starting point that economics aims to identify regularities that are presumed to exist. Boland (1989) took case studies to illustrate the process of method choice. Mayer (1993) advocated a particular set of criteria based on the distinction between pure and applied theory. He advocated internal, formalist criteria for deductive theory and client satisfaction for empirical theory. But without any epistemological explanation for the need for a range of methods, given a unitary, or monist, ontology and epistemology, a body of thought made up of pure theory and applied theory, with no explicit connection between the two, simply appears incoherent.

It might seem that pluralism of method could be justified by a pluralist epistemology. Since reality may be understood in a variety of ways, and there are no independent grounds for preferring one understanding over another, there are no grounds for choosing one method of acquiring knowledge over another. The rhetoric/hermeneutic approach has taken an agnostic position (different methods are taken on their own merits but there has been no advocacy of pluralism, indeed there has been a denial of prescriptive methodology in general). The postmodernist approach might be interpreted as advocating a plurality of methods; one of its most notable features was the denial of general theories. Yet, as has been suggested above, any postmodern position on method is self-contradictory; the essence of postmodernism is to eschew normative statements, and indeed theory in general.

The advocacy of a range of methods is entailed by the open-system epistemology of approaches such as that adopted by Post-Keynesian economists, or institutional/evolutionary economists. But this is not pluralism of method in the eclecticism sense, although it is commonly misunderstood as such. It is entailed by an open-system epistemology that knowledge is acquired by gathering evidence and constructing arguments in order to build up rational belief. These contributions to knowledge are incommensurate in the sense that they do not build up to a single probability statistic, that is, they do not fit into closed-system theorising. Certainly, the choice of a range of methods depends on the nature of the problem and the context. But the choice is guided (and thus limited) by reason, by convention and by vision/worldview/ontology; it is differences in these that account for different schools of thought which have in common open-system theorising (see Dow, 1990b). To distinguish this approach from that of the eclecticists, it must be emphasised that reason, conventions and vision all take on a particular meaning and play an explicit part in open-system epistemology (terms do not have unitary meaning). Closed-system reason is only a subset of open-system reason (see Carabelli, 1988). Conventions are a necessity in building up knowledge in Keynesian logic (see Hodgson, 1988), while in mainstream epistemology they lack logical foundation, as Boland (1982) has tirelessly pointed out. Finally, vision (or ontology) determines how problems are identified and interpreted (see Dow, 1990b). Given an open-system ontology, there is a range of possibilities; given a closed-system, unitary ontology, there is only one.

Methodological pluralism

Methodological pluralism is a meta-methodological position; it advocates that methodologists study a range of methodologies (by means of rational reconstruction). Critical pluralism involves the criticism of this range of methodologies by means of a range of criteria. This position has been advocated most notably by Caldwell (1982, 1986, 1988). The underlying reasoning is that there is no independent basis for deciding on one methodology. Rather than devoting fruitless efforts to finding the best methodology, methodologists should devote their efforts to promoting methodological understanding among economists by clarifying the nature of the different possibilities and demonstrating their strengths and weaknesses according to different criteria.[5]

Although this positive role for methodology counters the anti-methodology position of the rhetoric/hermeneutic approach, Caldwell (1990) embraced the hermeneutic idea of taking each approach on its own merits to promote a better understanding among practitioners of different approaches. The critical element is additional, however, and represents the fundamental meta-methodological difference from the hermeneutic approach. The rhetoric/hermeneutic approach accepted plurality of understanding and plurality of method as a description of reality, but refuses to make any normative judgement about the nature or extent of those pluralities; postmodernists positively welcomed plurality of understanding and method (the more the better, as a reflection of a fundamentally fragmented reality). Caldwell, rather (from his Popperian starting point) appeared to regard a wide plurality of methodologies as a regrettable necessity, and looked forward to the outcome of methodological pluralism as being a narrowing-down of possibilities (see Caldwell, 1989).

---

[5] Boland (1982, 1991) at times also seems to be a methodological pluralist as well as a pluralist of method. Redman (1991) advocated a critical rationalist version of methodological pluralism.

But, as it was pointed out in the discussion of Caldwell's (1988) paper (see de Marchi, 1988, pp. 53–6), Caldwell does not spell out the epistemological foundations of his methodological pluralism (or its ontological foundations). What is the reason for a range of methodologies in the first place? Is it in the nature of knowledge (and reality) that it be so, as the open-system approach suggests? Or is it a temporary limitation on our understanding, as the eclecticist approach suggests? Or is it pure folly that methodologies and methodologists persist at all in spite of the fragmentation of knowledge (and possibly reality) as the rhetoric approach and postmodernists suggest?

Critical methodological pluralism explicitly aims to go beyond description. But as with eclecticist pluralists, the question arises as to the criteria for criticism. Caldwell particularly advocated criticism in a methodology's own terms as a way of promoting greater understanding of a particular methodology. Such an effort is clearly preferable to the all-too-common criticism of one methodology by the criteria of another (see Caldwell, 1986). But it is only feasible up to a point. If the justification of methodological pluralism is epistemic, then, just as facts are theory-laden and theories are methodology-laden, so must the knowledge of methodologists be coloured by their own vision of reality and of how knowledge is constructed. Epistemic pluralism, after all, involves recognition that there are different understandings of reality, but in general, any one economist or methodologist only has one understanding. I can attest from personal experience of trying to present a range of schools of thought in their own terms (Dow, 1985) that it is not possible to switch fully satisfactorily in a detached fashion from one ontology-plus-epistemology to another. But without a pluralist epistemology, what is the justification for methodological pluralism?

While I wholeheartedly share Caldwell's view that trying to understand different methodologies in their own terms is a worthwhile exercise and should serve to promote more constructive debate among economists, the scope for that understanding is always conditional on the methodologist's own ontological and epistemological position. This applies even more strongly to the application of external criteria, which must be chosen according to some further criteria if the exercise is to have meaning.

Caldwell's statements of methodological pluralism have tremendous appeal in their advocacy of civilised, reasoned, non-self-serving behaviour. However, methodological pluralism, as presented so far, lacks force because of its lack of epistemic and ontological foundations. In traditional epistemic (that is, dualist) terms, methodological pluralism can be interpreted as non-methodology because it does not establish standards. Understood as the dual of traditional monism, methodological pluralism may be understood as according with the rhetoric approach, which denies prescriptive methodology any role. Yet understood as a means of improving knowledge, where knowledge is understood as an open system, methodological pluralism is fully justifiable. Methodologists cannot escape their own preconceptions any more than anyone else can. However, an ontological and epistemic awareness can enhance awareness of these preconceptions, which in turn can enhance awareness among economists at large of their preconceptions and improve mutual understanding.

Conclusion

I conclude, therefore, that methodological pluralism in a pure form, like pluralism of method, pluralist epistemology and pluralist ontology, is untenable as a basis for knowledge (see further Chapter 10). Pure pluralism is taken here to be the dual of the traditional unitary, or monist, position of mainstream economics. Further, the justification of methodological pluralism or pluralism of method is not at all clear when either is combined with a unitary, closed-system epistemology and/or ontology. On the other hand, the recognition of the inevitability of a range of methodologies and the advocacy of the employment of a particular range of methods is the logical outcome of an open-system epistemology and ontology.

This chapter is offered as an exercise in open-system meta-methodology. It offers an attempt at a rational reconstruction of a range of positions with respect to pluralism, in the full knowledge that these reconstructions may be flawed, not least because of my own preconceptions. But this is how knowledge progresses: offering arguments provides scope for feedback to correct misunderstandings and to direct modifications in thinking. Within an open-system approach, there is no contradiction involved in arguing for one's own viewpoint while respecting and being open to the viewpoints of others.

9
The Non-neutrality of Formalism

Jointly authored with Victoria Chick

The emphasis of mainstream economics on a methodology of deductivist mathematical formalism has been a powerful force in the development of economics, and it is now a critical factor in determining what appears to be possible for new economic thinking. It is often argued that mathematics simply translates verbal argument into a more precise and rigorous form which aids both understanding and theory development. But the argument developed in this chapter is that the translation is not neutral in that it changes the nature and content of the original verbal theory. Pluralist methodologies drawing on non-classical logic are discussed as an alternative, in which formal mathematics is one among many methods.

Introduction

In the view of many, perhaps most, economists, to state a theory in terms of a formal model is an unambiguous improvement, rather than, as we see it, a matter of costs and benefits. The benefits (greater rigour, more precision, demonstrable results), are widely understood, while the costs are underexplored. The costs are associated with the way in which formalising an argument can change its meaning, that is, with its non-

---

The original version of this chapter was published under the title of 'Formalism, Logic and Reality: A Keynesian Analysis' in the *Cambridge Journal of Economics*, 25(6), 2001, 705–22. It benefited from comments made by participants at the Association Charles Gide Conference on Formal Models and Economic Theory: History, Analysis, Methodology, Paris, September of 1999, the methodology seminar at the University of Roskilde in October of 1997, the Faculty of Economics seminar at the University of Catania, Brian Loasby, Peter Skott and two anonymous referees.

neutrality. This chapter will focus on the particular costs of formalism, associated with the obstacles formalism poses for translating from (formalist) theory to practical application.

It has been argued (by Backhouse, 1998a; Chick, 1998a and Dow, 1998) that analyses which today would be described as informal turn into something quite different when formalised. In this chapter, we elaborate further on reasons for this non-neutrality. Although these reasons are interrelated, they can be grouped under four headings: the choice of assumptions or axioms, the choice of method, the type of logic employed and closure. The present chapter will concentrate on the last three of these, as the first has been extensively explored in the literature. 'Formalism' is taken here to mean mathematical formalism, that is, a methodology which requires that all arguments be expressed, or at least be expressible, in mathematics.

While for some economists it is sufficient to construct a world of internally consistent logic, most profess the aim of generating results of relevance to real-world problems. To us the most interesting question is how to move from results obtained with formal methods under conditions of closure to the reality one is attempting to model. This question raises the central issue of the match of method to one's ontology; we will argue that formalism requires a particular understanding of the nature of reality. Here we consider how, taking our rather different understanding of the object of study as a starting-point, we may choose a different method of analysis, based on a different type of logic. Our argument is thus that formalism as the starting point defines its own domain of application. Correspondence with reality then depends on one's understanding of the nature of the real social world.

We proceed now to consider method, logic and closure in turn (although all are interconnected). This allows us to consider the issue of the relative generality (extent of domain) of formalism compared with a more pluralist methodology. We end with a consideration of the issue of partial closure (segmentation) within the pluralist approach.

The formalist method

The history of economics has been dominated by a search for universal principles or invariant laws, following the methodology of science, especially physics, in the nineteenth century and before (see Mirowski, 1989). That methodology looks for event regularities, which are the starting point for the 'covering-law' understanding of causality (see Runde,

1998). As Lawson (1997a) has made us aware, to observe (or theorise about) event regularities requires that the system under observation (or the object of theory) must approximate a closed system. Such a system is defined by the extrinsic condition that it be isolated from outside influences and an intrinsic condition that the agents 'inside' the system behave in a consistent manner. Closed systems are often amenable to mathematical expression, with such disturbances as remain being accounted for by an error term. (In such a case, we have quantifiable probabilistic knowledge rather than exact knowledge.)

Of course, some branches of science have a trump card which is missing from the economists' pack: the ability to conduct experiments. Experiments can be constructed so as to conform closely (if never perfectly) to the conditions of closure. In an experiment, the extrinsic conditions are assumed to be achievable by engineering controlled conditions and the intrinsic condition of stability of behaviour is assumed on mechanistic grounds (atoms don't think). Where these assumptions are justified, experiments may verify or falsify theories. The successes of experimental science led to the view that it is the purpose of science to discover or confirm event regularities in ideal conditions. The results then obtained can be modified in real-world applications (allowance is now made for the friction removed by the experimental conditions, for example). However, the two-slit experiment[1] showed that the answer obtained from a question could depend on the question asked, thus destroying the independence of the observed from the observer, in particular the observer's *quaesitum*. Until that point, science could claim that its constant reference to 'the facts' kept its theory in touch with the real and objective world of observation. However, this experiment showed that, even in the physical sciences, closure by experiment is not complete; it is not sufficient to generate unambiguous knowledge. The two-slit experiment thus shows the interdependence of methodology and how the subject matter is conceived. Accordingly Prigogine and Stengers (1984, pp. 204–5), reporting advances in chemistry, physics and biology which challenge the nineteenth century view of science, argue that

> We come to problems where methodology cannot be separated from the question of the nature of the object investigated. We cannot ask the same questions about a population of flies that reproduce and

---

[1] A beam of light passing through a single slit in a screen produces a pattern consistent with light as particles. Opening a second slit nearby produces interference, which indicates that light is a wave. The way the question is asked determines the answer. (See Bohm 1957, pp. 40–1, for example.)

die by millions without apparently learning from or enlarging their experience and about a population of primates where each individual is an entanglement of its own experiences and the traditions of the populations in which he lives.

Economists are acutely aware that they have few equivalents of experimental conditions against which to test their theories.[2] The reaction to this fact, however, varies.[3] It could be argued that, since we cannot generally appeal to experimental evidence, the only criterion of theory appraisal which ensures that we do not fall into error is internal consistency. But internal consistency can only be assessed in a closed system.[4] If we cannot generally construct closed systems experimentally, then we must rely on closed theoretical systems, and the question posed by such a procedure is, what relation does this 'thought experiment' of a closed theoretical system bear to our concept of reality? In other words, what is the relation between our theory and our ontology?

Nevertheless, the focus on internal consistency is extremely appealing. After all, who would support the opposite: logical inconsistency in theoretical structures? And closed systems have the immense appeal of delivering definitive solutions. As Hahn (1991, p. 47) described this approach to economics: 'an activity congenial to those who prefer proof to speculation and who derive satisfaction by subjecting their thinking to the discipline of the demands of consistency and coherence'.

However, not only does the normal usage of the term 'consistency' refer to a particular and restrictive form of logic, but also the criterion of internal consistency does nothing to ensure the relevance, or correspondence to reality, of the theory: avoidance of logical error does not prevent errors of application. The absence of closely controlled empirical systems against which to test theories leaves theory appraisal open to criteria derived from fashion, authority and ideological preference, for there is no reality check available.[5] We know that, even in the

---

[2] See Harvey (1999) for a social science argument about the contextual contingency and observer-dependence of observed 'facts'.

[3] There has, of course, been a tremendous amount of effort in recent years devoted to building up experimental evidence, with specific attention given to techniques to close off the experiments from outside social influences on the behaviour of subjects.

[4] See Coddington's (1975) related critique of Hahn's criterion of 'precision'; see also Chick (1998) and Chapter 4.

[5] See Lawson's (1997a) exposition on the problems experienced by econometric analysis founded on closed-system principles applied to an open-system reality.

physical sciences, when the decisive experiment is available, the promotion of theory is subject to forces usually analysed under the category of the sociology of knowledge; how much more vulnerable to these forces must economics be if the only criterion is internal consistency. Stiglitz (1991, p. 136) sums up the achievements of the last century as follows: 'The economists of the twentieth century, by pushing the neoclassical model to its logical conclusions, and thereby illuminating the absurdities of the world which they had created, have made an invaluable contribution to the economics of the coming century.'

Stiglitz prefaced this judgement by reference to progress in the form of the rejection of testable hypotheses arising from this logical framework. But, as he pointed out, the difficulty lies in identifying exactly what has been rejected. So difficult has it proved to achieve anything conclusive by an appeal to 'the facts' (themselves now well understood to be theory-laden) that some would instead advocate the highest level of abstraction as the goal of theory. They regard the job of economic theory to be the provision of a logical framework, an internally consistent syntax, the purpose of which is to guard against logical error when the syntactical structure is later filled with meaning.[6] This stance is equivalent to the Hilbert programme in mathematics (see Weintraub, 1998). It has been espoused by, for example, Debreu (1991). There is intellectual satisfaction in constructing a closed, logical system and 'living in it consistently' (a favourite phrase of Paul Davidson). But it has been noted (Coddington, 1975, pp. 550–3; Chick, 1998) that the practitioners of the syntactical approach are not distinguished for their attempts to imbue their structures with meaning; yet that is what is required if you believe that economics ought to say something about the real world. If there is no check on the realism of the assumptions/axioms, the method of theory construction, the applicability of the type of logic employed (always classical logic in these cases) or the closure chosen, the result can be a structure which can equally easily either illuminate or falsify the characteristics of the real world. There is nothing to keep the system from 'going off the rails'.[7]

---

[6] Hahn (1973) makes this case for the general equilibrium method without reference to the theory-ladenness of facts; for him the purpose of theory is to make claims precise enough for definitive empirical testing.

[7] Instrumentalism, as advocated by Friedman (1953), that is, the reliance on predictive success as the appraisal criterion, was espoused also by the New Classicals, in spite of the forceful critique from conventionalists (see Caldwell, 1984, ch. 3). But neither Friedman nor the New Classicals actually practised pure instrumentalism, relying on other forms of justification for their theories.

A classic example of abstraction losing track of reality is the system of Walras (1926), which apparently suffered from an inconsistency in its logical structure (quite apart from issues of empirical counterparts): the measure of available labour time. Walras himself was not sympathetic to abstraction for its own sake, but rather had his eye constantly on the characterisation of real-world markets, and in particular on disequilibrium behaviour (see Walker, 1987). However, since the system begins with available stocks, against which to measure excess demands and supplies, the question of the maximum available labour time is immediately begged. The system is not perfectly closed: the labour quantity admits of a fixed answer only by arbitrary choice (and we know that 'normal' working hours have declined secularly with society's wealth). While Walras (1926) allowed for the choice between productive and idle labour and Arrow and Hahn (1971, p. 75) acknowledged the ambiguity, for Debreu (1959), the quantity of labour is simply measured by the time worked at a particular date. The ambiguity surrounding the 'stock' of labour or its services has not been resolved; therefore it must be the case that Walrasian neoclassical economics commands support on grounds other than perfect logical consistency, which grounds are better analysed in Kuhnian terms.[8]

It can be argued, for example, that formalism in economics arose from a belief that nature is entirely mechanical and closed (see Maas, 1999, who made this argument with respect to Jevons). Yet if that type of belief is no longer current, then the methodology of formalism is not justified by ontology. If the mechanical model is now understood to be inadequate when applied to some aspects of nature, still less does it apply to the social sciences. If human nature and the social world more generally are understood as an open system in the sense that economic agents learn and innovate and that the institutions and conventions which shape economic actions evolve through time, then it is necessary to explore the relationship between results obtained under conditions of closure to this open-system reality. Such an understanding of reality raises the possibility that, as institutions change, theory must also change. Doubt is cast on the possibility of finding immutable laws applicable to, say, feudalism and capitalism alike, or even to capitalism in various stages of its development. From this perspective, a theory can be 'right' at one time and become 'wrong' (more accurately, outdated) at another. The

---

[8] Eichner (1985) criticised the lack of meaning in pure general equilibrium theory in similar terms; see further the ensuing exchange with Dasgupta and Hahn.

notion of imbuing a closed theoretical system with meaning is thus not an objective procedure; it requires the exercise of judgement.

We have discussed here the issue of the stage at which real world 'meaning' has its impact: before or after theorising. In the next section, we consider the concept of meaning more generally, and its relation to the form of logic employed.

Meaning and logic

We have characterised mainstream economics as the outcome of constructing theory according to the strictures of classical logic; for consistency, these strictures must continue in place when the theory is applied to the representation of the real world for the purpose of empirical testing and deriving policy implications.

One of the key strictures of classical logic necessary to this exercise is that the meaning of scientific terms is fixed (see Hacking, 1981, pp. 1–2). In particular, meaning must be consistent within the theory; the meaning of a variable such as 'the general price level' must be the same in each partial analysis so that the parts may then be assimilated into a complete system. However, meanings do change over time; meanings have changed in mathematics itself (see Weintraub, 1998). During the twentieth century, when mainstream economics took on its modern form, the conceptualisation of 'unemployment', 'rationality', 'equilibrium' and so on has changed. But, given the mainstream positivist view of science, such change as is admitted would be regarded as refinement, part of the progress of science. Indeed, much of the change has been the outcome of the reductionist programme designed to ensure compatibility between macroeconomics and microeconomics by means of consistency in the use of terms.

One of the attractions of fixed meanings, for many mainstream economists, has been the apparent capacity to apply a theoretical system to a wide range of conjunctural and historical circumstances. This requires that the common, constant meaning of terms has universal application. At the level of empirical testing in the positivist mode, the issue of meaning refers to the identification of data series which correspond to the theoretical concepts. Clearly, this identification poses challenges for applied economists, who also recognise that series change their content (the consumer price index and the monetary aggregates are obvious examples). Yet more significant for our discussion is the possibility that the concepts actually have different meaning in different contexts (over space and time).

Two examples which may serve to reinforce this point are the concept of human nature and the concept of money. With respect to the former, it is now well established (see for example Winch, 1997; Tribe, 1999) that Adam Smith understood human nature in a different way from modern mainstream economics. Yet leading mainstream economists claim to have formalised and extended Adam Smith's system of markets, ostensibly based on his initial premises about self-interest but actually based on axioms of rationality which embody a different concept. This whole question of changes in meaning between different generations of economists is an issue central to the history of thought (see Dow, 1998) and to the problems of communication between adherents of different schools of thought (Dow 1985).

The goal of constant meaning is also subverted by the evolutionary change of institutions. An example is money, which used to be full-bodied coin and which is now a network of debt. While the changes in the volume of money of the first type might be considered exogenous, the changes in the second clearly cannot. In order for monetarist theory to preserve conclusions developed under money of the first type, the exogeneity appropriate to outside money had to be maintained; hence Friedman's resort to the famous helicopter device.

More powerfully, perhaps, the example of money suggests that terms may have different meanings simultaneously. Neo-Austrians for example (see Hayek, 1979, ch. 3) make the argument that, from a subjectivist viewpoint, money consists of those assets which are perceived by the individual holder to be perfectly liquid. Since individuals may differ in how they regard the liquidity of different types of bank accounts, for example, the project of contemplating an aggregate measure of money is doomed from the start: the conceptual meaning of the term 'money' in general is constant, but its real-world counterpart is unidentifiable. Clearly, this is an extreme position, but less extreme positions which recognise the subjective element in assessing liquidity, or the ambiguity of such terms as general acceptability or means of payment, must concur with the proposition that the identification of the real-world counterpart of the theoretical concept of money is highly problematic. These problems are bound to be compounded when studies are extended to different societies or over extended periods of time.

Problems of meaning have been addressed by some who advocate formalism, though they concentrate on the specific issue of whether methodologists share meaning with practitioners, and thus what is the appropriate role for methodology (see for example, Weintraub, 1989 and Backhouse, 1997, ch. 3, 4).[9] Implicit in the work of those who are aware of issues of meaning but who pursue a formalist agenda, is a presumed goal of approximating to correspondence and fixity of meaning. The goal of the exercise reveals that this work is still embedded in the structure of classical logic, with its requirement of fixity of meaning within theoretical discourse.

Problems of identifying the real-world counterparts of classical logic can be expected if the real world does not in fact conform to classical logic in the first place. We consider now the possibility of different types of logic which may be better adapted to the problems economists face. There is a range of expression of alternatives, for example intuitionist logic (Tennant, 1987) and fuzzy logic (Coates, 1997). In economics, the most thoroughly researched alternative logic is the ordinary (or human) logic of Keynes (see Gerrard, 1992), which has recently been linked to the older tradition of common sense logic (Coates, 1996; Davis, 1999b). According to this tradition, as expressed for example in Smith's (1759) *Theory of Moral Sentiments*, knowledge is socially constructed; it follows that meaning itself is context-specific. Lawson (1977a, 1977b) has developed this idea as the concept of 'situated rationality', in which individuals make decisions in the context of their social and economic position. What is rational for the entrepreneur may not be rational for the worker, for example, and conflicts between different interest groups are thus not evidence of the irrationality of either side.

In the *Treatise on Probability*, Keynes (1921) sought a logic which would provide reasoned grounds for belief in propositions as a basis for action when certain or complete knowledge is only a special case and it is normally not available. This logic was to be applicable to everyday belief and action, as well as to 'scientific' knowledge and resulting policy recommendations. In the common sense tradition, the inevitable limitations on human knowledge had to be made up for by a grounding in a more fundamental belief (in the existence of the external world, for example) if action were to be justified. (The inevitability of knowledge limitations arises from the perceived organic nature of the real world.) This belief was predominantly conventional, shared by communities (social or scientific), and it was an integral part of the formation of knowledge. Keynes argued that we form hypotheses, and thus more

---

[9] The issue of meaning within theory and between theory and observation has more often been explored by the postmodern critique of methodology and by rhetoricians such as McCloskey (1983), who first challenged traditional methodology on rhetoric grounds.

context-specific beliefs, on the basis of available evidence, which in general is insufficient to provide a conclusive demonstration of truth, supplemented by indirect knowledge based on (ordinary) logic. Even evidence in the form of direct knowledge does not correspond to the logical positivist vision of 'the facts'. It consists of 'sensations which we may be said to *experience*, the ideas or meanings, about which we have thoughts and which we may be said to *understand*, and facts or characteristics or relations of sense-data or meanings which we may be said to *perceive*' (Keynes, 1921, p. 12, emphasis in original).

Ordinary logic in turn generates knowledge which is imperfect, partial or vague. This 'imperfection' is inevitable, as it concerns an organic whole of which complete, precise knowledge is impossible (see Gerrard, 1992). Organicism here refers to the evolving complexity within systems which are themselves open, and which involve heterogeneous entities (firms, governments and so on).[10] Keynes's espousal of this type of organicism is well documented, by Carabelli, 1995, for example). The issue of meaning for Keynes was thus less a matter of linguistic interpretation (as in Wittgenstein's later thought) than a matter of correspondence with an organic conception of the real world. As Davis (1999, p. 511) puts it, '[v]agueness…. had an ontological foundation in the very form of reality, and those intent on formalising economics, who "assume strict independence between the factors involved" in the economic world, only escape vagueness in Keynes's view by constructing ontologies appropriate to "symbolic pseudo-mathematical models"'. Thus, an organicist understanding of the subject matter justifies the adoption of an ordinary (human) logic; this logic generates knowledge which may at best be vague, in contrast to classical logic, which generates precise knowledge in terms of a closed system. But, as we elaborated earlier, the latter method leaves open the connections to be drawn between these precise theoretical conclusions and the organic nature of reality. We thus return to the question of closure in the next section.

Organicism, atomism and closure

A condition for the application of classical logic which is not unrelated to fixity of meaning is the separability of terms and of relationships between terms. Separability, of which the most extreme form is pure atomism, allows for the construction of a closed, axiomatic system

---

[10] This sense of organicism is not to be confused with the biological notion of functional totalities, in which boundaries are clearly specified.

such that the whole system is an aggregation of its independent parts. Atomism is the dual of organicism. The extrinsic and intrinsic closure conditions necessary for a system to be constructed in this way (Lawson, 1977a, noted above) are thus not met by organic systems; Carabelli (1991b) explained Keynes's critique of the formalist orthodox method explicitly in terms of organicism versus atomism.

The condition for intrinsic closure is that the elements of any large system or subsystem of relations retain a fixed identity throughout the period of analysis (whether in real time or logical time); they themselves are closed, albeit subject to causal forces. They cannot therefore themselves change as a result of interactions with other elements. Thus, the nature of the elements and their responses to external stimuli – just as the meaning of terms – remain fixed throughout. This condition too is not met in organic systems, in which the units of analysis (individuals and all the institutions of society: families, firms, governments and so on) evolve interdependently, changing society and creating new conventions of behaviour.

The implications for classical logic of the conditions for closure not being met therefore are similar to those of the absence of fixity of meaning: not only is meaning not fixed, but the objects of meaning are not fixed, due to the process of interdependent evolutionary change, a process which itself evolves.

Nor can it be supposed that the problem of closure is merely technical: rather, the choice of closure can determine the character of the resulting theory. Sen (1963) made this point by means of a five-equation model of a one-commodity economy, embodying quite standard attributes: a production function, equality between the wage and the marginal product of labour, a distribution of income between profits and the wage bill, a reduced-form equation in which investment is equated to a distributional determination of saving *à la* Kalecki and Kaldor and an independent investment function. There are four unknowns, so the system is over-determined. Neoclassical theory gives up the independent investment function, Kaldor gives up the marginal productivity equation and it is also possible to relinquish the full employment assumption. Each of these choices will close the system, but the theory which results from each choice will necessarily be different. Marglin, Taylor and Dutt have pursued the same strategy to categorise growth theories and comment on the implications of choosing one closure rather than another (see Dutt, 1990; Caserta, 1993). It can be seen that the choice of closure is not neutral, arbitrary or merely practical.

The question of closure is related to the choice of exogenous and endogenous variables, but even this is not the whole story. A system even simpler than Sen's model is the following IS-LM system, in which * indicates exogeneity: $S(r,Y) = I^*$, $M^* = L(r,Y)$. This model could be either 'monetarist' or 'Keynesian' depending on whether M^* or I^* is chosen as the driving force of the system.

Togati (1999) delineated two sorts of exogenous variables: primary, or causal, exogenous variables, which have a direct influence on the level of activity; and secondary, exogenous variables, whose values, for the purpose of the theory in question, can be taken as given or treated as constants. He argues that the choice of primary exogenous variables is not arbitrary but it is governed by a deep-level methodology. Employment, as determined in the labour market on the basis of preferences and technology, is the primary exogenous variable of classical macroeconomics. Employment then, determines output, and saving and investment together determine the interest rate. By contrast, Keynes begins with money and expectations, from which comes the principle of effective demand, which in turn determines employment and the real wage. The money wage, technology and the capital stock are secondary exogenous variables. Note that this interpretation of *The General Theory* differs from the usual one in which money and expectations are taken as given and ascribed no particularly exciting role, the key exogenous variable being investment. Togati's typology highlights the determinants of investment.[11]

The classical choice of primary variables is based on the familiar assumptions of atomistic choice in markets in which agents have equal power (or rather lack of it), with given available resources (labour, technology). The market will then produce a unique equilibrium. Money and expectations, Togati argues, are secondary exogenous variables in this system precisely because they are inherently not atomistic: whatever acts as money has to be generally acceptable, that is, it is a social institution. Expectations too have a social dimension, whether this is ascribed to the role of convention or to the recognition that even a small producer must take account of the firm's position in its industry and economy.

Keynes's model is an open system in two senses. 'Spatially', the appeal to conventions and routines indicates that in his theory the system needs elements beyond the market in order to work, while the classical

---

[11] His typology has affinities with Carabelli's (1985) distinction between *causa essendi* and *causa cognoscendi*.

model is 'closed' to that suggestion. The other sense has to do with time. Keynes's theory is one in which the causal structure just outlined has a temporal dimension. Money, liquidity preference and long-period expectations determine the demand for investment, which feeds into aggregate demand. Wages (money wages), other prime costs and short-period expectations together determine output, and demand later determines prices and profits; expectations can be mistaken and later be revised, and so on. If one knew all the interactions, one could describe *The General Theory* as an open-ended, path-dependent dynamic system. One doesn't know all the interactions, however, so an equilibrium is found, among all the possible outcomes, and this tells us something useful about the interrelations of which the theory is composed. This equilibrium is a kind of temporary closure, which will break down as time goes on.

The matter of closure in the context of open systems raises the very question of what it means to theorise about a system, like the economy, which is always evolving. As mentioned above, one response is to escape into the exploration of syntax, to derive relations which are not only institution-free but completely devoid of economic content. Another strategy, also designed to free theory from historical contingency, is to imagine initial conditions for the economy; for example, the debate over whether money derives its power from the state or from social consensus can be couched in terms of money's origin (Wray, 1998, for example). A further example is the modelling in circuit theory of the finance of firms' working capital: if firms are imagined to start from scratch in their present form, they will need capital from outside.[12] This assumption contrasts with Keynes's implicit assumption that firms' working capital comes mainly from last period's sales; this assumption implies that the firm has been and is a going concern (Chick, 1997). In the latter case, the theorist 'dips into history' at some point and models what is seen without worrying overmuch about how the institutions came to be as they are. Historical contingency is accepted. It follows that the theorist also accepts that, as institutions or behaviours change, the theory will be rendered obsolete. This approach requires a period in which institutions are sufficiently stable to be analysed; the development of theory requires some tranquillity in the real world (a point made by Laidler, 1991, in the context of classical monetary theory).

---

[12] 'The first step in the economic process is the decision taken by banks of granting credit to firms in order to enable them to start production' (Graziani, 1990, p. 12). See also Cencini (1995).

Note that, in this form, closure is neither arbitrary nor abstract. Rather, the process of theorising starts with an appreciation of the chief characteristics of the economy itself. Selection of these characteristics represents a kind of closure: a slice of history with sufficient stability is extracted from the evolutionary process and it is made the subject of analysis 'as if' that process had come to a temporary stop. It can be seen as a subset of a continuous process which is treated as if it meets the intrinsic and extrinsic conditions for closure. The chosen closure should be recognised as provisional or transitory.

A similar problem is posed by organicism. There is a view that organicism precludes any form of closure. This view arises from a duality in thinking which poses issues in terms of fixed meaning/multiplicity of meaning, certainty/ignorance, rationality/irrationality, atomism/organicism. This dualism implies that the only available choice is between logical positivism and no science at all: 'nihilism' (Amariglio and Ruccio, 1995). This perceived choice between duals is itself the product of classical logic. Ordinary logic, outwith the strictures of classical logic, recognises the interconnectedness of organicism but it does not regard it as impenetrable or inextricable. Rather, ordinary logic provides the basis for procedures to segment interconnectedness in order to generate knowledge.

Ordinary logic was offered (by Keynes) as a logic with general applicability as a basis for action, including 'scientific' application. What is normally understood by the term 'scientific' is some form of generality, in which that generality derives from abstraction.[13] It is precisely what is entailed in generality that is at issue here, and thus what is entailed in the abstraction. Given an organic reality, how should theory be constructed, segmenting that reality, in order to generate general statements, and what is meant by 'generality'? In the next section, therefore, we consider the reasons, and conditions, for segmentation of some form in order for knowledge to be generated.

Segmentation and atomism

Keynes's ordinary logic offers an alternative to classical logic which provides reasoned grounds for belief which are nevertheless not conclusively demonstrable. The choice in favour of such logic derives directly

---

[13] Coddington (1975) makes clear that the issue of formalism is not one about abstraction *per se*, since that is required by theory, but about the form of abstraction.

from a view of the real world as being organic: variables are interrelated, and both variables and their interrelations evolve in such a way as to evade capture by a closed system of logic. Ordinary logic is not the dual of classical logic, which would lead to the conclusion that no general (that is, scientific) statements are possible. Rather it generates general (scientific) statements, but the methodology underlines their contingency.

A particular feature of this logic therefore is that it cuts swathes through the recognised interconnectedness of things in order to generate (contingent) general statements. The organicism of the real world is not regarded as uniform, so some segmentation is justifiable. Even if it were uniform, some segmentation would be required if action is to ensue. The interconnectedness of even limited systems like university timetables can be said to approach uniformity, but a start has to be made somewhere and so some priorities have to be established and precedent, that is, history, is useful. More generally, the issue of segmenting activity within the management of firms, in spite of interconnectedness, poses similar issues in management economics.

While Keynes was for a long time characterised as posing a dual between certainty and complete uncertainty, research resulting from the publication of his *Collected Writings* has revealed his conception of degrees of uncertainty.[14] Correspondingly, some systems are less organically connected than others to the overall social system of which the economy is a part. Knowledge progresses by identifying (and justifying) subsystems which can be segmented off for special study, always bearing in the back of one's mind the ultimate interconnectedness. Indeed, Keynes was quite explicit on how this bears on the limitations of mathematical formalism, in a way highly reminiscent of Marshall's advocacy of short chains of reasoning:

> The object of our analysis is, not to provide a machine, or method of blind manipulation, which will furnish an infallible answer, but to provide ourselves with an organised and orderly method of thinking out particular problems; and, after we have reached a provisional conclusion by isolating the complicating factors one by one, we than have to go back on ourselves and allow, as well as we can, for the probable interactions of the factors amongst themselves. This is the nature of economic thinking. Any other way of applying our formal

---

[14] Again, there is a parallel in the management literature when we consider scenario planning.

principles of thought (without which we would be lost in the wood) will lead us into error. It is a great fault of symbolic pseudo-mathematical methods of formalising a system of economic analysis...that they expressly assume strict independence between the factors involved and lose all their cogency and authority if this hypothesis is disallowed; whereas, in ordinary discourse, where we are not blindly manipulating but know all the time what we are doing and what the words mean, we can keep 'at the back of our heads' the necessary reserves and qualifications and the adjustments which we shall have to make later on, in a way in which we cannot keep complicated partial differentials 'at the back' of several pages of algebra which assume they all vanish. (Keynes, 1936, pp. 297–8)

Here Keynes was referring to the qualified judgement required in the process of constructing a mathematical argument. However, his other writing indicates that this passage could refer more generally to the combination of mathematics with other methods of analysis. Almost certainly, he would agree with Marshall on the limitations of abstract theory.

In my view, 'theory' is essential. No one gets any real grip of economic problems unless he will work at it. But I conceive no more calamitous notion than that abstract, or general, or 'theoretical' economics was economics 'proper'. It seems to me an essential but a very small part of economics proper; and by itself even – well, not a very good occupation of time. (Marshall, 1925, p. 437)

Marshall, too, had an organicist, open-system understanding of reality, involving, for example, the irreversible life-cycle of the firm, consumers embedded in their social setting and so on, and modelled it using the technique that Keynes also adopted in *The General Theory*, of dividing events into long and short periods. This technique is an attempt to deal with historical time and still get results. One could argue that Keynes completed a project which Marshall intended; consider the evaluation of Marshall by Loasby (1991, p. 16):

Marshall associated development with evolution and coordination with equilibrium, and attempted to incorporate both equilibrium and evolution within a single body of analysis; but he failed. He hoped his 'principle of continuity' would allow him to combine incremental novelty in an open system with the application of differential calculus while that system was provisionally assumed to be closed; but the general perception was of inexplicable hesitation in pursuing the logic of equilibrium.

Systems of simultaneous equations, such as Walras's model, IS-LM, or the Sen/Dutt models cited above, produce a completely different kind of closure. These models have one solution, called equilibrium, and they admit no dynamics once that position is reached unless there is a change in the initial conditions.

The methodology which Keynes espoused for economics was a case study in ordinary logic or human logic, whereby he employed a range of methods (sources of indirect knowledge) along with such evidence (direct knowledge) as was available in order to piece together an overall picture of the economy, his *General Theory*. However, and this has been the source of much misunderstanding of Keynes, the overall picture could not be rendered commensurate within a single closed mathematical system, not only because of its open structure, analysed above, but also because of the way in which it was built up using different methods. In particular, the segmentation he employed to focus on different aspects of the economic process and different arguments within the profession, could not be put together in a mathematical system precisely because of what had to be kept 'at the back of the head' during the segmented analysis, which was by definition not amenable to formal expression (or it would not need to be kept at the back of the head).

This segmentation has implications for the question of how we go about acquiring knowledge. For mainstream economics, the extrinsic and intrinsic conditions of closure, which are assumed rather than discussed, mean that economic relations can be separated off from other relations both at the disciplinary level and within the discipline. But for an organicist economics, the interrelations cut across disciplinary divides at both the macro and micro levels. Even if interdisciplinary boundaries were well defined, the organic nature of economic behaviour itself means that the conditions for closure are not met within economics itself.

The question of the relationship between complex wholes and closed-system analysis is not unique to economics. An actual economy is an open, evolving, complex system; so too is the universe, which it is the job of physics to model. We have seen in physics, if not in economics, the success of the atomistic method, in which results gained from study of a small part of the whole can be generalised to the whole. We have also seen that this success is only partial and that Newtonian results are now understood to apply to only a subset of circumstances. Newtonian mechanics are now nested within a larger system of thought. More importantly, the limits of applicability of those mechanics have been specified. In the macroscopic world, we have a similar phenomenon, in which entropy (which leads to uniformity) and self-organisation (which leads to differentiation) coexist. Although these forces are contradictory, the problem is not the contradiction but identifying the boundaries so that the appropriate theory can be applied. Prigogine and Stengers (1984, p. 204) put the resulting difficulties for scientists as follows. 'In complex systems, both the definition of entities and of the interactions among them can be modified by evolution. Not only each state of the system but also the very definition of the system as modelized [sic] is generally unstable, or at least metastable.' We have already seen that a closure can be found within a dynamic, open system by devising ways to isolate a period of time for analysis. The next question is the extent to which organic unities are 'decomposable' into units which can be analysed separately.

In Walras (1926), we can see this decomposition being attempted. He started with exchange, then introduced production, then accumulation and finally money. There are, to our knowledge, no clues as to Walras's choice of this ordering. We also see rather quickly that his scheme conforms to Togati's placing of money and expectations as secondary exogenous variables in the classical system. So one point is very clear and indeed it has been commented upon by many: the way the Walrasian system has been compartmentalised results in modelling production as if it were exchange and relegates money to an afterthought, procedures which mainstream economics continue to follow today. Therefore, his scheme and *The General Theory* can never be made compatible. Those who think that Keynes got it right would argue that the question of the order in which problems are tackled is of the utmost importance. We have no criteria about how that should be done, except for the remarks of Keynes about the monetary production economy (Keynes, 1973a, pp. 408–11).

Although we have shown that Keynes did proceed by compartmentalisation, (though not the one of Walras), that was not the perception of one whose instincts were neoclassical. 'Pigou (1936, p. 121) stresses...that Keynes's desire to reach a stage of generality is so high that everything must be discussed at the same time while the Classical's approach is to deal with "pure" cases and go from the simpler to the more complex (that is, proceeding by stages toward real life) (Togati, 1999, p. 13, n. 2).

Pigou seems to be arguing that Keynes's methodology, founded in organicism, is insufficiently segmented to be tractable. There is, in fact, confusion inherent in the concepts of 'at the same time' and 'proceeding by stages' which correspond to the historical time of the real world and the logical time of abstract analysis, respectively. This confusion stems from Pigou's not appreciating the significance of Keynes starting with the real world and generating general statements about it which would take different forms when applied to different real-world contexts. As Carabelli (1991, p. 116) put it:

> For Keynes, a general theory was one which did not tacitly introduce hypotheses of 'independence from'. Thus, his use of the word 'general' is truly connected with his methodological criticism of the classical theory. ... A theory which, at the beginning of its analysis, avoided introducing limiting assumptions of independence, was truly general. Theories – like the classical theory – which did not were simply special cases of the former.

Thus, it is more than an irony that, while Keynes put forward his macroeconomics as a general theory, the neoclassical synthesis purported to show Keynes's theory to be a special case, arising from special assumptions about behaviour in the labour and money markets. That this apparently conflicting interpretation persists is evidence that there is some difference of view as to what is entailed in generality. The neoclassical interpretation arose directly from the application of a formal, closed system to Keynes's system, with which it is incompatible (see Torr, 1999). While Keynes's theory was therefore general in not assuming independence, it was not general in the sense that Pigou implied, of considering everything at once. Keynes chose his own way to segment the subject matter (keeping the rest of the whole 'at the back of his head'). Wherever segmentation occurs, formal analysis may be applied to a theoretical segment. Segmentation occurs at the level of the identification of variables for consideration in the first place. Lawson (1997a, pp. 204ff.) explains the motivation for identifying possible causal processes in terms of what he calls 'contrastive demi-regularities' or 'demi-regs':

> Although the social world is open, dynamic and changing, certain mechanisms may, over restricted regions of time-space, be reproduced continuously and come to be (occasionally) apparent in their effects at the level of actual phenomena, giving rise to rough and

ready generalities or partial regularities, holding to such a degree that prima facie an explanation is called for.... The patterning observed will not be strict if countervailing factors sometimes dominate or frequently co-determine the outcomes in a variable manner. But where demi-regs are observed there is evidence of relatively enduring and identifiable tendencies at play. (Lawson, 1997a, p. 204)

Keynes in effect identified a demi-regularity in the relation between consumption and income which he expressed formally in the consumption function. Yet he listed a range of other factors which might interfere with this regularity in particular contexts, employing non-mathematical analysis. In *The General Theory*, also, he took the money supply to be given, segmenting the consequences of monetary expansion from the mechanisms by which it was brought about. Yet in other writing, notably the *Treatise on Money*, the focus rather was on the mechanisms. Putting together the segments of analysis of bank behaviour, central bank behaviour and credit and asset market behaviour, analysed using a range of methods, allows an analysis of the underlying causal mechanisms at work in a particular environment, with implications for appropriate policy (see Dow, 1997b). It is significant that the Bank of England (1999) presents its policy-making rationale in these terms, albeit somewhat cloaked in the formalism of the official discourse.

The monetarist model also employed the closure of assuming the money supply to be exogenous. As a result of further presuming the separability of money from real factors, the inference was drawn that controlling the money supply would be both necessary and sufficient for controlling inflation. This was interpreted as a universal theory, applicable equally to, say, Chile and the UK. But, in a real-world organic system in which the money supply is not in fact exogenous and separable, the particular assumptions of the closed system were not satisfied and the policy did not have the anticipated results. A Keynesian analysis would have kept 'at the back of the head' the provisional nature of the segmentation and, in the case of activist monetary policy, brought to the fore an analysis of the potential for the monetary authorities to exert causal force. Such analysis would inevitably be context-specific. More generally, a Keynesian would argue that the organic nature of reality creates uncertainty (for agents, as for economists), and thus the need for an asset confidently viewed as safe, that is, money. Which assets are viewed as safe is also clearly a context-specific matter.

In some cases, the difference between segmentation and atomism may not be readily apparent. Atomism requires analysis at the smallest possible level, defined as units which are independent and isolated from outside influences, that is, it requires that the intrinsic and extrinsic conditions for closure, respectively, be met. When the partial analysis is combined with other partial analyses, if these conditions are met, there need be no further change to the partial analyses. Segmentation and partial analysis in the tradition of Marshall and Keynes, however, are rather different. Neither of them achieved the construction of a system like that of Walras (nor did they falsify reality as he did), precisely because their recognition of the organic nature of reality and the provisional nature of their segmentations precluded a formal fitting together of partial analyses into a whole; the process of altering the segmentation itself would have repercussions for the partial analyses because of the interactions held 'at the back of the head', the pound of *ceteris paribus*.

Conclusion

We have argued here that mathematical formalism is non-neutral because the method itself requires important assumptions to be made about the nature of the subject matter, if connections are to be made between theory and the real world. Understanding of the implications of mathematical formalism has been clouded by the presumption that classical logic is coterminous with logic. But it is in fact a highly restrictive logic, requiring certainty about the truth value of premises if truth is to be attached to the conclusions. In a social world which in general precludes certain knowledge about premises, classical logic is of limited application. Put another way, classical logic is only applicable within closed systems, which are the ones which can yield certain knowledge.

Mercifully there are alternative logics which are compatible with open systems and which permit theorising which generates knowledge, albeit knowledge not held with certainty ('vague' or partial knowledge). While our starting point is an understanding of the social world as being organic, this does not preclude segmentation in the form of provisional closure in order to generate theories. These theories may well be expressed mathematically (but not necessarily). They are general in the sense that they are designed for application to open social systems; this means that specific applications will require specific detail on context. Closed system theorising is thus not general in that it only applies to the special case of closed, atomistic systems, which have very limited practical application.

The open nature of reality, therefore, poses problems for the application of formalist theory. There is a variety of responses by applied economists, depending on whether or not their starting point is pure theory. Each of us may be confident in our capacity to keep the necessary qualifications to pure theory at the back of our minds. However, these qualifications are of central methodological significance and therefore require to be made explicit. Thus, as Keynes (1973b, p. 306) argued in his critique of Tinbergen's econometrics, the *onus* is on the economist to justify treating a particular context as a closed system when this can at best only be an approximation. What we keep 'at the back of our heads' must at some point be brought to the fore.

The ordinary logic of Keynes, which we have touched on here, provides some guidance as to how to bring intuition and judgement to the fore. This logic supports a methodology which encompasses a range of methods in order to build up knowledge. Mathematics is only one method; other, non-mathematical methods are required in order to address the complexity of social systems. By definition, these methods together are not commensurate (or they could all be reduced to mathematics). Therefore, the method of exclusive mathematical formalism inevitably limits scope for application, and thus is non-neutral.

10
Structured Pluralism

> *The argument developed in this volume is both that it is useful
> to understand economics in terms of the different methodologies
> employed by different schools of thought and that this diversity
> allows much better scope for contemplating new economic thinking.
> But much of the discussion of pluralism, curiously, has discouraged
> thinking in terms of schools of thought, due in part to a tendency to
> apply categories in a dualistic way. This chapter aims to reinforce
> the non-dualistic understanding of pluralism and the usefulness of
> thinking in terms of schools of thought and indeed of (permeable,
> evolving) categorisations in general as a guide to thought. These
> categorisations provide pluralism with the kind of structure which
> makes it workable.*

Introduction

Methodological pluralism, understood as the advocacy of plurality, has
become commonplace among methodologists. Indeed, Salanti (1997,
p. 7) went so far as to state in his introduction to the pluralism conference volume that 'all people interested in economic methodology seem
to be, in a broad sense, ready to endorse one kind or another of "pluralism"'. More recently, the plurality and pluralism of modern methodological thought is set out in Hands's (2001) account of what he calls the
'new economic methodology'. Indeed, the idea of pluralism has been

The original version of this chapter was published in the *Journal of Economic
Methodology*, 11 (3), 2004, 275–90. It benefited from the comments of John
Davis, John Finch and other participants in the INEM Conference at Leeds, and
from exchanges on the subject with Victoria Chick and Rob Garnett.

taken up more widely, not only within economic methodology, but also within economic practice itself. There is now a grouping of around 40 international organisations in ICAPE, the International Confederation of Associations for Pluralism in Economics. At the theoretical and policy levels too, there has been an explicit expression of pluralism.

Alongside this development, there has been a growing reluctance to refer to schools of thought in economics. On the face of it, it is curious that this should be the case when schools of thought have been one of the most obvious modes of pluralism within economics since the 1960s. It is not necessarily the case that the notion of pluralism is antipathetic to the notion of schools of thought as such, although that argument has been made, and we address it below. Hands (2001, pp. 402–4) points out that non-mainstream economics has provided much of the impetus for the new methodology and argues that this methodology can provide a congenial home for non-mainstream schools of thought within its broader arena. However, there is no suggestion from Hands that schools of thought have any particular role to play in methodological pluralism.

Further, while methodological pluralism has probably been most strongly advocated by economists associated with non-mainstream schools of thought, some are now putting a greater emphasis on shared methodological pluralism rather than differences between schools of thought. This is particularly noticeable in the critical realist approach, for which schools of thought are secondary categories within the primary categorisation of open-system/closed-system thought. The emphasis thus seems to be shifting to the distinction between new economic methodology and old economic methodology, between pluralists and monists, between open systems and closed systems.

For methodological pluralists, there is clearly a danger that these categories might be treated dualistically. In a way, this gets to the heart of the issue with pluralism which we will address in this chapter: the status of categories in a pluralist system. The issue is addressed here in terms of a particular focus: to consider whether there is a continuing role for categorisation according to schools of thought in economics within methodological pluralism. This requires, first, a discussion of the methodological status of schools of thought, and, in particular, the role of criticism. Methodological pluralism itself then requires further discussion. What is entailed by the broader notion of pluralism? Does it require some limitation in order to be workable, and if so, what is the basis for limitation? The case is made here for what is termed 'structural pluralism'. This approach is outlined with reference to thinking on open systems. It is then illustrated with a discussion of the current nature, status and implications of the conceptualisation of economics as consisting of a collection of schools of thought. The argument draws on a discussion of Kuhn's conceptualisation of paradigms.

It is important to the argument developed here that we are ultimately concerned with a reality of which language is a part. The way in which we understand words and concepts is rooted in our ontology, and these understandings in turn have real consequences for action. Yet the role of language for knowledge is crucial. Different understandings of terms are very important – not least the term 'pluralism' – for expression of this argument as well as its content, since they reflect different theories of knowledge. There is no escape from this reflexivity. The specific arguments expressed here, and the language used, inevitably draw on a particular understanding of schools of thought, pluralism, the work of Kuhn and so on. There is reflexivity specifically in the argument that incommensurability of language is only partial, and therefore that communication of sorts is deemed to be possible. Indeed, we shall see that this issue is one which is addressed by structured pluralism.

Schools of thought

The term 'school of thought' has been used widely in economics, referring to differences within and between both mainstream and non-mainstream economics. But, while there had been differences in perspective in earlier periods, the notion a school of thought only really gained force during the second half of the twentieth century. This coincided, and it may arguably be explained by, the growth of mathematical formalism as the dominant methodological feature of economics (as documented by Morgan and Rutherford, 1998). Indeed, it was also during this period that economics as a subject came to be defined by some by its method(ology).

There have been, however, different understandings as to what defines a distinctive school of thought. In the 1960s and early 1970s, schools of thought could be identified in terms of differences expressed within a common methodological framework. The textbook version of the Cambridge capital controversies focused on the possibility of factor re-switching in terms of a common formal framework, as did the textbook version of the Monetarist/Keynesian debate. Thus, schools of thought were understood initially in terms of theoretical differences. With the growing fragmentation of mainstream economics, the term school of thought continued to be used in this way (by Phelps, 1990, for example). However, there was a growing awareness that differences between Cambridge England and Cambridge, MA, and between monetarists and Keynesians in fact stemmed from much deeper methodological, epistemological and ultimately ontological differences (Dow, 1985; Mair and Miller, 1991; see further Chapter 2). It was a reflection of the 'old methodology' approach that this was identified by some simply as ideological difference, arguing that ideology was, and should be, separable from economics; see for example Hahn (1984, p. 4). This current persists in modern critiques of thinking in terms even of mainstream/ non-mainstream, far less schools of thought (Goodwin, 2000).

The awareness of the possibility of legitimate difference in approach to economics was informed by the work of Thomas Kuhn (1962), whose concept of paradigm can be used interchangeably with school of thought. Kuhn picked up on Popper's focus on scientific communities to develop an explanation for the apparent lack of adherence of scientists to common sets of rules arising from philosophy of science. Emphasising not only the absence of a universal set of standards, but also the absence of a shared use of language, Kuhn challenged the view that it was feasible to agree on a demonstrably valid universal philosophy of science (the 'old methodology' in Hands's terms). Rather, scientific communities form around shared ontological beliefs, epistemologies and methodologies, out of which emerge distinctive sets of methods and theories, expressed in terms with meanings shared by the community. Arguably, elements of ideology inevitably are embedded in what is ultimately a belief system, in such a way that they cannot be separated out. These paradigms are incommensurate in that there is neither an independent set of principles by which to judge them, nor a shared set of meanings of language by which to discuss them. Normal science conducted within these paradigms, together with extraordinary science which from time to time challenges ruling paradigms by focusing on reassessing foundations to address anomalies, is how Kuhn understood the way that science proceeds.

It is important to recognise that, within this framework, there is a role for reasoned advocacy of a particular methodology embedded within each paradigm. An 'old methodology' advocacy would consist of the argument that that methodology has the status of being universally valid, conclusively superior to alternatives. A 'new methodology' advocacy consistent with Kuhn's framework recognises that no such claim can be made for any one methodology; there is an awareness of alternatives, a sense of 'otherness' (see Kaul, 2008). We generally now understand that reason isn't all – indeed, David Hume and Adam Smith reached the conclusion now current in 'new methodology' that, while it was the extensive use of reason which characterises science, reason in turn rests on the sentiments and beliefs (of individuals as social beings) which provide the foundations of science (Dow, 1999a). It is important not to associate forcefulness of argument across paradigms necessarily with presumption of correctness in any absolute sense; persuasion is part and parcel of methodological pluralism.

Extraordinary science, in Kuhn's scheme, is the locus of such argument. If scientific revolutions take place, then some persuasive communication must have been possible (Kuhn, 1962, pp. 202–3). In spite of incommensurability, reasoned arguments may therefore be constructed, expressed and in some sense understood from outside the paradigm, in favour of the preferred alternative methodology. While each paradigm may be understood as a social system, there is a larger disciplinary social system (economics, for example) of which each is a subsystem. There are some shared focuses and understandings which allow some communication (whether expressing agreement or disagreement).

It has been a common argument against the applicability of Kuhn's framework to economics that, where we might possibly identify a paradigm shift, there is evidence of continuity between one paradigm and another; no 'revolution' in economic thought is purely discontinuous (see for example Blaug, 1976). Indeed, this was the subject of more general controversy (Lakatos and Musgrave, 1970). However, Kuhn's view of revolutionary change in ideas was not that it is a dualistic switch from one set of ideas to the next. Kuhn's argument was rather that meaning changes during a revolutionary episode, such that what comes after is incommensurate with what went before, if snapshots were taken, as it were, ten years apart. Indeed, Kuhn (1977, Preface) demonstrated how awareness of paradigmatic change and an effort to understand the language of another paradigm, even as far back as Aristotle, can reveal meaning and thus understanding (albeit imperfectly). Similarly, there will be some continuities (of cultural and educational context for example) between paradigms extant at any one time which allow *some* communication and *some* mutual understanding to take place.

It follows then that in Kuhn's framework incommensurability does not mean an absence of communication, but rather difficulty in communication. As Kuhn (1962, p.202) put it, 'what the participants in a communication breakdown can do is recognise each other as members of different language communities and then become translators'. Again, the starting point is recognition of difference, from which communication can build – an exercise in hermeneutics. Thus, criticism across paradigms is possible, and it can be fruitful. The incentive to engage in such communication is to be exposed to new ideas, new arguments and new perspectives on one's own paradigm.

But criticism needs to be understood in terms both of the meanings and methodological principles employed. Thus, criticism of paradigm A may be conducted in terms of the meanings and methodological principles of that paradigm, pointing out some internal inconsistency. Yet the fact that much non-mainstream criticism of mainstream economics has been couched in the terms of mainstream economics, for example, as an exercise in communication and persuasion, does not signify acceptance of the paradigmatic principles of mainstream economics. Alternatively, the meanings and methodological principles of paradigm B may be employed in order to analyse paradigm A, so that the criticism is at the level of paradigmatic difference. In this way, those who belong to paradigm B present the reasons, in terms of paradigm B, for adhering to that paradigm's principles. Criticism is inevitably conducted from the perspective of one paradigm or another. However, one of the important legacies of Kuhn was to increase awareness that communication across paradigms required a particular effort of translation, whichever paradigm's 'language' was used.

This methodologically aware criticism occupies a middle ground between criticism from a monist perspective on the one hand, and a complete absence of criticism on the other. As to the first of these, there have been arguments that methodological pluralism is not firmly enough embedded in practice, and that Kuhn's ideas have encouraged too much criticism. Indeed, some have identified this as a dualistic form of criticism, that is, rejection, in interparadigmatic relations (see Chick, 1995). Garnett (2006) argues that attachment to schools of thought has at times been associated with a tendency to be overly critical of alternatives (especially across the mainstream/non-mainstream divide) and overly assertive of the case for supplanting other schools of thought (what he terms 'paradigmism'). He is concerned that this evolution from criticism to a 'separation' of paradigms departs from the spirit of methodological pluralism. (Indeed, Davis, 1997, suggests that there is a danger of theoretical monism within schools of thought.) Garnett argues, therefore, for a move beyond old ideas about schools of thought in order to create a more constructive environment for theory development. And a study of actual theory development in economics, particularly by younger scholars, indeed suggests that, whether understood explicitly or implicitly, methodological pluralism has already had an increasing influence, encouraging more constructive communication across paradigmatic divides.

On the other hand, Fullbrook (2003) argues that Kuhn's ideas have encouraged immunity to criticism. Paradoxically, they have given licence to an 'anything goes' approach on the part of mainstream economics; they provide protection from criticism from outside, emasculating non-mainstream criticism. Methodological pluralism in this sense is understood as removing any need for reasoned justification. This development, I would contend, is more the outcome of the way in which Kuhn's ideas have developed in the 'new methodology' rather than Kuhn's ideas themselves. In particular, the issue is the dualistic interpretation of methodological pluralism. We therefore consider pluralism more generally in the next section.

Pluralism: the issues

The monist view on schools of thought, inevitably, is that they serve no useful purpose, in that one approach can be identified as superior, for example as fitting what are understood as the best rules of science. Alternatively, it might be argued that schools of thought reflect only theoretical difference, not methodological difference. What is more interesting is to consider further the criticisms of the notion of schools of thought which have arisen from pluralism. These criticisms have arisen from two quite different standpoints, which reflect two different types of argument for pluralism, which we now consider.

Salanti (1997) drew the helpful distinction between pluralism as an ethical principle (elaborated on by his co-editor, Screpanti, 1997) and pluralism as a normative methodological principle. It is on the first that there is greatest agreement, while the disagreements centre on the reasons for advocating pluralism as a methodology (pluralism of method), or indeed as a meta-methodology (methodological pluralism) and on what that pluralism means (see further King, 2002).

Methodological pluralism as an ethical principle was evident in the practice of key figures such as Warren Samuels. Yet for him, too, there were epistemological grounds for methodological pluralism (Samuels, 1997, 1998). If for whatever reason no one methodology can be demonstrated to be superior to all others (in the extreme, this could derive simply from empirical observation of economic methodology rather than epistemological argument), there is good reason for a range of methodologies to co-exist. Since schools of thought are distinguished substantially by their methodologies, the argument carries forward to support the co-existence of a range of schools of thought. If none can dominate on grounds of reason, ethical argument suggests tolerance of this diversity and equal access to economic discourse. (For a monist, the issue of tolerance of methodological diversity does not arise, since it is believed that the superiority of one methodology can be demonstrated.)

The ethical argument for tolerance of methodological pluralism has been central to the rhetoric approach, but in deliberate opposition to any prescriptive epistemological argument (McCloskey, 1994). However, because it is argued that no one epistemology can be demonstrated to be superior, this can be seen to apply equally to pluralism. Giving primacy to ethics, what is important is effective communication as the basis for effective persuasion. Schools of thought, with their linguistic and methodological differences, can be seen as potentially creating an ethical challenge by putting up barriers to good conversation. However, effectively the epistemological argument is being made that good communication is actually possible across the discipline. This was supported when McCloskey (1994, ch. 24) demonstrated how 'neoclassical economics', 'Marxian economics', 'Austrian economics' and so on can be used as categories in constructive conversation.

While not normally accompanied by explicit ethical argument, the same type of epistemological argument against prescriptive methodology is central too to the approach to both methodology and historiography associated with science studies. This approach understands the work of the methodologist and historian as being primarily descriptive. Since any description employs categories and themes, there is a plurality of histories, as Weintraub (1999) has argued with respect to the history of economics in the twentieth century. Methodological pluralism in the form of schools of thought enters into the frame only insofar as plurality of methodologies provides one of these themes. Again, methodological pluralism is understood as something broader than schools of thought. If communities of economists work within schools of thought, then that is simply part of the architecture of economics which is the subject matter. But the schools have no general epistemological role.

The more positive epistemological argument for methodological pluralism goes further; as well as being good ethics, pluralism is required by the absence of conclusive demonstrable arguments in favour of any one methodology. Variety is seen as producing a more robust basis for knowledge than any single, conclusive, methodology. The argument similarly applies at the meta-methodological level. Yet there is a danger of logical contradiction, that the argument for methodological pluralism itself denies any general basis for such an overarching argument.

There is the danger, in other words, that truly generalised methodological pluralism actually erodes any basis for discourse. This argument has been more fully developed by Davis (1999a, p. 166). He makes the case for what he calls 'principled relativism', in which 'our ability to explain the relative character of discourse turns on the principles involved in reading across discourses'.

Let us consider further the difficulties posed by a generalised methodological pluralism. If there is a reasoned argument for methodological pluralism itself as well as pluralist methodologies which can be communicated successfully across methodological differences, then that pluralism must have some identifiable characteristics. It is therefore not unlimited, or unconstrained. There is some common ground for discourse, and not just over pluralism. It is of crucial importance, therefore, in trying to understand what is entailed by pluralism, to discuss its structure. And indeed that has been the subject of much of the methodological pluralist literature. For example, Caldwell (1988), who spearheaded this literature, has developed the notion of critical pluralism, which focuses on critical analysis of economic methodology, explicitly from the perspective of one methodology or another.

The role of criticism was highlighted also by Samuels (1998, p. 301) as one of the ways of avoiding 'methodological anarchy' in spite of the absence of metacriteria for choice of methodology. Further, emphasis is to be placed on 'the process by which knowledge and the credentials of knowledge are pursued'; this has provided much of the agenda of the science studies approach. However, the most important emphasis, according to Samuels, needs to be placed on 'the identification of the precise nature, grounds and limits of particular methodologies'. Together, these pursuits provide some structure for methodological pluralism.

Having argued that 'pure', or unconstrained, pluralism is logically as well as practically unsustainable, I had earlier used the term 'modified pluralism' to refer to the middle ground between monism and pure pluralism (Dow, 1997/Chapter 8 and 2001), or 'moderate pluralism' (Dow, 2002). Here the term 'structured pluralism' is put forward as more accurately reflecting what is entailed. This concept is explained further in the next section, and the role of schools of thought is then explored in these terms.

Structured pluralism

In considering further the form taken by pluralism, it is important to push further back to the reasons for a pluralist epistemology. Why exactly is it that there is widespread agreement that we have no conclusive basis for agreeing on one best epistemology, and therefore we must accept that science will be pursued pluralistically? Were it defensible, a monist approach would be more satisfactory. The explanation must refer to the nature of the subject matter, which in the case of any social science includes human knowledge.

The argument for methodological pluralism is that, if certain knowledge about reality is not in general possible, that is, knowledge is in general held with uncertainty, then there is no basis for identifying one best way of building knowledge (see for example Samuels, 1997). It must therefore be the case that this subject matter is not such as to yield law-like behaviour and definitive theories and methods to capture causal mechanisms or their manifestations. We can understand the conditions for a subject matter which does or does not support monism in terms of closed and open systems, respectively. A system which yields certain knowledge, and thus supports monism, must be closed in the sense of having all of the following characteristics (Dow, 2002, pp. 139–40, as paraphrased in Chick, 2004; see further Chapter 11 for further refinement):

1. 'all relevant variables can be identified;
2. the boundaries of the system can be specified, so that it is clear which variables are exogenous and which are endogenous; these categories are fixed;
3. only the specified exogenous variables affect the system, and they do this in a known (or predetermined) way;
4. relations between the variables are either knowable or random;
5. the components are separable (independent, atomistic) and their nature is constant;
6. the structure of the relationships between the components is known (or predetermined).'

If the reality we study is not such a system, then it must be open to some degree and in some way, depending on which of the following conditions are met (any one being met ensures that the system is open):

1. 'It may not be possible to be sure, in a complex system, that all relevant variables have been identified;
2. the boundaries of the system are semi-permeable and/or their positions are not perfectly clear and/or may change; this implies that the classification into exogenous and endogenous variables may not be fixed;

3. there may be important omitted variables and/or their effects on the system may be uncertain;
4. there is imperfect knowledge of the relations between variables; relationships may change, for example owing to human creativity;
5. there may be interrelationships between agents and/or these may change (for example agents may learn);
6. connections between structures may be imperfectly known and/or may change; structure and agency are typically interdependent.'

It is the presence of any of these latter characteristics of economic systems which requires methodological pluralism. No one epistemology can be conclusively shown to be superior to all others in trying to establish reasoned conclusions about an open-system reality.

But we can gain clues as to the character of methodological pluralism by considering the subject matter further, and in particular, the fact that human knowledge is part of that subject matter. The reality we study, and the causal mechanisms at work, involve physical entities, and actions have physical consequences. Yet the system within which these operate is essentially a social system which has evolved by embodying human knowledge. Human action in turn (whether at an individual or social level) requires reasoned justification, just as do the conclusions of scientific enquiry. Keynes (1921) investigated the grounds for reasoned belief as the basis for action in general (in philosophy and science, as in practice). He explored the possibilities for a (pluralist) logic which, unlike classical logic, addressed circumstances which could only yield uncertain knowledge. And the end point of action is critical; the key issue was how to cut through the uncertainty in order to take decisive action. The parallel in methodology is the key issue of how to cut through methodological uncertainty in order to decide how to go about building (uncertain) knowledge in practice.

Keynes's epistemology developed on the basis of an ontology of open social systems with the characteristics outlined above. While real social systems are open, they are not chaotic (Chick, 1995). In order to provide a basis for action, institutions and habits of behaviour evolve. Thus, the emergence of the firm, the establishment of posted prices, contracts, rule of law and so on provide important elements of stability (Loasby, 2003). They provide boundaries which allow for segmented decision-making. Within such a system, knowledge is held with uncertainty, but it is knowledge nonetheless. Thus, in the particular case of science, knowledge develops within disciplines, segmenting what needs to be understood. Theories within disciplines segment particular aspects of the subject matter for detailed scrutiny. Even the terms we use require some segmentation, separating one thing from another which may, in reality, not be completely separate (see Hausman, 1992, on separability). Language itself is a mechanism for segmenting our reference to reality, as well as reference to ideas. Similarly, building knowledge (under uncertainty) only becomes possible when we segment some aspect off from the rest for scrutiny. The only way to avoid this, as in general equilibrium theory, is to assume a closed system, such that economist and economic agent alike can feasibly hold certain, or 'certain-equivalent', knowledge.

But these boundaries and segmentations, it must be emphasised, are provisional and mutable. They may serve a purpose for a while, but they become impediments to progress when conditions change. It is boundaries that define social systems – indeed, which give them their systemic character. Firms, for example, are systems which require a stable structure in order to develop strategies. But systems change. For example, changes in the external environment eventually require a reassessment of institutional structures. Strategies are required to create a more stable structure. Such change may also require a change in knowledge structures, including language. Language changes to mould itself to changing realities and changed understandings of that reality. Indeed, there is, accordingly, virtue in 'vagueness' of language (Kuhn, 1970; Coates, 1996, 1997; Davis, 1999b). What we have seen, therefore, is that real economic systems evolve in such a way as to produce structures, which are not rigid and which change from time to time. Just as pure pluralism is unworkable, therefore, so is the view that the economic system is open in some absolute sense (see further Chapter 11).

Critical realism has focused specifically on the central importance of open-system ontology (Lawson, 1997a, 2003). However, Lawson identifies schools of thought primarily according to whether or not they start from such an ontology. It is this binary classification (open/closed) of ontology which is most significant for critical realism. Schools of thought then are only differentiated according to the questions they ask within that ontology – their 'ontological commitments'. Yet, just as real social systems require some structure in order for social life to proceed, so an account of ontology requires some structure in order to be serviceable as a basis for knowledge.

It is a central tenet of critical realism that reality is structured. But this structure is provided by the epistemological categories employed in order to conceptualise ontology, and there is scope for different types of categorisation. Categories are employed too in order to provide the knowledge basis for agency, and indeed, there is feedback between agency and structure. In particular, as soon as language is employed in order to refer to ontology, the possibilities open up for different forms of categorisation. Effectively, then, different schools of thought can be identified with different categorisations and conceptualisations of either an open-system or a closed-system ontology (Dow, 1990b, 1999b). Given the requirements of social organisation and the requirement in particular for effective communication within paradigms, there is a practical limit to the number of paradigms which may be extant at any one time, so that the pluralism represented by schools of thought is structured.

The privileging of the openness of systems and the plurality of methodologies has tended, as we have seen, to lead to criticisms of a focus on schools of thought, on the grounds that it tends to discourage pluralism. Here it is helpful to go back to Kuhn's concepts of normal and extraordinary science and the process of paradigm change and the contemporary debate on these concepts. For Kuhn, in a mature science, extraordinary science is an unusual activity which only comes to the fore at times of crisis. Normal science, in which foundations are not questioned, is the norm. By not questioning foundations, those engaged in normal science effectively accept the paradigm's principles as being the best. Further, theory evolves within a given mode of categorisation and ascription of meaning to language. It is extraordinary science which opens up the possibilities of different methodological directions, the adoption of different categorisations and different meanings. This creates an almost dualistic scenario which seems to limit the scope for methodological pluralism and justify a monist approach within normal science. Kuhn was not dualistic about the process of paradigm shift, which he saw as an incremental process beginning with normal science. But the normal science/extraordinary science divide nevertheless appears too sharply drawn.

Further, Kuhn's picture of a mature science has never fitted well with social science, which accords better with his picture of immature science, or the arts – a situation where several paradigms persist simultaneously and where extraordinary science is accordingly more prevalent. For a social science, there is good reason, in the nature of the subject matter, to argue that plurality would be the norm no matter how mature the discipline. For our purposes, what is more at issue is to consider specifically whether normal science and extraordinary science might be understood differently, in Kuhn's framework, for an 'immature' science. Rather than opening up discussion to foundational questions only at times of crisis, interspersed with long periods without such discussion, the situation we are considering is one in which alternatives are always present. Communication issues do not apply only during brief periods of crisis, but from day to day when discourse is undertaken across paradigms. The distinctions between normal science and extraordinary science then become blurred. Thus, normal science with no account being taken of paradigmatic foundations may occur within a paradigm, but it cannot go far without coming up against methodological issues when communication is attempted outside the paradigm. More important, it is arguably when theory develops by making new connections across paradigms that most breakthroughs occur. This Smithian view of the growth of knowledge by means of new connections is one which Kuhn (1962, p. 200) specifically associated with paradigm shifts. This is precluded for Kuhn's mature sciences, except during unusual periods of scientific revolution.

Kuhn (1970) specifically addressed disputes over the relative roles of normal and extraordinary science which were represented in the same volume. For other philosophers of science, particularly Popper (1970), normal science appeared to lack the crucial, critical, feature of science. Popper's argument would appear to favour universal extraordinary science, with everything open to question. Rather than the science studies approach on the one hand, which emphasises description over criticism, and the support which Kuhn's normal science appeared to give to protection from criticism, Popper identified science fully with criticism. In his response, Kuhn put the emphasis on the crucial feature of meaning change as a result of a paradigm shift, which is absent in the theory development of normal science. He then drew the helpful distinction between understanding another language and translating it. Incommensurabilty means that there is no fully satisfactory way of translating language from one paradigm to the next (just as more generally something is always lost in linguistic translation). Yet it is still possible to learn other languages in such a way as to allow communication. This is what facilitates the transition from one paradigm to the next. For pluralist social sciences, in which we are concerned with contemporaneous rather than consecutive paradigms, this distinction has particular import. While it would be an unreasonable (Popperian) distraction to have all economists engaged at all times in efforts of extraordinary science in the form of translation, it is nevertheless reasonable to have all economists capable to some degree of understanding the meanings of other paradigms' languages (or, at the very least, conscious that there is an issue of linguistic difference).

What we find, then, is that, if we construct a particular understanding of normal science and extraordinary science to suit the social sciences, we address the concerns of those who see Kuhn's framework as actively discouraging pluralism. Paradigms, or schools of thought, provide the structure by which we categorise different approaches within a pluralist epistemology. However, practitioners cannot stray far from extraordinary science in a pluralist environment, since sensitivity to the need for translation is necessary for successful communication and, potentially, persuasion, across paradigms. We come back to the ethical argument for pluralism – mutual respect is the basis for civilised behaviour in a pluralist environment. But the epistemological argument is equally compelling, that we cannot expect anything other than methodological pluralism, and it needs to be structured in order to have meaning. Schools of thought provide some important elements of that structure. Indeed, the biological metaphor of diversity of strains within species being necessary for the survival of the species can be seen to carry over to epistemology, such that methodological pluralism is positively welcome.

Conclusion

We have been concerned here to reassess the role of schools of thought within methodological pluralism. While it might have been expected that the wide adherence to methodological pluralism would have enhanced the usefulness of categorisation according to schools of thought, this has not been the case. Rather, the categorisation has been treated on the one hand as being innocuous – simply part of the architecture of economics which might be referred to in descriptive accounts. On the other hand, it has been regarded as putting up barriers to the openness of discourse which follows from practicing methodological pluralism.

Going back to the ontological foundations for methodological pluralism, the structuring of social reality (and the language which plays an important part in that reality) suggests a structuring also at the epistemological level. Structured pluralism, then, is the advocacy of a range of methodological approaches to economics which, like the range of social structures, is not infinite. The structure is provisional; schools of thought change, not least because of their interactions with each other, as well as with the changing subject matter. A methodological approach, just like social structures, requires a community with shared beliefs about the nature of reality, a shared focus on a particular segment of that reality, shared categorisations, and shared understandings of meanings of terms. No matter how much of a genius, no individual can persuade others to accept new ideas without some common ground of understanding, some scope for making a connection with the audience (an argument which goes back at least to Adam Smith, 1762–3). In other words, the functioning of science requires paradigms, or schools of thought.

The argument has referred extensively to Kuhn's framework, not least because of his emphasis, in defining paradigms in terms of incommensurability, on language. This reinforces the role of schools of thought in defining the purview of particular categorisations and understandings of terms. Many of the benefits of methodological pluralism, such as the making of new connections across paradigms, can only be derived if there is sufficient awareness of, and understanding of, language difference that some communication is possible. Some languages are closer than others, making mutual understanding easier. But, without some categorisation of language itself, within a framework of schools of thought, there would be no point of reference on which to base efforts to communicate.

11
The Meaning of Open Systems

Jointly authored with Victoria Chick

The concept of open systems appears increasingly frequently in the literature but, as with other concepts we have discussed, it has different meanings depending on the underlying approach. This chapter is an attempt to clarify some of the meanings given to open and closed systems, demonstrating that the distinction is not a dualistic one. Different understandings are possible, just as different responses are possible in the form of different approaches to theorising. As an indication that what is being discussed is not some dualistic mainstream/non-mainstream opposition, we focus on different understandings and applications of open systems within non-mainstream economics.

Introduction

Thinking about the economy in terms of systems has a long pedigree, but the terminology of openness and closure in economics is attracting increasing attention. It is apparent that these terms are being employed differently, not only between mainstream and non-mainstream economists but also within non-mainstream economics. The purpose of this chapter is to tease out these differences in meaning and, more important, the underlying methodological approaches which account for these differences. This exercise is offered as a contribution to clarifying the debate.

The original version of this chapter was published in the *Journal of Economic Methodology*, 12(3), 2005, 363–81. We are grateful for the comments of Andy Brown, John Davis, Geoff Hodgson, Jesper Jespersen, George Krimpas, S. G. (Fieke) van der Lecq, Tony Lawson and Menno Rol. They are not responsible for the errors and omissions which may remain.

In the first two parts of the next section, we discuss the two concepts and propose criteria for openness and closure. Differences of opinion have arisen not only because terms are used differently, but also because of confusion over the different levels at which openness or closure is being considered: the level of reality and the level of theory. At the level of theory, there are the further distinctions between models, theories and systems, which we consider next. We also address the question of how far openness and closure at different levels can be nested in each other.

Critical realists have taken as the hallmark of closure the constant conjunction of events (if x then y, perhaps stochastically) and the absence of such regularity as the test for openness. In the fourth part of the next section, we assess the consequences of concentrating on the outcome of openness or closure (event regularity or its absence), as the critical realists do, rather than on the conditions of openness or closure. There is no one-to-one correspondence between conditions and outcome. This reveals a potentially important difference in how closed and open systems are understood. We then compare the critical realists' conditions for closure with ours. The issue of boundaries emerges from that comparison as an important potential source of misunderstanding. We put forward the argument that the very notion of a system entails boundaries of some sort: a system must have limits as well as connections. This means that our own use of the term 'open' when combined with 'system' involves some modification from a 'pure' openness; openness is not the dual of closure. We suggest that some of the reason for difference in approach lies in the personal intellectual backgrounds of the main protagonists.

In the third section, we briefly explore the appropriate relationship between theory and reality as perceived by mainstream economics, critical realism and ourselves. The question of boundaries is seen here as part of the discussion of different meanings of terms such as abstraction, isolation and idealisation.

Some of the different usages which we uncover may simply reflect terminological differences which can easily be resolved upon further enquiry and discussion. But others may be more deep-seated. We conclude by attempting a review along these lines.

Open and closed systems

Systems defined

Let us start with the concept of 'system'. The *Oxford English Dictionary* offers many variants, of which the following are closest to what an economist usually means:

1. within the category *'an organized or connected group of objects'*: 'a set or assemblage of things connected, associated, or interdependent, so as to form a complex unity; a whole composed of parts in orderly arrangement according to some scheme or plan'
2. within the category *'a set of principles, etc.; a scheme, method'*: 'the set of correlated principles, ideas, or statements belonging to some department of knowledge or belief; a department of knowledge or belief considered as an organized whole.'

Clearly, the defining characteristic is interconnection within a collection of things or ideas which can be regarded as having a recognisable coherence or unity.

A network of ideas is identified by the set of connections it comprises. Loasby (2003), drawing on Potts (2000), has pointed out that a general-equilibrium theoretical system, where 'general' in this context means that all the elements in the system are connected with all the others, is the exception rather than the rule. In general, the set of connections in any system is incomplete. The particular set of connections and absence of connection 'is what differentiates one system from another and gives them a sense of both character and order' (Chick, 2004, p. 5). There is a nice demonstration of this principle in Dutt (1990): he takes a basic model and, by the choice of the last equation (the last 'connection', which also determines what is left out), derives models with, successively, neoclassical, Marxian and Post-Keynesian characteristics.

There is a parallel understanding of social systems. The following is a possible definition: 'A system is a network, a structure with connections, within which agents act, mostly in ways which reproduce and reinforce the system, but sometimes in ways which lead the system to evolve' (Chick, 2004, p. 5). Typically, the connections are not complete. Institutions are a powerful source of both connections and barriers, both constraining and enabling decision-making and action. They define the parameters within which certain activities take place, and some activities are excluded; hence, we speak of the capitalist system, the market system, a university system and so on. Many other institutions, to which the word 'system' is seldom applied in ordinary speech, are systems in the sense used here: companies, hospitals, the family. Systems are a subject of study in their own right, though the results and methods of systems theory are not central to our purpose here: it is only the use of the term 'system' to denote a type of organisation which is important.[1]

It is an important issue for our discussion that in general the connections and absence of connection that characterise a system need not be fixed. They are in general mutable; institutions and behaviour evolve. Ideas change in response to changes in the real world, to discourse and by the exercise of imagination; new ideas can lead to new connections.

Open and closed

Let us again consult the *Oxford English Dictionary*:[2]

> '*open system*, a material system in which the total mass or energy fluctuates; an incomplete or alterable system (of ideas, doctrines, things, etc.).'

> '*closed system*, a complete and essentially unalterable system (of ideas, doctrines, things, etc.); a material system in which the total mass or energy remains constant; a self-contained realm, unaffected by external forces.'

The first thing to note is that the definitions refer to three characteristics: the degree of completeness, mutability and relation with 'the outside'; and two levels: reality and ideas. These features are reflected in the conditions, originally derived without reference to these OED definitions, by Dow (2002, pp. 139–40) (see also Chapter 10) and developed

---

[1] Systems theory (Bertalanffy, 1968 is the *locus classicus*) has found principles that are common to systems regardless of their content, although for some purposes distinctions might be made between institutions and systems. Systems theory has been applied to economics by Boulding (see 1956, for example).

[2] One commentator pointed out that this is a definition from thermodynamics and asks, 'why go to the dictionary when you can tailor to needs'? Apart from the fact that, since the definition refers to systems of ideas as well as to the natural world, the scope of the definition goes beyond thermodynamics, there is an important issue of principle here. A similar point was made by Hicks (1965, pp. 15–6, 23) concerning equilibrium. He maintained that economics should have its own definition, which he thought should be the meeting of preferences. First, such a tactic breaks continuity with the use of language across disciplines and cultural life in general. We do not favour a private language for economics, even if it were generally agreed within the subject. Our second objection is that, in the face of a lack of consensus, no single individual, even one with a considerable constituency, should have the right to 'tailor to needs', that is, to determine definitions for the subject as a whole.

further below in Table 11.1. The first set of conditions applies to characteristics of perceived reality and the second to theories about reality. The theoretical conditions follow from the conditions pertaining to reality. It is important to note that satisfying any one of conditions (i) to (iv) is sufficient for openness in reality, and any one of conditions (v) to (viii) for openness of a theoretical system. Furthermore, it is in the nature of open systems that this list should not be taken as exhaustive.

Table 11.1 Conditions for open systems

Real-world systems
  i. The system is not atomistic; therefore at least one of the following holds:
    a. outcomes of actions cannot be inferred from individual actions (because of interactions);
    b. agents and their interactions may change (for example agents may learn).
  ii. Structure and agency are interdependent.
  iii. Boundaries around and within the social or economic system are mutable for at least one of the following reasons:
    a. social structures may evolve;
    b. connections between structures may change;
    c. the structure-agent relation may change.
  iv. Identifiable social structures are embedded in larger structures; these may mutually interact, for the boundaries of a social system are in general partial or semi-permeable.

Implications for theoretical systems
  v. There may be important omitted variables or relations and/or their effects on the system may be uncertain.
  vi. The classification into exogenous and endogenous variables may be neither fixed nor exhaustive.
  vii. Connections and/or boundaries between structures may be imperfectly known and/or may change.
  viii. There is imperfect knowledge of the relations between variables; relationships may not be stable.

We take it as read that an actual social or economic system is open; when this ontological question is addressed in the literature, there seems to be general agreement on this point. In other words, there is general agreement that at least one of conditions (i) to (iv) is satisfied. In economics, it is at the level of theory that issues of the characteristics of systems are more commonly addressed. It is this undue focus on theory and lack of attention to the ontological presuppositions of theory which has been the subject of the critical realists' critique. It is their contention that the use of closed modes of theorising or modelling presupposes a closed-system ontology. We explore the relation between theory and ontology below.

It follows from the sufficiency of any one of the above conditions for open systems that *all* the conditions set out in Table 11.2 are *necessary* conditions for a closed system, and together they are sufficient. They apply at the theoretical level. Open systems and closed systems, as defined above, do not constitute a duality, but a spectrum (Mearman, 2002, 2005). While closure of an epistemological system requires that all of conditions (1) to (8) be satisfied, openness only requires *any one* of conditions (i) to (viii) to be satisfied. While any system which is not closed is therefore open, no system is perfectly open. There is scope for a wide range of types and degrees of openness.

Table 11.2 Conditions for closed theoretical systems

1. All relevant variables can be identified.
2. The boundaries of the system are definite and immutable; it follows that it is clear which variables are exogenous and which are endogenous; these categories are fixed.
3. Only the specified exogenous variables affect the system, and they do this in a known way.
4. Relations between the included variables are either knowable or random.
5. Economic agents (whether individuals or aggregates) are treated atomistically.
6. The nature of economic agents is treated as if constant.
7. The structure of the relationships between the components (variables, subsystems, agents) is treated as if it is either knowable or random.
8. The structural framework within which agents act is taken as given.

An open system is characterised by some (partial, mutable) boundaries *in order for it to be a system*. The use of the descriptor 'open' in conjunction with 'system' alters the sense of 'openness'; complete openness is incompatible with the system remaining recognisable as a system (see Capra, 1975).

Mearman identifies the origin of these conditions in mathematics, but the two sets are different. While the closure conditions are compatible with – indeed are the conditions for – mathematical modelling, that is not the case for the conditions for openness. While there may be scope for openness in fuzzy mathematics and complexity theory, conventional mathematics cannot encompass the kind of fluidity involved in openness.

Systems, theories and models

The practice of thinking of the economy, and knowledge about the economy, in terms of systems is not new. Skinner (1976) makes much of Adam Smith's systemic approach to the economy and our understanding of it. The way in which general equilibrium theory (re)interpreted Smith's understanding of systems has been well documented (see for example Winch, 1997). Keynes, and the literature on Keynes, have also influenced our understanding of the economy, and of knowledge under uncertainty, in terms of systems. Here we address the epistemological status of systems, theories and models.

Models and theories are systems; the former is an interrelated set of formal propositions, often expressed as equations, and the latter is an interrelated set of ideas or hypotheses. In economics, we use the terms 'theory' and 'model', often loosely, to indicate approaches to interrelated ideas. Most mainstream economists indeed do not differentiate: for them, models are theories. For example, Lucas (1980, p. 697) stated that 'a "theory" is not a collection of assertions about the behavior of the actual economy but rather an explicit set of instructions for building a parallel or analogue system.' But we remember a time when there was a clear difference: models were thought of as aids to thinking but falling short of the explanatory power which would give them the dignity of theory.

A model is a formal structure defined by its assumptions and definitions. While the model is being employed, these restrictions are complete and fixed. Theories are broader than models. They may be either formal or informal and they may encompass several models. A well-documented example of a theory encompassing models is that in Keynes's *General Theory* (1936), within which Kregel (1976) found three models, each based on different assumptions about expectations. The theory is expounded in the book as a whole; the models have a role in the development of the theory but they are less than the theory. At the epistemic level, the term 'open system', as we are using it in the present context, is a close approximation to what we understand by 'theory'.

Serious confusion may also arise between system and model. Van der Lecq's (2000) distinction between open and closed systems, on the one hand, and open and closed models, on the other, is particularly helpful in considering the open/closed distinction from the perspective of mainstream economics, in which models predominate. She explained that 'openness', applied to models, means something different from openness with respect to a system: whereas the criteria above suggest that (formal, mathematical) models are always closed systems,

[c]onfusingly, in [mainstream] economics the terms closed and open are applied to formal models. A model which consists of only endogenous variables is called a closed model, whereas a model in which exogenous variables are included in order to solve it, is called an open model. The term open model reflects the idea that the model would be indeterminate without information from outside. ... In the terminology [of systems], both closed and open models are examples of a closed system approach. (van der Lecq, 2000, p. 161)

She proposed a third category of system to cope with closed models (where everything is endogenised): the isolated system. This usage conforms to that in physics: a physical system is closed if the boundary is proof against the transfer of *either* matter *or* energy, while in an isolated system *neither* can cross the boundary. Thus, isolation is a stronger condition than closure: isolated systems are a subset of closed systems.[3] This addition is an improvement but it still leaves a linguistic mare's nest: a closed model is an isolated system, and an open model is a closed system.[4]

Subsystems

In general, not only can a system of ideas be defined in terms of connections within partial and provisional boundaries, but also there may be subsystems within such systems, as defined by the connections which mark out an area as semi-separate or amenable to further closure by imposing additional conditions. These subsystems may be closed models within the larger, open system (or theory). Closure is then (conceptually) nested within openness.

The type of theorising which emerges from this procedure depends on whether or not the theorist keeps the features of the larger system (of which the subsystem is a part) 'at the back of one's head' (Keynes, 1936, pp. 297–8). The distinction is between ignoring for the time being aspects of reality, on the one hand (because this is necessary for model closure, in van der Lecq's terms), and actively assuming something known to be false which precludes later relaxation, on the other (the process of isolation, in van der Lecq's terms). The first is a method for partial analysis within open-system theories which is widely referred to

---

[3] The term 'isolation' is another which is given different meanings. It is most closely associated with the work of Mäki (1992), to which we refer below.

[4] An additional source of confusion is the reference to closed-economy and open-economy models to indicate whether international trade and payments are, respectively, excluded or included.

as abstraction. The second is part of the method of closed-system modelling, which involves idealisation.[5] Theory can adapt to incorporating the omitted feature in the first case but not in the second. An example of the first case is Kregel's (1976) account of three different assumptions about expectations in Keynes's *General Theory* to which we have already referred. These assumptions defined three models, in which (a) no expectations changed, (b) only short-term expectations changed and (c) all expectations could change, respectively. An example of the second case is the typical New Classical model where, given the axioms of individual rationality, expectations are fully defined by the model itself, leaving no room for expectations to be held constant in spite of an exogenous change, or to change without identifying some exogenous cause (a change in the available information, for example). This feature is intrinsic to the model and it cannot be altered.

It is this lack of adaptability of models of the second type that causes some open-systems theorists to be reluctant to think in terms of models at all. We think this position is both extreme and unnecessary, for we believe that closed-system models can be compatible with open theoretical systems (see Chick and Dow, 2001/Chapter 9 and the penultimate section below). The key is how far the theoretical system is identified by its models. Within an open theoretical system, there is scope for changing the assumptions, boundaries or *ceteris paribus* conditions to suit the theorist's immediate purpose, as for example assuming that long-term expectations are fixed in one model but not in another. Theorising extends beyond the models in order to take account of what has been 'kept at the back of one's head'. A closed theoretical system, on the other hand, tends to be identified by its models. Hodgson (2004), in making the case for situating models within a larger context, can be understood in our language as arguing that closed system models need to be embedded in theories or open systems.

---

[5] These two approaches can be classed as partial representation and idealisation (Rappaport, 1996, p. 217) or legitimate and bogus abstraction (Lawson, 1997a, pp. 232–7), respectively. Mäki's (1992) distinction between isolation by omission and isolation by idealisation does not correspond directly to these two approaches, since they are discussed only in terms of isolated systems, and for him abstraction is a subset of isolation. We discuss the debate between Lawson and Mäki on the method of isolation further in the second part of the subsection on Lawson, below.

Lawson's critical realism

The litmus test: event regularities

For Lawson (1997a, 2003, 2004), a closed system is fully identified by the occurrence of event regularities, and, conversely, openness is equated with an absence of event regularities. The latter, he argues, corresponds to reality as we know it. However, identifying closed systems at the empirical level, Lawson (2003, p. 15) has to address the possibility that event regularities may occur, not as the result of causal connection, but either by chance or as a result of common cause; this he classifies as 'closure of concomitance'. Event regularities which occur for these reasons do not require the assumption of atomism. Indeed, such event regularities can be useful for explanatory work since, having no necessary reason to persist, their breakdown can provide a point of interest for the contrastive analysis which Lawson advocates. However, it is event regularities due to 'closure of causal sequence' which are the focus of mainstream economics. Theory then is designed to represent causal connections that either predict or explain event regularities; for these theories or models, the assumption of atomism is required.

As is well known, Lawson gives priority to ontology. He has argued consistently and vigorously that the closed-system approach of mainstream economics can only be justified by closure at the ontological level. Cases of closure are rare in the social realm, and therefore the closed-system theorising that characterises the mainstream is almost always inappropriate. This position raises the question of the relationship between theorising and reality, which we take up in the next section. However, first we wish to look at the relationship of Lawson's litmus test to Dow's criteria as given above.

It can easily be seen that if a theory/model meets the Dow conditions for closure, it will predict regular outcomes following from the behaviour and relationships of which it is composed. Predicted event regularity is a conclusion which follows from the conditions for closure. If and only if the theory is correctly structured in terms of causal mechanisms, these systematic predictions will be borne out in practice. It is in that case a matter of indifference whether correct closed theoretical systems are described by their predicted event regularities or by the structure which gives rise to those regularities. By definition, however, theory cannot predict or explain chance correlations. And at the level of actual events, one can observe and make use of regularities without a theory of their causation. Nor is there any reason to suppose that theories are correctly specified. Thus Lawson's criterion cannot say (nor does he claim to say) anything about theory, its correctness or appropriateness.

The choice between Dow's conditions and Lawson's criterion is not neutral when applied to open theoretical systems either. The Dow conditions for openness may or may not give rise to event irregularity. Consider criterion (v), in which variables whose importance or effect is unknown to the theorist (otherwise they would have been included) are omitted or variables which are known to be important are not modelled. The latter case may also be found in closed-system models. The event regularity which would follow if these variables had been included will not in general be confirmed in practice. The second case is familiar even to first-year students learning about shifting demand curves. An example from *The General Theory* is, again, the treatment of expectations: theoretical results alter when long-term or short-term expectations, which are included but not modelled, change: they act like exogenous variables.

However, event regularity can be consistent with an open theoretical system as we define it. For example, the hypothesis 'if income rises, consumption will rise', is a postulated event regularity, though understood to be subject to lags and individual variation. It is fundamental to Keynes's theory, which models real-world features (i(a)) and (iv) and as a theory it is open according to condition (vii): its borders are not closed, especially to time.

The difference between the case of omitted variables and the consumption example rests on the conditions for openness which apply in each case: the first has to do with condition (v) (open) or (1) (closed) (omitted variables); the second example has to do with condition (iii) (open) or (2) (closed): shifting boundaries. The propensity to consume survives the shift from short period to long period and even, though qualified by Keynes to allow for lagged adjustment to change, the transition from one level of activity to another. Indeed, it is the engine of that adjustment once the 'disturbance'– a new level of investment – has taken place. More generally, without some regularities of this kind, in our view, theory cannot really proceed. Lawson recognises this in his 'demi-regularities', correlations which, though not exact, are sufficiently regular to allow theorising (see Lawson, 1997, p. 204).

In summary, we have shown that at the theoretical level there is no one-to-one correspondence between event regularities and the Dow conditions. This seems to us a good reason for concentrating on the conditions rather than, as Lawson does, on the outcome. Lawson does provide conditions, to which we now turn to compare them with Dow's criteria.

Extrinsic, intrinsic and aggregation conditions

Lawson (1997a, pp. 77–81) states three conditions which produce closure (and by implication, in their absence, openness): an extrinsic condition, an intrinsic condition and an aggregation condition. His extrinsic condition is that potential influences on the dependent variable other than those explicitly taken into account (omitted variables) must be uncorrelated with the variables focused on. This condition is similar to but less stringent than the combination of Dow's closure criteria (1) and (3). The 'intrinsic' closure condition, that relations within the system be known and predictable, correspond to Dow's criteria (4), (6), (7) and (8). The aggregation condition, which precludes interdependencies within the system, is Dow's criterion (5). There is thus a correspondence with all of Dow's criteria except the reference to boundaries (criterion [2] for closed systems; see also criteria [v] and [vii] for openness), to which Lawson has now (2004) taken explicit exception, despite the fact that the very words 'extrinsic' and 'intrinsic' imply a boundary. For Lawson, a boundary, either within or around open systems, is identified as 'distorting' reality, something which critical realism wishes to avoid.[6] We take it that this idea of distortion comes from the proposition that theory should mirror reality. This conception might also account for his antipathy to the *ceteris paribus* method,[7] though perhaps it is rooted instead in the misuse of *ceteris paribus* to rule out variables which should be included. This is a problem for another time.

Boundaries

An antipathy to the idea of boundaries would seem not entirely consistent with Lawson's own description of social reality. Lawson's analysis of social ontology refers explicitly to social structures (conventions, institutions and so on). Structures imply connections and boundaries (the limits to structures); these are the characteristics of systems. As long as social ontology is understood in terms of system, or structure, then surely boundaries on complete openness are implied.

A second difficulty has the same nature as the first, in terms of finding a way between extremes (duals): in the real world one rarely, outside the controlled experiment, encounters perfect event regularity (even

---

[6] 'To study an open system by using any form of closure ... disfigures the landscape of an open system' (Nash, 2004, p. 76).

[7] Expressed by him as a discussant to Chick's INEM, 2002, paper, now Chick (2004).

stochastically) or its complete absence. Nash (2004) points out that Lawson's recognition of 'demi-regularities' implies that systems cannot be completely open (with which we entirely agree, but for structural reasons). The very activity of attempting to understand reality presumes that there is *some* regularity. However, 'some regularity' is very different from the complete order of a closed system or its dual, chaos.

Some support for this view that the problem lies in the scope for dualism found in the debate between Lawson and Mäki as to whether 'isolating closures' provide the basis for theorising. Mäki (1992) argues that an open-system ontology can be and routinely is analysed by a closed theoretical system by applying the method of isolation. Lawson does not take exception to the use of the term 'isolation' if all that is meant is 'abstraction' (Lawson, 1997, pp. 131–3) (nor indeed of the term 'closure' if all that is meant is 'theorising'). But he understands the intent of isolation in Mäki's usage as being to identify separable relationships, with an implied direct correspondence between ontology and theory which he claims has no justification in reality (Lawson, 2003, pp. 307–8, n.4). Indeed, Mäki (1992, pp. 348–9) points out that it is important whether social systems are closer to the mechanical or the chemical analogy. He argues that the method of isolation applies more closely to the former, since mechanical causes have additive effects (that is, they meet the aggregation criterion), while qualitative, emergent change can occur when chemical causes are combined and interact. He concludes therefore that 'strong isolations' are indeed unsuited to open systems. We have already seen the very restrictive nature of the concept of an isolated system in the physical sciences: such a system is only approximated by laboratory conditions, and it is quite unattainable in the actual social world, though not, of course, in thought experiments. Yet Mäki's use of the expression 'strong isolation' implies that a weaker version of isolation is also possible, which might correspond more closely to Lawson's meaning of the term 'abstraction' (Lawson, 1997a, pp. 131–3), so that it is no longer a dualistic issue of choosing between isolation and not-isolation.

While we do not wish to explore further here any difference of meaning with respect to 'isolation', the debate is suggestive that the disagreement with Lawson over boundaries may reveal a misunderstanding of what we mean by boundaries. For us, boundaries are not always fully isolating but, rather, in general semi-permeable and mutable. Very simply, if Lawson understands boundaries in terms of rigid, isolating barriers, this assumption may seem to him too strong, and we would agree. Runde (2002), another leading critical realist, speaks quite happily of the fact that individuals 'cut up' reality in order to understand it. 'Cutting up' holds the strong implication of imputing boundaries. At the ontological level, structure implies boundaries.

The difference between us and the critical realists lies in defining openness and closure in terms of the structure of the system versus its manifestation or outcome. For closed systems, the choice is only neutral if the system is 'perfect', that is, conditions (1), (3) and (4) are met. If the closure conditions are met and the theoretical system is correctly specified (that is, it captures reality quite closely), event regularities in theory and empirically are a consequence. However, if for example important relationships are missing from a theory (there are omitted variables), the behaviour of the dependent variables will not exhibit event regularity in practice, whether the theoretical system is open or closed. And some regularities will survive the shifting boundaries of some open systems. So, the choice is not neutral, as we have seen. Our approach gives the structural foundation for event regularities or their absence. Lawson only gives criteria for closure, but unlike the outcome of event regularity or its absence, our criteria for openness are not simple duals of the criteria for closure but explicitly encompass a wide range of possibilities for and degrees of openness.

Personal intellectual backgrounds

We believe that it is possible that the differences in perspective explored here have to do with the different starting points of the participants.[8] All three of us share dissatisfaction with much mainstream analysis on the grounds of its detachment from reality as we perceive it. The present authors have come to open and closed systems from theoretical and methodological considerations, respectively. Chick's characterisation of Keynes's *General Theory* as a play (Chick, 1983, pp. 27–32) and other work on Keynes's method (Chick 1998b) and equilibrium conditional on constraints or boundaries (Chick and Caserta, 1997a),[9] established the importance of shifting boundaries within theory. Dow's work on modes of thought (1985) contrasted the fixed categories of Cartesian thought and the greater (but not complete) fluidity of categories in a Babylonian approach (see further Chapter 4). The two approaches came together through conversations on how to theorise if the subject of theory was a complex organic unity. Our answer was to use temporary and partial

---

[8] To seek insights in this way is consistent with Searle's (1995) emphasis on 'deep background' as a determinant of framing as well as a focus on mode of thought (see further Chick, 1995).

[9] The seeds of this idea were planted as early as the mid-1970s (in a lecture given by Chick in Perugia).

closures to make analysis of a complex system tractable. Lawson's concentration on the manifestation rather than the cause may stem from his background in econometrics, in which finding event regularities is the core concern. His critique may have been provoked by the inability of econometric analysis to capture the irregular, but nevertheless real, relationships which constitute social and economic reality – an inability which is shared by much mainstream theory, owing to its closed-system character.

Theorising and reality

Some of the differences we have explored in this chapter have to do with the assumed or appropriate relationship between theory and reality. In critical realism there is, as explained above, a general presumption that the approach taken to studying the economy should be determined by ontology.[10] But although that sounds to us like common sense, it is a belief or judgement not universally held. We contrast attitudes below.

Mainstream economics

Since mainstream economists mainly theorise in terms of models (as isolated or closed systems), critical realists suggest that their conclusions can only apply to closed ontological reality. It is the falsification of open reality that is the foundation of their critique. In actual fact, this question of mapping onto reality does not seem to be of much importance within the mainstream. Though Lawson accuses mainstream economists of 'bogus abstraction', that is, 'the pretence that economic phenomena are, after all, generated under conditions equivalent to those achieved through experimental control' (1997a, p. 235), we doubt that this is the deliberate stance of many. Rather most mainstream economists probably accept that they are abstracting from many aspects of reality, as do we all. And for those who adopt the 'as if' method, if the conclusions 'work', the realism or otherwise of the assumptions is not seen to be important. For many, the economy is unknown territory: it is the axioms of rational behaviour and the equilibrium method that shape the theory. We portray this stance in Figure 11.1. The direction of the arrows indicates that what can be said about reality is inferred from the level of theory. The detail at the 'reality' level is not filled in, while at the theoretical level we find a core set of axioms and a number

---

[10] The resulting correspondence between theory and reality is, however, not direct, since reality is understood to be stratified, and there is no necessary synchronisation between the different levels.

of models, not connected by any larger scheme (see Hodgson, 2004). Mainstream economists will say this is a caricature, of course, but so is the critical realist claim that by entertaining closed-system theorising they are presupposing a laboratory economy. Indeed, any form of abstraction entails some form of caricature.

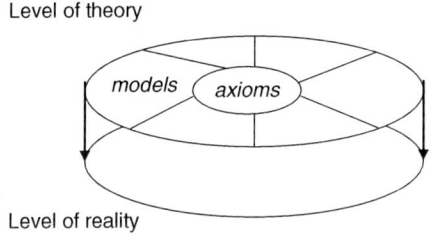

Level of theory

Level of reality

Figure 11.1 Mainstream economics

Critical realism

Just as closed theoretical systems imply for critical realism a closed ontology, the conception of the economic system, and social systems generally, as open implies that theory should be constructed as open systems, with the exception of rare occurrences of ontological closure, which can be modelled by closed systems, as illustrated by Figure 11.2. In this diagrammatic representation, the open-system ontology is shown by a dotted line as a boundary. From this, it follows that knowledge is also an open system. At the level of theory, open-system theories are likewise shown in terms of dotted boundaries, that is, they are neither closed nor completely open; the *boundaries* are provisional and semi-permeable. The term 'theory' is being used here broadly to encompass explanation in terms of a range of (possibly countervailing) tendencies, rather than in the mainstream sense of a unified, law-like explanation.

Lawson (2004) has argued that even the (provisional, semi-permeable) boundaries which define theories (and groupings of theories into

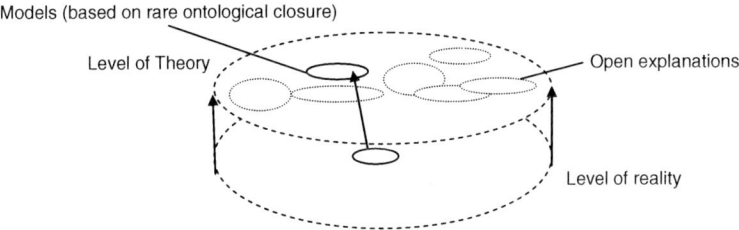

Models (based on rare ontological closure)

Level of Theory

Open explanations

Level of reality

Figure 11.2 Critical realism

schools of thought) are distortions of that reality. Yet this reaction again, it seems to us, reflects a misunderstanding of our use of the term 'boundary' as something fixed and complete, rather than as something provisional and semi-permeable. Critical realists dissociate themselves even more from the idea of using models, which are defined by a formal closure which is generally absent from reality. While it is accepted that there could be, in principle, rare instances of closure which would justify the use of models, in practice, critical realism is characterised by the complete absence of models.

Our position

Like critical realists, we understand social systems as open and mutable but structured by institutions, habits and so on. We also agree that the primary focus should be on ontology, from which our approach to pursuing knowledge follows. Our difference with critical realists is that we see no need for such a strong reluctance to acknowledge the need for boundaries (in our open-system sense); such boundaries serve as a means of building theories, including models as one tool of theorising (see Figure 11.3). Indeed, we see great virtue in devices, such as *ceteris paribus*, designed to keep some aspects of reality at bay temporarily, thus allowing analysis to proceed. We have no objections even to complete closures so long as these are in place only temporarily; thus, models are shown with continuous boundaries, although these closures are provisional. We accept that these closures distort reality: the most obvious example is the suspension of time in the short and long periods. The ability to treat these closures as temporary depends on their being part of a larger scheme, which we call a theory; theories are open systems. Similarly, theories may be grouped into schools of thought, in which the boundaries which define schools are provisional, semi-permeable and possibly overlapping.

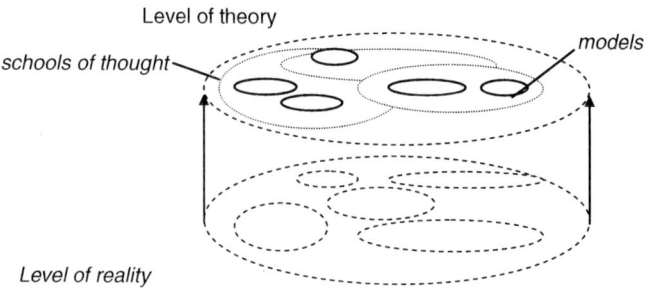

Figure 11.3　Our position

Conclusion

Our examination of the language of open and closed systems has revealed that the words do not always have the same meaning or apply at the same level. A mainstream economist might consider a model open because of the presence of exogenous variables and/or stochasticness, while a non-mainstream economist would regard any model as closed since the identity of all relevant variables (endogenous and exogenous, random or not) must be established in order to define the model.

Such models may, however, be embedded in theoretical systems, which may be open or closed. When the theory is defined by models, then the theoretical system must in turn also be closed. However, closed models can also be embedded in open theoretical systems which provide what is being 'kept at the back of one's head' when considering models. There is scope, and indeed the necessity, for analysis also of these factors when appropriate. Open theoretical systems are constructed precisely to allow different (provisional, semi-permeable) closures for application to different economic situations or problems. Closed theoretical systems in contrast have boundaries (between rationality and irrationality for example) which cannot be changed without completely changing the system.

While most economists would probably agree that the real social system is open, not everyone would agree that ontological openness precludes theoretical closure. However, if by closure one understands 'isolation' (in the sense of 'strong isolation'), this may have led to a misunderstanding of the idea of boundaries which may be complete but temporary, or semi-permeable.

To us, the fact that an economic system has some (provisional, partial) structure provides the basis for theoretical structures, even with closed models. If like critical realists we were to see these boundaries (structures) as 'distorting', then this would apply equally to the identification of individual causal powers. We think this term 'distortion' conjures up an unfortunately dualistic conception of openness which implies a complete absence of regularity, as the dual to law-like behaviour. We have tried to explain openness as something other than the dual of closure.

By finding the origins of an open theoretical system in an open ontological system, the way in which we construct theories and models is conditioned by the nature of reality. Thus, in an open-systems approach, consistency is understood as a relation between theory and reality, rather than internal to theory, as in a closed-system approach.

Even in econometrics, in which external consistency is important, the predominant mainstream approach is geared to establishing the validity or otherwise of closed-system models. In order to construct models, restrictions are necessary. These are bound to be 'distorting'. Yet the important issue is how this is done; reality has to be 'cut up' in some way for analysis, and some cuts make more sense than others do.

Disagreement remains over the role of event regularities. For Lawson, these define closed systems, while for us they are a consequence of the structure of closed systems. Some closures do not lead to the outcome of observed event regularities, and open systems can contain stable, reliable relationships. In the second case, the issue is whether the regularities can be relied on as the outcome of a persistent structure (as in a closed system) or *in spite of* a mutable structure.

The difference between our understanding of open and closed systems and that of the critical realists seems to stem primarily from different use of language, different starting points and different emphases. But the difference with the implicit understanding of open and closed systems in mainstream economics seems to stem more from an underlying difference in mode of thought. In the methodology of mainstream economics, the focus is at the theoretical level. At this level, the difference between us is between attempting to understand a complex reality by an open-systems technique which allows for uncertainty and mutability, and the method of closed models based on axioms and which fully specify external and internal forces, respectively. This is not to say that mainstream theory does not evolve. New variables and new relationships may be identified to reflect new theory and changing reality. However, the new variables and relationships are introduced in new models; the models are not subsets of a larger theory. Rather the models are intended as full representations of the theories. Those aspects of reality from which the theory is isolated (such as unquantifiable uncertainty, evolving institutional structures, behaviour that does not conform to the rationality axioms and so on) are not 'kept at the back of one's head'. In terms of the criteria listed above, the closure is complete. This difference is deeper and, we expect, more difficult to resolve.

12
The Issue of Uncertainty in Economics

Central banks, which are required to act in spite of uncertainty, have been making increasing reference to uncertainty in their public statements. The significance of uncertainty has come to much wider attention with the financial crisis, for policymakers and for economic agents. But economists too need to consider the implications of the uncertainty that they also face. Here, we examine further the different meanings and sources of uncertainty as something pervasive in some degree, even in the absence of crisis. A pluralist approach to knowledge is considered as a way to address uncertainty.

Introduction

Policymakers are required to act, even if the action is a continuation of the status quo. The institutional structure within which monetary policy is made requires that a decision be taken at regular intervals as to the repo rate to be set by the central bank. This decision has to be taken on some grounds, and the focus here is on the grounds which economics provides.

It is clear that such decisions are not made under conditions of certainty. The Minutes of the Bank of England Monetary Policy Committee, for example, reveal that the arguments put forward by each member involve more or less uncertainty, but also that the arguments among all

The original version of this chapter was published in P. Mooslechner, H. Schuberth and M. Schuerz (eds), *Economic Policy-making under Uncertainty: The Role of Truth and Accountability in Policy Advice* (Cheltenham: Edward Elgar), 2005, pp. 191–203.

the members can be quite diverse.[1] Indeed, the Bank of England's inflation forecast is expressed in the form of a 'fan', whose amplitude is an indicator of uncertainty surrounding the core forecast.

That this uncertainty should be made so explicit, and so public, is an interesting development in itself, contrasting with such periods as the 1980s when policymaking was made apparently with great confidence on the basis of large macro models. Experience showed that much of this confidence was misplaced.

But if we cannot be certain as to the outcome of policy actions, what is their justification? There is a long tradition of Austrian, or neo-Austrian, economics within which the scope for policy action is limited on the grounds that the knowledge base of policymakers is insufficient, relative to that of economic actors. Indeed, the macroeconomic aggregates on which policy is designed to impinge are seen as having limited meaning.

The purpose of this chapter is to explore further the concept of uncertainty and how it affects the foundations of policy-making in economics. We start by considering what we mean by uncertainty, and its source. We will consider first the distinction between uncertainty as a property of the real world, and uncertainty as a property of our knowledge about the real world. We then consider the distinction between uncertainty as a subjective concept and as an objective concept. Economic actors and their knowledge of the real world are the subject matter of economics; in the third section, we consider their knowledge and uncertainty in relation to the knowledge and uncertainty of economists about them. We consider how both economists and economic actors can deal with uncertainty, introducing partial, provisional closures in order to construct knowledge about an open system. We conclude by taking further the explicit question of monetary policy-making under uncertainty.

The nature and source of uncertainty

By uncertainty, we mean here unquantifiable risk, although quantifiable risk is often referred to in economics as uncertainty. If risk is quantifiable, we can insure against it. It is of limited interest because it allows the focus to continue to be on the core prediction. Thus, much of the macroeconomics which provided the foundation for policy advice, for a long time, effectively ignored the size of error variance. As long as

---

[1] See Aikman et al (2010) for a recent discussion of the increasing frequency of references to uncertainty in central bank publications.

the error term had zero mean and it was normally distributed, the stochastic nature of the system could effectively be ignored, and certainty equivalence assumed.

However, greater quantifiable risk is relevant to decision-making when the potential loss arising from outlying outcomes is taken into account. Indeed, much of the monetary policy literature dating from Brainard (1967) and Poole (1970) focused on the significance of higher variance in the error terms of equations representing the transmission of monetary policy. But as attention to Brainard's idea of parametric (model) uncertainty increased, the robust control theory solution was found in ever-more elaborate structures for the error term, that is, continuing to allow quantification of uncertainty as risk (see further Dow, 2004b).

Quantifiable risk more generally has been the main focus of economics, rather than unquantifiable risk, because of the attractions of mathematical formalism.[2] However, the possibility of unquantifiable risk needs to be addressed, not least because its existence is evident (and its importance enhanced by the crisis). Keynes (1921, p. 3) introduced his *Treatise on Probability* by pointing out the limited scope for conclusive argument in 'metaphysics, in science, and in conduct'. Most arguments outside the use of 'academic logic ... are admitted to be inconclusive in a greater or lesser degree', that is, to be uncertain to some degree. Considering the source and extent of uncertainty gets to the heart of economics and its philosophical foundations.

Uncertainty is a property of knowledge. Yet a distinction is drawn in the literature regarding the source of uncertainty, that is, between aleatory and epistemic uncertainty (see Lawson 1988, for a full discussion). The former is uncertainty which arises from the nature of the real world, while the latter arises from our capacity to have knowledge about the real world. If there is randomness in nature, for example, so that an economy experiences random real shocks, then our knowledge of these shocks is inevitably incomplete, and therefore our ability to predict is limited accordingly. Randomness, however, is measurable and entails certain knowledge that shocks are random, so that this representation of aleatory uncertainty in fact corresponds to quantifiable risk. Aleatory uncertainty in the sense of unquantifiable risk is much less easy to pin down; we may not have any basis for knowing that the real world conforms to a stochastic system.

---

[2] See Backhouse (1998b) for a modified advocacy of this position, and Blaug (1999) for a historical account.

Epistemic uncertainty arises from an inability to know the real world. In the monetary policy literature, epistemic uncertainty can arise because of lags in the availability of data, or because of an inability to measure variables such as potential output (see Goodhart, 1999). More generally, epistemic uncertainty understood as bounded rationality refers to limitations on the human ability to compute. The presumption is that in principle the economic structure and the mechanism for the transmission of monetary policy are knowable, but in practice we cannot fully access this knowledge. The implication of much of the discussion in the theoretical literature is that it is simply a matter of time before impediments to knowledge are overcome (see for example, Blanchard and Fischer, 1989, p. 505). The policy literature is less sanguine. This type of epistemic uncertainty is less amenable to capturing in a random error term, so the (policy-focused) model uncertainty literature has addressed this type of uncertainty by considering policy rules which are robust across a range of possible representations of the real world (see for example, Bray et al. 1995).

However, it may be that the nature of the real world is so complex that we cannot have full knowledge of it, even in principle; this may be one way of understanding the human condition. Indeed, David Hume's theory of human nature involved this inevitable limitation on knowledge; this was the source of his (commonly misunderstood) problem of induction (Dow, 2002). Observation gives us clues to underlying causal mechanisms and we build knowledge as best we can, but we have no direct access to knowledge of these mechanisms.

Further, since human knowledge and action based on this knowledge are central to the real world of social systems, the distinction between aleatory and epistemic uncertainty becomes blurred. To pursue this idea, it is helpful to consider what the uncertainty is about. In most of the monetary policy literature, the goal is to construct a model which represents the economic structure and the transmission of monetary policy within that structure. What cannot be pinned down is classified as uncertainty. If the structure the economist is trying to capture is stochastic but unquantifiable, uncertainty is aleatory. If there are difficulties in pinning down the structure, uncertainty is epistemic. This classification presumes that the economic system is such that it can be captured in a model. If on the other hand the real world is complex and organic, with behaviour and institutions evolving over time, sometimes gradually and sometimes with discrete shifts, then it cannot conceivably be fully captured in a model. Models will capture aspects of that complexity and thus add to knowledge. Yet that knowledge is inevitably partial and provisional. It is not just that there are limitations to human knowledge. These limitations are inevitable not only because of human failings, but also because of the nature of the real world about which we are trying to build up knowledge, and of which human nature is a central part. The creativity of individuals as well as the evolving social patterns of behaviour and institutions mean that the economic structure changes in inevitably unpredictable ways.

It is helpful to recall Popper's (1982) three-way classification of the universe: world 1 is the physical world, world 2 the psychological world and world 3 the product of the human mind. The first two constitute one of the conventional understandings of the subject matter of economics to which the concept of aleatory uncertainty may be applied. World 3 is the province of epistemic uncertainty. But, as Popper argues, the three worlds are all interdependent, with human constructions being both the product of worlds 1 and 2, and in turn affecting them. Popper concluded that, taken together, the three worlds produce an indeterminate whole. The indeterminacy is not stochasticness, but a more profound indeterminacy which means that the universe is an open system. Once we understand the universe as an open system, according to Popper, it cannot be represented by a deterministic (even if stochastic) model. It is therefore no longer appropriate to talk in terms of the 'true' model about which we are uncertain. There is no such thing (other than hypothetically, as something known by the deity). Epistemic uncertainty therefore follows from, and in turn contributes to, the openness of the real world.

A more appropriate distinction may then be between subjective uncertainty and objective uncertainty. Subjective uncertainty refers to the individual perceptions of the real world, and the different psychological states of different individuals. This can be distinguished from some independently established degree of uncertainty which it is in some sense rational to hold with respect to a given body of knowledge. This distinction is important for the (neo-)Austrian approach to knowledge. Methodological individualism emphasises the subjective.

However, the Austrian approach stems from a particular understanding of the nature of the real world as an open system (a particular ontology). It is therefore logically compatible with a less subjectivist approach, which sees objective grounds for uncertainty arising from the openness of the economic system. This was Keynes's view – that there would be different degrees of uncertainty depending on different contexts (including different psychological states), which were nevertheless objective in that they were reasonable given the relevant context. The sharp subjective/objective distinction thus breaks down. In fact, the focus on such duals is itself more compatible with a closed-system approach. By exploring an open systems approach here, we emphasise more the totality of uncertainty as arising from the openness of the real world, rather than dualistic categories (see further Dow, 1990/Chapter 4).

In order to function in this real world, individuals do build up knowledge, albeit uncertain knowledge. Indeed, it was central to Menger's (1963) contribution that institutional arrangements evolve in order to provide a reasonably stable foundation for knowledge. So the economic structure itself is conditioned by knowledge limitations and attempts to surmount them. Similarly, the project of science can be understood as an exercise in reducing uncertainty about the real world, and in turn, impacts upon the real world. Epistemic uncertainty and efforts to address it become bound up with the real economic structure and thus with sources of aleatory uncertainty. In the next section, we focus on the parallelism between the efforts of economic actors to reduce uncertainty and the efforts of economists (see Dow, 2003b, for a more full account).

Uncertainty of economists and uncertainty of economic actors

As a social science, economics is concerned with individual and social action, within social structures. Economists therefore aim to build up knowledge about this action and these structures. This provides the basis for policy action and the design of economic structures. But knowledge in turn can be understood to be central to both action and structures within the economy, so that issues of uncertainty can be seen to impact both on the subject matter and on economic science. In the passage referred to above from Keynes's *Treatise on Probability*, he clearly sees the issues as applying to economics ('science') and to economic behaviour ('conduct').

Knowledge has been even more central to the Austrian understanding of the economic process. Drawing on this tradition and the Marshallian tradition, there is a large modern literature which sees knowledge at the core of economic reality. A key contributor to this literature, Brian Loasby, draws explicit parallels between the way in which knowledge is generated in the firm and in markets, and the way in which it is generated among economists (see for example Loasby, 1999). He goes back (more recently in Loasby, 2003) to Smith in a way which resolves the objectivity/subjectivity dualism which has the potential to threaten a blending of the Austrian and Marshallian traditions. Drawing on Hume, Smith accepted that truth was not demonstrable. He turned, therefore, from a rational account of science to a psychological account, focusing on the motivation for science and the basis for reasoned persuasion to accept (provisionally) one account of reality over another. Although science was explained in psychological terms, it was not seen as subjective (as the dual of objective) since it was grounded first in a belief in the existence of the real, and second in practice (both scientific and non-scientific). Indeed, the methodological individualism of Austrian economics has accordingly been conditioned by its blending with evolutionary economics, such that individual behavior is seen as conditioned by pre-existing institutions (see for example Caldwell and Boehm, eds, 1992).

Loasby (2003) further explores the role of closed models in building up knowledge of an open reality. For firms, some closure is a necessary feature of knowledge as the basis for action; for example, planning requires some expectation as to the outcome of innovation (some closure in what we might think of as an inherently open process). The firm itself is a form of closure. Action is based, and institutions are designed, on the basis of the identification of patterns, of connections which are understood to be present as opposed to absent. The very notion of a system entails incomplete connectedness of reality. Similarly, as economists, we build theoretical systems on the basis of patterns which we understand to be present in nature.

A fixedly closed system precludes uncertainty (as opposed to quantifiable risk); it requires internal relations to be given, and external forces to be random. In reality, a perpetually closed system is generally unsustainable; firms come and go, institutions evolve. But provisional closure is necessary for action, while perpetual attention to change from within and without leads to paralysis. Further, provisional closure itself reduces uncertainty for other actors. The existence of labour contracts, of posted product prices, of stable institutions all serve as a set of patterns within which action can be taken. Periods of crisis are those in which familiar patterns break down, uncertainty is rife and paralysis sets in.

Chick and Dow (2001/Chapter 9) argue that the methodology of employing partial, provisional closures in order to build up knowledge of an open reality allows for generality. It reflects the generality of uncertainty, while allowing different partial closures to reflect different contexts. Further, this kind of pluralist analysis may simultaneously employ different closures, even when addressing a single context. Thus, one part of the analysis may take the money supply as given, while another part explores the process which determines the money supply. The provisional closures within which actors make decisions in the economy can be thought of as models. They are human constructs which facilitate the economic process. When actors are uncertain they can be thought of as being uncertain about whether there is good reason to continue with the models they provisionally employ as the basis for action. There is apparently a direct parallel with the model uncertainty of economists which for a time became a major focus for central bankers (see Dow, 2004b). The critical issue, however, is what the uncertainty is about. We need to distinguish between uncertainty as to which is 'the best model' and uncertainty as to which is 'the best collection of provisional, partial models', that is between monism and pluralism.

The model uncertainty literature in general avoids this parallelism between economists' knowledge and the knowledge of economic actors. The literature which assesses the relative merits of a given range of leading macroeconomic models makes no comment on the fact that these models depict individual economic actors as displaying no such uncertainty. Similarly, the Bank of England (1999), which in other respects has been most outspoken on the need for pluralism as the basis for policy decisions, nevertheless employs models which presume certainty equivalence among economic actors. The major exception is work in which Sargent plays a leading part, such as Sargent (1999); he is concerned with symmetry of treatment between economist and agent. Yet to make agents' uncertainty and the uncertainty of economists tractable, it is depicted for both as a complex stochastic process which is subject to predefined limits. What is expressed as uncertainty is in fact risk with respect to knowledge of the true model of the economic structure.

Keynes (1921) explicitly addressed the question of how individuals (in the economy, or economists or whatever) establish reasoned grounds for belief such as to provide a basis for action; this found an echo later (Keynes, 1937) when he encapsulated a key element of *The General Theory*, the theory of liquidity preference. In the absence of a true model which individuals or economists could aim to access, given the openness of the real world, no one best route to knowledge can be identified. Action, according to Keynes, is based on reason (understood as rational grounds for belief), subject to a psychological force (intuition and/or animal spirits). Classical logic alone is insufficient to justify action since we cannot be certain of the outcome of our actions, far less the environment within which they will be played out. For Keynes, reason is based instead on ordinary logic, or human logic, which does not require certainty as to the truth or falsity of premises.

Ordinary logic, for economic actors and for economists, consists of multiple strands of reasoning, drawing on a range of sources of direct knowledge. Both actors and economists employ a pluralist methodology. Recourse is made to convention. In the absence of adequate knowledge derived from individualistic rationality, conventional knowledge is built up at a societal level. When forming expectations under uncertainty, individuals use what individual knowledge they have, but also refer to expert sources and indicators of societal expectations. The framework within which knowledge is formed and action taken is a set of conventions and institutions built up over the years in response to the need to cope with uncertainty, ranging from the rule of law to conventional market behaviour. But by the same token, expectations, lacking a rationalistic foundation, are subject to periodic discrete shifts. A change in conventional understanding, due for example to a highly publicised event or an expression of a new expectation by a leading pundit, can have widespread consequences for expectations, for the degree of uncertainty with which they are generally held and for ensuing action.

The same is true of economists. One of the major insights of Kuhn's (1962) approach, taken forward by the sociology of scientific knowledge, or science studies, is that scientific communities' normal research is built on a conventional foundation shared by the members of the community. The modern rhetoric approach, echoing Smith's theory of rhetoric, focuses on what is conventionally persuasive in the presentation of new ideas. Further, these conventions are embedded in an institutional structure set up to provide a basis for scientific activity: journals, textbooks, conferences and so on. Were scientific knowledge not subject to uncertainty, then rationalistic arguments could compete in a world akin to perfect competition. Yet, just as that world is impractical for markets in general in a world of uncertainty – markets require conventional behaviour and institutions in order to function – so too, scientific communities require some underpinning. This introduces some closure which allows science to proceed. But there is an inevitable circularity in the conceptual framework conventionally adopted by a particular community or paradigm, the way it understands the economic system and the way it understands arguments about that system (see Loasby, 2003). A fixed closure is unsustainable and science is subject to paradigm shifts just as conventional expectations are subject to discrete shifts. Economic paradigms do evolve over time, responding to experience of reality which challenges a particular choice of closure. Monetary policy provides an excellent example of such a challenge. We turn in the next section to consider where this discussion takes us in considering the methodological foundations for monetary policy.

Uncertainty and monetary policy

The conventional closure involved in basing policy on one large macro model, treated as the 'true' model, was confronted by the experience of predictive failure (see for example Clements and Hendry, 1995). One response was the Bank of England's (1999) professed embracing of pluralism (although there was still an emphasis on one core macro model).[3]

The 1980s can be understood as a period in which policy was based on a form of humanism. There was optimism that the large macro models provided an adequate guide to policy action, which could be expected to yield the predicted outcomes. This optimism was gradually punctured when these expectations were confounded. The prevailing paradigm of New Classical Economics had relied on certainty equivalence on the part of economic actors and economists alike. Within this paradigm, there emerged the Lucas critique which challenged one of the closures within the model structure: that behaviour was invariant in the face of policy action. Lucas (1976) argued that rational individuals in fact respond to policy action in such a way as to make it impotent. The conclusion was that policy action could only have an impact on the economy if it was random, that is, there was no point in policy action.

This conclusion found support from a line of argument which took a very different starting point. Far from individuals and economists knowing too much, the problem with policy action might derive from unknowability resulting from radical uncertainty. Thus Hayek, for example, expressed the radical uncertainty of the Austrian approach as grounds for an argument against humanism:

> If man is not to do more harm than good in his efforts to improve the social order, he will have to learn that ... where essential complexity of an organised kind prevails, *he cannot acquire the full knowledge*

---

[3] See Dow (2004b) for a discussion of a pluralist methodology in response to model uncertainty, and Downward and Mearman (2008) for a discussion of the Bank of England's methodology in terms of triangulation.

which would make mastery of the events possible. He will therefore have to use what knowledge he can achieve, not to shape the results as a craftsman shapes his handiwork, but rather to cultivate a growth by providing the appropriate environment, as the gardener does for his plants. (Hayek, 1975, p. 42, emphasis in original)

This argument attracted support from a wide range of perspectives which were influenced by the emergence of postmodernism, which more generally challenged humanism. Thus, for example, while starting from a closed-system theoretical perspective based on certainty-equivalence like Lucas, Hahn (1983) denied the empirical validity of the New Classical approach – the knowledge requirements could not in practice be met. Like those coming from a radical uncertainty perspective, Hahn therefore raised questions as to how policy intervention could be justified.

The Keynes uncertainty approach is aimed more at a middle ground (an argument developed in detail by O'Donnell, 1989). Uncertainty itself justifies government intervention, since it can serve to provide an element of stability for economic actors. O'Donnell explains this role in terms of knowledge and institutions:

> State activity was thus a *precondition* of successful individualism, improving the efficiency of resource utilisation and eliminating some of the hazards of pure *laissez-faire*. By attacking remediable sources of uncertainty, providing data banks and by reforming institutions, it could improve the environment in which individual rationality was exercised. (O'Donnell, 1989, p. 303, emphasis in original)

The role is extended by the content of Keynesian fiscal and monetary policy; both are designed to provide a sound basis for investment by reducing uncertainty. In the case of fiscal policy, the government may actively intervene by engaging in its own capital projects to boost confidence. In the case of monetary policy, the focus is on maintaining stable low interest rates to reduce uncertainty for firms with respect to finance, and regulation and supervision of the banking system to ensure a more generally stable financial environment as a backdrop for decision-making. In both cases, the aim is to encourage investment by reducing uncertainty from various sources.

The implementation of this policy approach arguably was so successful that the relative stability of the 1950s and 1960s encouraged inattention to issues of uncertainty and expectations. The neoclassical synthesis of that period ignored these central features of Keynes's economic theory. This coincided with a high level of confidence in the capacity of the state to manage the economy and a continuation of closures in theorising which became increasingly untenable, leading to the New Classical revolution.

There was a dualistic swing away from humanism, followed by a return to seek out some middle ground. Yet conflicting understandings of the economic crisis have now reopened old dualistic arguments about the role of government. This is evident in discussions about banking reform. An ontology of beneficent market forces promoting stability, as implied by mainstream theory, suggests reduced regulation as the appropriate cure (the crisis being identified as the outcome of past government interference encouraging excessive risk-taking through moral hazard). Yet the urgency of the crisis at the time required central bankers to disregard professed theoretical positions and take action to reduce uncertainty and restore confidence in markets. Even in the face of their own uncertainty, it was clear that some action was required.

Before the crisis, central banks, including the European Central Bank, were addressing methodological issues as they grappled with the uncertainty of their knowledge in the face of the requirement to act. It was a time of rather uncomfortable transition, as old closures (such as certainty-equivalence on the part of economic agents) bumped up against the actual uncertainty of policymakers. The Bank of England had taken a lead by pointing to pluralism as the methodological route to follow. But much still needs to be done to spell out what that entails for how the knowledge foundations of monetary policy are constructed.

Conclusion

We have addressed here the fundamental issues raised for economics by a consideration of uncertainty in its broadest sense. These issues get to the heart of what it is that we do as economists, as well as what we do as economic actors. There is a danger of falling into one or the other of two sharp categories with respect to knowledge: the certainty equivalence of closed-system models on the one hand and the radical uncertainty of completely open systems on the other. Both inhibit policy action. But by considering the middle ground where some closures are introduced (by individuals, by social institutions, by government, by theorists) in order to reduce uncertainty, we can see how social structures do manage to function in spite of uncertainty, and how actions to affect behaviour and institutional design may serve to reduce uncertainty.

The methodological approach implied by this middle-ground is a form of pluralism – not 'anything goes', but a recourse to a range of methods and types of knowledge suited to the problem at hand and the type of economic structure within which it is understood to occur. This seems to be what central bankers tend to do anyway, being closer to the real world and more compelled to action than academic economists. But there is still an uncomfortable juxtaposition between this practice and the approach which is often professed by central bankers as well as academics: modelling as the exclusive method within a closed-system approach, rather than in the partial, provisional way of the pluralist approach. A fundamental rethink at the methodological level is required to produce an approach to the knowledge base of policy which is philosophically consistent in a world profoundly coloured by uncertainty.

13
Variety of Methodological Approach in Economics

There was an interesting bout of reflection on the discipline around the Millennium, out of which emerged a view that, while mainstream economics might have been monolithic in the past, it had now branched out in pluralistic fashion, so that the notion of schools of thought no longer applied. Mainstream theory and methodology have certainly evolved, with increased variety at the theoretical level. But we conclude here that there is still methodological commonality (including shared conceptualisations and shared meanings of terms) which constrains the forms that this new variety (and future developments in the mainstream) can take. New economic thinking is therefore not benefiting nearly as much as it might from drawing on a range of methodological approaches, that is, from methodological pluralism. This chapter draws together the different strands of analysis developed earlier in the volume.

Introduction

In this chapter, we take stock of economics in methodological terms. The discipline of economics is continually changing, requiring a re-examination of the concepts of mainstream economics and non-mainstream economics. The particular feature of recent change which this chapter examines is the appearance of increasing variety, or plurality, in economics, in particular in economic theory, and what this implies

The original version of this chapter was published in the *Journal of Economic Surveys*, 21 (3), 2007, pp. 447–19.

for non-mainstream economics. In the process, we revisit a range of themes addressed earlier in the volume.

In this exercise, we can benefit from the unusual degree of reflection on the state of economics during the recent millennium. Weintraub's (1999) approach to the subject explicitly drew on modern developments in historiography, which acknowledge that different histories can be written from different perspectives; no historical account can claim to be the one 'true' account. The emphasis therefore was on the variety of perspectives in economics and, by implication, variety in economics itself. Indeed, such an account provided implicit support for pluralism, that is, the argument for, or celebration of, variety. But if economics is pluralistic, how are we to understand it as a discipline? And does plurality spell the end of methodology on the one hand, or set out an agenda for a new methodological discourse on the other? Does plurality mean that criticism has no role ('anything goes'), or does it require a redrawing of the framework for criticism? What opportunities are offered by pluralism?

The role for variety had already arisen in earlier exercises in looking forward to the future of economics. In 1991, the *Economic Journal* marked the occasion of the first issue of its second century by inviting leading economists to reflect on what the future held for the discipline (see further Chapter 7). Among the prescient themes which emerged were the following, each of which was explored by several contributors:

- the opening of economics to input from, as well as input to, other disciplines, notably sociology and psychology (see also Allen, 2000);
- increasing specialisation within economics (and thus of conferences, journals and so on) leading to fragmentation of the community of economists;
- increasing cohesion around methodological and theoretical principles, with a move away from the type of divide seen in the Monetarist-Keynesian debates.

John Pencavel (1991) concluded that these seemingly opposing trends would be compatible if we think of economic ideas as being diverse and competing freely in competitive markets. He used the term 'pluralistic' to describe the outcome, which he welcomed as reducing the scope for '[p]rofessional tyranny' (ibid, p. 87), by implication an imperfection in the market for ideas. Yet plurality is not universally welcomed, since it raises concerns as to how the different types of theory can be put together. Blanchard and Fischer (1989, p. 505), for example, had referred to it as being 'logically uncomfortable'.

The concept of plurality has been explored more widely in recent years, both within and beyond economics. It is conventional now to remark that we live in a pluralist society, for example. Since economics is a social science, and particularly given the greater interface with sociology, it would not be surprising to find evidence of plurality also in economics. But there has further been the development in the economic methodology literature of the argument for plurality, that is, pluralism. This literature, further, has clarified the different meanings of the term, out of which we might understand the different identifications of, and attitudes towards, plurality, as well as its implications (see Chapter 8). These developments in the field of methodology are just part of the increasing specialisation within fields in economics, which itself raises issues of meaning and thus of communication.

The purpose of this chapter is to try to overcome some of the communication difficulties across specialisations (including methodology) in order to consider variety in economics. First, we review the evidence on variety. We then probe further what is meant by plurality at different levels which need to be distinguished (reality, methodology, method, theory), and then review the arguments for and against pluralism, starting with Caldwell's (1982) seminal contribution to the modern discourse. This discussion throws the spotlight on a range of important issues, including the relation between mathematical formalism and plurality. We also consider schools of thought as a particular form of plurality. Here it is relevant to consider the role of Kuhn's analysis in relation to plurality and pluralism. In particular, while the arguments for plurality are strong, it is argued further that unstructured pluralism or eclecticism, understood as an absence of selection criteria, or 'anything goes', is antithetical to the building up of knowledge.

It is concluded that it would be helpful – for our understanding of the current state of economics with its variety of approaches to theory and evidence, for communications between different approaches and for future developments in the discipline – for the scope for both openness and constructive critique to be more widely discussed. This would imply that more economists be aware of, and discuss more, the architecture of the discipline. Indeed, it will be argued that, while we observe variety at the level of theory and evidence, the reasons for such variety also justify variety at the level both of method and of methodology. While their characteristics may change, the concepts of mainstream economics and non-mainstream economics are still relevant as a way of capturing variety at the meta-methodological level.

Evidence of plurality in economics

We start by considering how far, and in what way, economics may be said to be pluralistic, drawing on the wide range of commentaries which have appeared in the recent literature. In order to consider how far modern economics is fragmented, it is useful to compare it with the recent history of economics, and indeed most of these commentaries have taken such an approach.

The conventional account (see for example Colander, 2000a, and Goodwin, 2000) characterises the 1970s and 1980s as a period of fierce debate between different schools of thought, often epitomised by the Monetarist-Keynesian debates. The differences are characterised as being policy-focused and, ultimately, ideological. But contemporary accounts from that period identified a wider range of schools of thought, which were differentiated more by methodological approach than by ideology alone: mainstream economics, Post-Keynesian economics, institutionalist economics, neo-Austrian economics, Marxian economics and so on. There were differences as to how to characterise mainstream economics. Weintraub (1985a) and Backhouse (1991) saw it as being unified in terms of the principles of general equilibrium theory (see also Dow, 1985). But Phelps (1990), Mair and Miller (1990) and later Snowdon, Vane and Wynarczyk (1994) could identify schools of thought within mainstream economics (such as monetarism, new classical economics, real business cycle theory and new Keynesian economics).

The most notable change identified in the literature some 20 years later has been a process of increasing fragmentation within mainstream economics, going beyond the schools of thought identified earlier. Colander (2000b), for example, focused on the movement of economics in the direction of handling increasing complexity. He noted a growing divergence from formal general equilibrium models for policy purposes, which was inevitably a force for fragmentation, and predicted a move towards more contextual microfoundations, which would reinforce that trend. He had already announced the 'death' of neoclassical economics as a useful category (Colander, 2000a). As predicted in the centennial *Economic Journal* issue, the growth of game theory, experimental economics, evolutionary economics, behavioural economics, complexity economics and so on had meant that the mainstream of economics could no longer be identified as a single theoretical system.

Davis (2006) offers an explanation for this development in terms of a cyclical process of trade in ideas, whereby variety emerges when imports exceed exports. Thus, many of these developments in mainstream economics can be seen as an adaptation designed to incorporate ideas from other approaches in economics (which had been questioning the rational economic man concept, for example) or other disciplines (such as psychology and biology). Since many of these developments have encroached on the middle ground between mainstream economics and non-mainstream schools of thought, Goodwin (2000) questions whether there is any continuing relevance in these two categories (see further Coats, 2000). The character of plurality in economics had changed.

This plurality of theories is also evident in their content, and the changing nature and scope of evidence, reflecting an increasing understanding of plurality in the subject matter. Thus, by considering the possibility of different information sets among different categories of economic actor, rational expectations theory generated multiple equilibria. This outcome jeopardised the clear implications which had earlier been drawn from the strong rational expectations hypothesis. Similarly, behavioural economics took on board different attitudes to risk in order to explain more complex behaviour in financial markets. Game theory took on the implications of interaction between different interest groups, and so on. This increasing focus on heterogeneous agents reflects a movement away from the idea of the representative agent in an effort to capture more effectively a complex reality (see for example Kirman, 1992). Thaler (2000) predicts a continuation of this trend. In the meantime, theory change has been prompted by new types of evidence that have been gathered on the basis of experiments (Morgan, 2005, Sugden, 2005). Further, happiness studies have gathered new survey evidence which challenges conventional utility theory (Frey and Stutzer, 2002). Survey evidence similarly has also opened up labour market analysis to concepts (such as self-worth) outside the conventional framework (Bewley, 1995).

Nevertheless, some see the resulting complexity of the disciplinary landscape as being unified by the shared purpose of a general systematisation of agents' rational behaviour (however defined) under certainty and uncertainty conditions, including interactive behaviour (Giocoli, 2003). Indeed, while there is a consensus that there has been fragmentation in terms of theory and evidence, there is also a consensus in the literature that there has been a growing cohesion at the level of approach, specifically in terms of method selection. Thus Blanchard, who with Fischer had drawn attention to the plurality within macroeconomics in 1989, as we noted above, had by 1997 come to emphasise the commonality at the level of framework (Blanchard, 1997, p. 582). More generally, Goodwin and Colander point to the increasing requirement for theory to be expressed in terms of formal mathematics, which at the level of method reduces significantly the degree of plurality. Indeed the consensus identified by commentators (such as Morgan and Rutherford, 1998, and Blaug, 1999) has been that constructing, analysing and testing formal models are the core activities of mainstream economics.

Thus, game theory has evolved by formalising different notions of rationality (Samuelson, 2004). In behavioural economics, the notion of 'rational' behaviour has been extended to incorporate what had once been dubbed 'irrational', such as time inconsistency and self-control. But the outcome is still expressed in terms of optimising behaviour subject to constraints, such that it is amenable to formal treatment (see for example Samuelson and Swinkels, 2006). The conventional mainstream notion of uncertainty (that is, risk) has been refined, now incorporating experienced uncertainty, as well as decision uncertainty (see for example Kahneman and Sugden, 2005), but again still applied within a utility maximisation framework. Institutional and conventional considerations are being given more prominence in labour market analysis. For example, Thomas (2005) analyses labour market behaviour focusing on the idea of the fair wage (and thus wage relativities). But the analysis still rests on a utility-maximising framework where such considerations do not appear in the utility function. Similarly, it is not clear how the evidence on happiness will be translated into theory, not least because of the subjective nature of the evidence. We seem still to be in Blanchard and Fischer's 'logically uncomfortable' territory.

Samuelson (2005) explains the challenges such developments pose for a formalist approach, exploring in detail the difficulties in combining the apparently conflicting insights from experimental economics with theory. For example, how far are surprising results from experiments still conditioned by the abstractions of the theory to which they related, and therefore do not constitute independent evidence? How should preferences be modelled when going beyond a narrow conception of self-interest? The importance of addressing such difficulties is emphasised when he concludes that 'at some point some connections must be made between theory and behaviour if economic theory is not to fade into either philosophy or mathematics' (Samuelson, 2005, p.100). The key question will therefore be how far the requirements of mathematical modelling are given priority in resolving the emerging incompatibilities between theory and evidence. There are, after all, other approaches available outside the optimising-individual framework, as in Davis (2003) on rational behaviour, and the two different treatments of the labour market in Chick (1983) and Nelson (1996). These approaches differ in giving formal models a partial role alongside other methods of analysis (or even no role). Unlike conventional theory, the model solution is not regarded as necessarily the definitive solution. One critical consequence of defining economics by a particular methodology, as in mainstream economics, is that such alternatives may not be recognised as even falling within economics. The homogeneity of methodological approach is then self-reinforcing.

Given the importance, therefore, of unity of method (alongside plurality of theory and evidence), we turn now to analyse its justification, as well as significance and implications. In particular, it is important, given the diverging trends in terms of theory/evidence and method, that it be clarified what is entailed by plurality at different levels. We do this in the next section, and at the same time consider the arguments put forward for plurality, that is, for pluralism.

Variety at different levels

We have already seen evidence of a consensus that there is increasing plurality in the practice of mainstream economics and unity in terms of methodology. So we also need to consider the relations between the levels, the meaning of plurality at the level of reality, and distinguish between a plurality of methodologies, or approaches, on the one hand and a methodology which advocates a plurality of methods on the other (Dow, 2001).

We start with the subject matter of economics: reality, and the nature of social systems, of which the economy is a part. The nature of reality in turn determines what kinds of knowledge are possible. It is difficult definitively to separate the level of reality from the level of our knowledge about it. Nevertheless, it is possible to make statements about what we understand as the nature of reality, and about what that implies for possibilities for knowledge. The question at issue here is whether or not there is an underlying unity to social systems. If there is, then behaviour is law-like, and it is the task of economics to uncover those laws. There is little scope for diversity of opinion, or plurality in terms of knowledge, except in the transitional state during which laws are being uncovered. Put another way, closed social systems allow for the identification of laws on the basis of which predictions can be made with confidence.

On the other hand, if there is diversity in nature, that is behaviour is not law-like, then there is scope for variety of opinion (that is, plurality of knowledge), and thus a range of possible explanations for economic outcomes (Runde, 1998). This would also be the case, even if there is unity in nature, if there are difficulties in observing nature. Open systems, which allow for human agency (creativity, the non-deterministic exercise of choice and so on) and the (indeterminate) evolution of the institutional structure within which individuals exercise agency, do not have the invariant kind of causal mechanisms which yield up laws, and allow instead for a plurality of explanations and modes of explanation (Davis, 2003; Chick and Dow, 2005/Chapter 11). Many economists would agree with Popper (1982) that reality is an open system (or at least, if a closed system, that signals are too noisy to allow us to identify it). For example, such thinking lies behind Colander's (2000b) prediction that economics will increasingly focus on the particularity of institutional context, so that we can expect increasing variety in knowledge.

For world-truth realists, reality is the arbiter of opinion: knowledge can only be regarded as true or false by reference to reality (Mäki 1988). Positivism saw world truth realism as ensuring unity of knowledge through empirical testing (only one opinion could be correct). But it became clear that empirical testing was not definitive in settling disputes in science more generally or in economics in particular. The problems ranged from the difficulty of identifying precisely which element of a hypothesis accounted for falsifying evidence and should be abandoned (the 'Duhem-Quine problem'), to the inability to test all theoretical statements, to more practical issues such as data compatibility. In charting the decline of positivism in philosophy of science, Caldwell (1982, p. 244) concluded that '[t]he most significant contribution of the growth-of-knowledge philosophers was the demonstration that the quest for a single, universal, prescriptive scientific methodology is quixotic'.

Different methodologies can be seen to follow from different understandings of reality. Thus, for example, market economies can be understood to be inherently stable (such that deviations from trend are understood as resulting from shocks, as in the new growth theory) or inherently unstable (as in the Keynes/Minsky theory of the business cycle). From each view of reality follows a different view of how best to build knowledge about it. A stable New Keynesian system with all variables, including shocks, identified (a closed system) lends itself to mathematical modelling which yields a precise conclusion. On the other hand, the focus of the Keynes/Minsky approach on the indeterminate nature of the timing and amplitude of the cycle, and the central role given to unquantifiable risk, explains the more partial role for formal models (without optimising behaviour) alongside other methods of analysis.[1] From these different methodologies stem different selection and use of methods, and different theories.

We can identify four arguments for variety in methodological approach, which we will discuss in turn below. The first is to accept its existence as a feature of knowledge systems on ethical grounds, whether or not it is justified. The second is to argue that no mechanism exists for unifying knowledge about reality, so we have no choice but to accept plurality of approach. The third is to argue that plurality of approach inevitably follows from the nature of the subject matter, and the fourth is positively to advocate plurality on the grounds that variety is essential to the survival of the discipline in the face of an evolving subject matter.

The ethical argument rests on what is seen as a fundamental aspect of knowledge (Screpanti, 1997; Mäki, 1997; McCloskey, 1994). If at a basic level we can construct knowledge in different ways, for whatever reason, and there is no agreed basis for identifying one best approach to knowledge, then there can be no justification in presuming that others' approach to knowledge will be the same as our own. To recognise this requires awareness that reality may be understood differently, terms may be used with different meanings, different criteria employed for deciding what is a good argument, and so on. The ethical argument then is to develop sufficient awareness of difference, first to recognise other approaches, and second not to reject them simply because they are different. This is not at all to rule out criticism. On the contrary, it is argued that critical analysis which is as 'objective' as possible requires some mutual understanding (of methodological principles, meaning and so on).

When Morgan and Rutherford (1998, p. 8) identified a change in the professional ethos of American economics away from interwar pluralism, they characterised it in terms of a move away from associating objectivity with even-handedness with respect to different arguments (and different types of argument). Even-handedness requires awareness of 'otherness'.[2] Morgan and Rutherford identify modern economics

---

[1] See for example Dow (1998); see Lucas (1980) for a different view.
[2] See further Kaul (2008).

with the rise of technocracy, and an association of objectivity instead with the adoption of a particular range of techniques. These techniques facilitate direct comparability of argument, but at the cost of precluding arguments which cannot be expressed in terms of these techniques. This approach is monist (that is, discourages variety) with respect to methodological approach. Further, the particular methodology itself is monist in content in making mathematical modelling the one general core method.

This increasing monism in terms of methodological approach has therefore allowed the emergence of a plurality of theoretical approaches, using different subsets of formal techniques. But at the same time, it has created a dualistic divide between theories which conform to these norms of development and expression and those which do not, discouraging mutual understanding and communication. There is an asymmetry in that, for mainstream economics, the formalist methodological approach defines the discipline, and thus excludes non-mainstream economics; for other approaches, economics is defined by subject matter, and thus includes mainstream economics. The ethical argument for pluralism suggests that even-handedness of treatment of different arguments should allow, not only for different theories within one definition of objectivity, but also for other concepts of objectivity. The partial role given to mathematical modelling (or even its absence), along with other methods of analysis, in other approaches indicates variety of methodological approach but also variety within those approaches.

In society at large, awareness of variety of approach to knowledge (as part of a more general awareness of otherness) rose in the 1960s, encouraged by Kuhn's philosophy of science, and later in more extreme form with postmodernism. Kuhn's (1962) paradigm framework was part of the movement away from positivism laying down the principles of best practice in science. Kuhn's history of science demonstrated that science evolves within communities with shared understandings of reality, shared views as to how to construct knowledge and shared understandings of terms. Interestingly, he suggested that the initial spur to his work came from the realisation that later astronomers claimed that Aristotle's reasoning was nonsense because they were applying their own, different, meanings to his terms; to understand Aristotle required an understanding of his different knowledge framework (Kuhn, 1990). According to Kuhn, science progresses within dominant paradigms, which are replaced with new paradigms when anomalies with respect to reality become insupportable. With the new paradigm, terms take on new meanings and criteria for good arguments change. Knowledge drawn from different paradigms is thus 'incommensurate'.

Kuhn was generally disregarded by those economists who misunderstood him as a relativist, advocating 'anything goes' (although the concept of paradigm shift has been widely used in accounts of economics in the twentieth century). The difficulty was that, if it is accepted that positivism does not provide a secure basis for knowledge, and there is no other incontestable candidate for the best approach, then it did indeed seem that 'anything goes'.

But there has recently been a revision to the view that Kuhn therefore had very limited impact on economics. Fuller (2000, 2003) argues that this extreme relativist (mis)understanding of Kuhn encouraged a withdrawal from methodological discussion altogether. Such a move was advocated most publicly by Friedman (1953), who argued that theories should be judged only by their predictive power. Making the case for an end to prescriptive methodology, McCloskey (1983) argued that economists persuade by means of rhetoric rather than methodological principle. The implication was that economists did not need to reflect on methodology, or to justify their theories with reference to any methodological principles. This may have proved to be telling for the subsequent fragmentation of mainstream economics, as well as the relative lack of discussion about it, but does not explain the increasing homogeneity at the level of general method.

In the meantime, postmodernism also influenced to some extent the content of economic theory. For those who understand knowledge of reality as being socially constructed, there is no independent account of reality which would allow a return to an empirical criterion, reinforcing the view that pluralism of approach is the only option (Samuels, 1998). Thus, Phelps (1990) for example identified the rational expectations approach with postmodernism, because of the subjective nature of expectations, something explored more thoroughly with respect to Sargent's thought by Sent (1998). Along with the view that there was no one incontestable understanding of the economy by economists, the practice developed of understanding the expectations of economic agents as also being subjective and thus open to variety, or plurality.

But there was also an argument for a more limited form of plurality of approach which did not adopt the methodological agnostic view (inappropriately) associated with Kuhn (Dow, 2004a). The emphasis here was on the limitations on variety imposed by the social nature of science, that is, focusing on Kuhn's emphasis (following Popper) on scientific communities. There is a limit to how far there can be plurality of understandings of the nature of reality, approaches to knowledge, and meaning, when knowledge needs to be developed within groups of researchers and communicated to others. Plurality in practice cannot be infinite.

Further, the emphasis on the social nature of scientific activity has encouraged attention on the sociology of the discipline, so that much of the activity within economic methodology now is some form of science study, concerned with understanding the choices made by economists in developing theory and the means by which they persuade others to accept their theories. This work draws on a rich seam in what is generally classified as the Sociology of Scientific Knowledge (SSK; see Hands, 2001, ch. 5, for a survey). A key concept in this literature, which has caused considerable problems for its application, is reflexivity. In particular, no commentary on an approach to economics can be objective in the sense of not itself employing an approach. The notion of a market for economic ideas, for example, is not objective, given the range of understandings of markets in the literature).[3] Thus, it is highly problematic to contemplate a market for ideas as a satisfactory arbiter of ideas about markets. Nevertheless, the SSK approach provides a vehicle for analysing the community of economists as a society, including the way in which methodological norms are adopted and propagated.

The third argument for a plurality of approaches rests on a specific argument about the nature of the subject matter as an open system (King, 2002; Chick and Dow, 2005/Chapter 11). The argument then is not just that there are limitations to the human capacity for knowledge which prevent us from identifying a single best approach to knowledge which would satisfactorily explain law-like behaviour. The argument is further that the nature of individual behaviour (with its social and creative aspects) is too complex to be predictable (even stochastically). Formal specification of the conventions and institutions which condition their behaviour to evolve in indeterminist ways, and of creativity which by definition cannot be known beforehand, cannot alone be expected to be adequate to the task. Further, while it is argued that it is part of the human condition not to have certain knowledge (or certainty equivalence), this in turn influences behaviour and the evolution of institutions. Policymakers are then better equipped to understand that behaviour, and its consequences, if knowledge is built up from a variety of approaches, and indeed a variety of questions asked.

---

[3] See for example Vickers (1995); Mäki (1999); Milberg (2001).

The fourth and perhaps strongest argument for variety of approach to economic knowledge comes from application of the biological metaphor. The argument refers to the subject matter only in the sense that theory has to adapt to new developments. In nature, diversity of species provides protection against unforeseen threats, such that if one strain succumbs to a threat, others are available to take its place. In other words, without diversity, the one dominant strain of ideas is highly vulnerable to unanticipated developments for which it cannot generate an explanation.

Within that diversity of approach, one possibility is a pluralist methodology, that is, reliance on a range of different methods, on the grounds that no one method is sufficient. These methods must be incommensurate, otherwise they would collapse into one method. Explicit adoption of this type of methodology typifies economics outside the mainstream, although there are differences with respect to the range and focus of methods employed. But McCloskey (1983) has demonstrated that, while the 'official discourse' of mainstream economics conforms to formalism in terms of a particular range of mathematical techniques for formulating theory and assessing evidence, the 'unofficial discourse' relies on a much wider range of methods of argument. And indeed variety of methods is implied by Collander's (2000b) prediction of greater context-specificity of economics, and greater focus on institutional variety. Nevertheless, the SSK approach emphasises the important sociological role played by official discourse.

The benefits of plurality of method have been promoted in the monetary policy arena by the Bank of England (1999) and the European Central Bank (2000), following the conclusion that single large formal macro models had proved to be an unsatisfactory basis for decision-making in the face of the complexity (or openness) of economic reality. This conclusion finds support and elaboration, not only in looking forward to future developments in economics (as in Collander, 2000b), but also looking back to Keynes's economic methodology. This was based on his study of probability in the sense of uncertain knowledge (Keynes, 1921) (see Dow, 2004a, and Chapters 5, 12). Keynes argued that in general, the confidence we have in particular conclusions increases, the more different types of argument, and sources of evidence, support it.

The relative benefits of a pluralist methodology can be understood in terms of a metaphor used by the pragmatist Peirce (Wimsatt, 1981). A pluralist methodology is represented by a rope, which is stronger than each individual strand; it is over-determined in that any one strand breaking will not bring down the edifice of a pluralist argument. A monist methodology (that is, reliance on one broad method which is necessary and sufficient for good argument, and which involves a shared set of terms and shared meanings) is another possibility within the range offered by variety of approach. The increasing reliance on mathematical formalism in economics in the mainstream can be classified as a monist methodology, and can be compared to a pluralist methodology in terms of relative costs and benefits. In Peirce's symbolism, a monist methodology is represented by a single chain, which is only as strong as its weakest link.

The mathematical formalist methodology clearly has strong attractions for many economists. One of the main advantages of a monist methodology is that all arguments are commensurate. The appeal of mathematical formalism is that it puts all arguments on an equal footing, allowing direct comparison, and a straightforward check on consistency (Allen, 2000). However, in an applied discipline (and even within pure mathematics), mathematical systems cannot be closed, so that internal mathematical consistency is insufficient; there inevitably remains scope for variety of opinion (Weintraub, 1998, 2002). And indeed, charges of logical inconsistency in practice have not proved decisive.[4] This suggests an increasing need for a different justification for arguments to be expressed exclusively in terms of mathematical modelling, if this approach is to be sustained.

The issue of justifying choice of methodology is just one of the issues which are associated with variety in economics. In the next section, we consider these issues, starting with mathematical formalism.

A review of some issues

Mathematical formalism

A discussion of mathematical formalism, in pure theory or as the basis for empirical work, can benefit from considering plurality at different levels, as above. At the level of choice of methodology, the preference for mathematical formalism which came to dominate economics from the 1950s is generally tacit among practising economists. Indeed, where it is still discussed, as in Allen (2000), it is generally in terms of the matter being settled. Yet the attitude to mathematical formalism could prove decisive for how the theoretical difficulties are resolved that we noted above as arising from experimental and survey evidence.

---

[4] Examples are the Cambridge controversies of the 1960s (see Harcourt, 1972), or critiques of the no-trade theorem, (see Sent, 2006).

At the level of choice of specific method (within a monist, formalist, methodology), there is a range of techniques which could be employed. The reason for any particular choice of technique is also generally left tacit; this is particularly so at the general level of choosing, say, differential calculus rather than set theory. However, inevitably such choice requires argument which is in some sense outside of mathematics. The choice requires reference to the nature of the subject matter and a weighing of the costs and benefits of possible methods of analysis in relation to that subject matter. The methodology then cannot itself be fully defined by mathematical formalism.

Similarly, we have drawn attention to something else which lies outside mathematics itself: the issue of meaning. The scope for different meanings itself is a source of variety, but one which is concealed if meaning is presumed to be held in common. Mathematical expression is often treated in terms of translation from verbal language to mathematical language, which is internally precise. Mathematical argument has the advantage that it can achieve more complex operations than verbal argument, retaining precision throughout. But while mathematical argument is internally precise, giving meaning to mathematics is not (Coddington, 1975). The vagueness of verbal language allows it to encompass shades of meaning, to evolve in meaning and to combine a plurality of types of argument. But if there is variety in meaning of verbal terms and variety in methods of argument, both are lost in an effort of translation into mathematics. Mathematical expression is therefore not neutral, but rather puts particular limits on the scope of subject matter and of argument (Chick and Dow, 2001/Chapter 9). Most importantly, meaning in application of theory further remains imprecise and open to variety of opinion. The rigour required for application is different from the rigour of mathematical argument, but no less important.

But, while inspection of the leading journals supports the view that mathematical expression is indeed a common feature of mainstream economics (Backhouse, 1998a), this is embedded to a greater or lesser extent within verbal argument, as McCloskey (1983) has pointed out. Indeed, the verbal content generally contains a range of types of argument. Nevertheless, since the requirement for mathematical expression is non-neutral as far as the content of argument is concerned, the verbal argument too is constrained.

But if mathematical argument needs to be supplemented by other types of argument, non-mathematical argument is required to explain why one methodological approach has nevertheless become the common source of homogeneity in mainstream economics. The explanation may be that the growing heterogeneity at the theoretical level can be counteracted by a common mode of expression, with sufficient commonality of meaning (of concepts like 'rationality') to allow understanding across subfields. This would be a particular form of the more general sociological explanation that scientific communities adopt a methodology which becomes an identifying feature (and we have seen that it is conventional now to say that mainstream economics is defined by its methodology). The community is perpetuated by means of education through textbook exemplars, by peer review, by hiring decisions and so on. While there is a deep background to knowledge which evades articulation (Searle, 1995), a community can serve to create and perpetuate a common background among its members and recruits to support a continuation of the methodological approach. All of this is the meat of Kuhn's analysis of paradigms.

'Anything goes'

The background to this growing homogeneity of method was the collapse of positivism, and thus of the possibility of setting up methodological principles for all of economics. The troubling implication was that the only alternative was that 'anything goes' (Salanti, 1997). It is natural for economists to seek firm foundations, and to be concerned at the sense that the discipline is developing in an *ad hoc* manner (Blanchard and Fischer, 1989; Colander, 2000a). In particular, there is a concern to be able to settle on criteria by which to gauge progress (Backhouse, 2000).

But one implication of pluralism is that it is not reasonable to expect to establish common criteria for progress. What is an acceptable explanation to one may not be acceptable to others, not just because there may be different preferred methods, but also because the nature of the subject matter is understood differently and terms are being used in different ways.[5] A 'pure' pluralist response would indeed be 'anything goes', but then it is not clear that we would be left with anything which could be called knowledge.

But in practice, since most economists tend to operate mostly in one of a limited range of (shifting, open) networks with shared underpinnings, the scope for plurality is limited. There is, therefore, a discrete

---

[5] One important example is the term 'rational' whose meaning in mainstream economics follows from its dualistic methodological approach, such that any behaviour which does not conform to the particular mainstream rationality axioms is 'irrational'.

number of approaches in economics. It is therefore feasible for any economist to learn enough about alternative approaches to engage in some communication and criticism, to good effect. Indeed it could be argued that most substantive developments in economics occur as a result of cross-fertilisation across school-of-thought boundaries (as in rational expectations theory growing out of an encounter with behavioural economics; see Kantor, 1979).

Communication is not perfect, as across language barriers, but it can nevertheless achieve some mutual understanding (Rorty, 1979). There is some common basis to all of economics (as in the structure of language, to continue the metaphor) which provides the basis for communication.[6] This hermeneutical argument supports the ethical argument for recognising plurality, and not rejecting simply on the basis of difference. But successful communication requires understanding not only of others' approaches to economics, but also of one's own approach.

If there is a limit to the scope for substantive overarching principles which apply to all of economics, then each approach to economics is incommensurate in the sense of not being directly comparable. But this should not be confused with internal inconsistency. As Hodgson (1997, pp. 148–9) put it:

> The role of diversity is not to sanctify or foster contradiction. Tolerance of the right of the scientist to practice, even when we may disagree with his or her views, does not imply tolerance of any method and proposition. ... Pluralism does not mean that 'anything goes'. ... We have to recognise the immense and enduring value of pluralism within the discipline without abandoning precision and rigour in our own work.

Surely most economists would agree with the necessity for precision and rigour. But the significance of methodological pluralism is that the meaning and application of precision and rigour may differ from one approach to another (just as Weintraub, 2002, has shown that they have changed within mathematics itself). In particular, there is a trade-off between different notions of precision and rigour in the application of theory (see Coddington, 1975). Consider a precise projection arising from a formal model with precise assumptions, within which classical logic has been rigorously applied. Precision and rigour

---

[6] There is some basis for this commonality in a shared subject matter of real economic experience, however differently this may be framed.

in this sense need to be weighed against precision and rigour as they are understood in the exercise of judgement, for example in relaxing assumptions which are unsustainable in practical policy application, such as *ceteris paribus*. Such matters are critical, for example, in making monetary-policy decisions (see for example Bank of England, 1999).

Schools of thought

If economics were to operate as a collection of loose communities, rather than an inchoate plurality, then it would seem that we would be returning to the configurations of the 1970s and 1980s. That period has been identified with ideological difference, distinguished from what is seen as the more open plurality which prevails now (Goodwin, 2000; Colander, 2000a).

Goodwin (2000) identifies the declining significance of ideology in economics with a growing disengagement from the policy process, which he regrets. But this does not address the role of values more generally. Values are an inherent part of Searle's (1995) deep background, which influences the way in which we understand the nature of reality, and build knowledge about it, and is thus endemic to our economic theorising. It is therefore inconceivable that differences in schools of thought would not have some value component. But there are different kinds of values, and it is arguably methodological values which are of greatest importance if we understand schools of thought in terms of methodological approach. As Backhouse (2005) argues, ideology may be understood quite differently in terms of the set of values which determine choice of methodology (in addition to ideology understood in terms of political preference). Mathematical formalism was seen by many as a mechanism for promoting pluralism while getting away from ideological debate. Yet mathematical formalism itself reflects what might be called an ideological choice.

Within this general mainstream methodology, it is possible to identify groupings, around endogenous growth theory, experimental economics, behavioural economics, complexity theory and so on. Each is developing a different set of mathematical tools and theories which effectively separates the discourse into sub-schools of thought. The dividing lines are not strictly drawn, not least because of the agreed adherence to mathematical formalism. Implicit here also is a shared view of human nature. While the old ideas of fully informed, rational, atomistic agents are increasingly being challenged by the idea of complex (learning, emotional and so on) heterogeneous agents (Thaler,

2000), the requirement to model behaviour mathematically is an effective constraint on what can be addressed. Mainstream economics as a whole still demonstrates methodological cohesion.

There are other methodological approaches in economics which can also be regarded as schools of thought, for example, the older forms of behavioural economics and institutionalism which quite explicitly chose an alternative to mathematical formalism in order to get round these constraints. These approaches too of course suffer from (different) constraints, yet they add to the plurality of methodology, of theory and method in economics.

The divisions between schools of thought are not rigid or impermeable, and indeed particular individual economists may be seen to work across such divides. But clarification of broad-brush differences in approach is a prerequisite for addressing difference (in meaning, and so on) in a constructive manner. It is also useful to use the basic classification of 'mainstream' and 'non-mainstream' to capture the distinction between economics being defined by mathematical formalism, and adoption of different methodological approaches, respectively (see Dow, 2008).

What is being portrayed here is what could be termed 'structured pluralism' (Dow, 2004b/Chapter 10). McCloskey (1994) has been concerned that we get away from structuring the discipline around schools of thought on the grounds that they inhibit discourse. But on the contrary, it can be argued that it aids discourse if there is some basis, first for identifying, and second for understanding, the principles and perceptions underpinning others' thought, something which is impossible with an unlimited and unspecified range of methodologies. It also provides the basis for effective criticism. Awareness of methodological difference is a precondition for engagement with ideas. Criticism inevitably comes from some perspective or other, without recourse to absolute principles. But, as Popper (1963b) argued, it is through criticism that knowledge progresses.

Conclusion

We have seen evidence that there are forces for heterogeneity in mainstream economics (at the level of theory and evidence) but much less at the level of methodology. Whether or not there is agreement as to the precise account of change within the discipline, it cannot be denied that there has been change. Yet this has attracted remarkably little critical scrutiny within the mainstream of economic discourse, as if whatever change occurs must be socially optimal.

One possible explanation which can be imputed from such methodological statements as have emerged (such as Pencavel, 1991) is that there is the presumption of some sort of invisible hand at work in a market for ideas. This is a powerful metaphor to use in economics, but one which itself requires further examination, not least because ideas are not traded; there is no price mechanism through which markets might adjust. Indeed this metaphor illustrates well its own limitations. Because, given the plurality in economics, there are different understandings of market processes within different schools of thought, each would understand the operation of a market for ideas differently. In particular, those who identify limitations to the social benefits of free markets, and thus contemplate intervention (including intervention to promote increased competition) would be inclined to question whether the unfettered production of ideas in economics did indeed produce the optimal outcome. While this argument is ultimately circular (depending on the perspective of market adopted), so is the argument that rests on the invisible hand. Indeed the scope for different understandings of key terms is central to the nature of plurality in economics.

It has been argued here that the growing plurality in mainstream theory and evidence, prompted by the desire to capture more of the complexity of the economy, raises questions about the sufficiency of mathematical formalism as a methodological approach. In other words, there is room also for non-formalist argument, with the mainstream methodological approach only one of a range of possible approaches. In particular, the issues posed for formal modeling by plurality in mainstream theory and evidence suggest that there is scope for more plurality at the methodological level. Economic theory is facing exciting new challenges which are open to a range of methodological treatments. The scope to take up these challenges would be severely limited if there were an overriding requirement to express all theory in terms of the kind of individual behaviour which can be captured in formal mathematics (that is, in deterministic form).

In practice, any discipline can only function with a limited range of approaches (within which there are understandings of the economic process, shared meanings, shared views as to what constitutes good theory and so on). An absence of universal methodological principles therefore does not mean that 'anything goes', but rather a limited range of sets of such principles. This implies that there is a continuing role for schools of thought as a way of categorising these difference approaches, aiding mutual understanding, and providing the variety on which economics can build.

But the main purpose has been to draw attention to the issues posed by current trends in economics and to encourage wider attention to them. To leave such issues unexamined is arguably to opt for 'anything goes'.

14
Afterword

The main theme running through this volume is an argument for economists becoming more aware of their own methodological approach. This is a precondition for methodological pluralism, that is, the willingness to consider a range of different approaches to economics when contemplating new economic thinking. When considering where economics should go next in the wake of the crisis, it seems unnecessarily restrictive to accept the limitations of the mainstream approach without examination and justification. Any approach has its limitations, but it is reasonable to think that economics would be more robust if it fostered diversity. What might suit one set of circumstances best might not suit another set of circumstances, and the argument in favour of any policy finding support from a range of approaches would thereby have higher weight. On the other hand, if different approaches come to very different opinions on policy, this should give policymakers pause for thought before leaping into action. (See further Dow, forthcoming, c).

What has held back such a development has been the fact that, in the terms of one approach, the analysis of another approach is unlikely to make sense and it is therefore ignored. Indeed, to ignore other approaches may not even be a conscious decision, given that we tend not to see what does not make sense to us. Thus, for example, mainstream economics has made only very limited use of theory developed within other approaches which already addressed issues of financial instability before the recent crisis; only those parts which could make sense within the mainstream framework were picked up. Similarly, attempts to incorporate uncertainty and behaviour which is not rational in terms of the rationality axioms into mainstream theory have been heavily constrained by what the framework does and does not allow. We have seen in this volume that this is an inevitable feature of different approaches.

What is required therefore, to help us address new economic problems as they arise, is enough methodological awareness (and academic courtesy) for economists to take the trouble to find out enough about each others' approaches in order to communicate (even imperfectly). That way debates become more constructive and creative new developments are more likely (possibly cutting across approaches, that is, creating a new approach).

Methodological pluralism is often misunderstood as an unacceptable relativism – 'anything goes'. Yet to interpret an absence of independent appraisal criteria as meaning *no* appraisal criteria is to apply a dualistic mode of thought, which itself requires justification. Any knowledge system needs some appraisal criteria. Thus, for example some approaches put higher priority on making theory specific to particular current institutional arrangements while others prioritise universal application. In principle, the range of possibilities is very large. However, in practice the need for a critical mass within scientific communities to support the various academic institutional arrangements of journals, conferences and so on, inevitably limits the number of approaches which can be sustained.

Methodological pluralism is also often misunderstood as involving all economists always actively considering a range of approaches. Not surprisingly, this is not appealing. Not only is it challenging to consider several ways of thinking at the same time, but also it would be very distracting constantly to be referring back to methodological issues. Instead, most of the work in providing critical accounts of different approaches would be done by methodologists. For practising economists, methodological pluralism consists instead of using the work of methodologists to inform awareness of the legitimacy of alternative approaches *in their own terms*. If their theorising is to be coherent, practising economists must settle on one approach or another. But methodological pluralism means that all economists should be equipped and prepared to justify what they are doing in relation to alternative approaches. However, to communicate across different approaches an extra effort is required to grasp differences of meaning and to understand what makes sense of different theories within these alternative approaches.

The purpose here has been to increase the scope of inquiry for new economic thinking by focusing on the foundational level, such that the value of doing so is better appreciated. Yet its achievement requires much more. Over recent decades, the challenges of mastering the techniques of mathematical formalism have increasingly come to dominate the education of economists. As a consequence, education in economic history, the history of economics and economic methodology have been squeezed out of the typical university curriculum. As a result, students in recent years will have been surprised to find that there have been previous episodes of banking crisis, that there have been theories of crisis at least since the nineteenth century and that there is no absolute methodological justification for the emphasis on mathematical formalism (but rather a large literature discussing a range of methodologies). Ideally, all three elements should be integrated into theory courses, rather than being relegated as minority specialisms. That way the theory makes more sense to students, they can better understand debates and they can become better equipped to address unforeseen economic developments. Students can thus learn how to form their own judgements when they come to develop theories and apply them to policy issues.

Beyond such long-term considerations as altering the economics education programme and increasing tolerance among economists, a move towards methodological pluralism would have concrete consequences for new economic thinking now. Once it is understood that other bodies of theory than one's own might actually make sense within their own methodological frameworks, the field would be open to a much wider range of existing theories on which to build. Once the nature of the alternative frameworks is understood, then ideas can more readily be shared and new ideas generated.

Obvious cases in point include 'old' behavioural economics and 'old' institutional economics whose difference from the 'new' versions is defined precisely in terms of methodological approach. These literatures are particularly informative on the behaviour of individuals and firms in different circumstances and on the nature, evolution and role of institutions. They put reform of financial regulation, for example, into a different perspective. The prevailing approach has focused on imposing constraints on rational optimising behaviour, for example by increasing capital requirements and ring-fencing retail banking. Building on different foundations, an old behavioural approach focuses rather on how individuals and institutions establish routines to cope with uncertainty in the environment of modern financial institutions, while old institutionalists focus on the historical evolution of the institutions of money and banking through cooperation between banks and central banks, and how confidence (as a social convention) in them became established. These analyses use a range of methods (case study and analytical-historical methods, for example, possibly alongside mathematics).

Such analyses focus on reinforcing the socially desirable functions of banking and building up confidence again. While the prevailing approach seeks to limit moral hazard understood as a rational response to central bank support, the alternative approaches seek to limit moral hazard with a different, broader meaning: that of a breakdown of *mutual* trust and cooperation between banks, central banks and the non-bank public. A key element would be a commitment by central banks to the lender-of-last-resort facility. (See further Dow, forthcoming, b and d.)

Another obvious set of literatures on which to draw in the wake of the crisis is the history of economic theory of crisis and modern theories of financial instability, which are deliberately not encompassed in general formal models because of the understanding of crisis as being non-deterministic (see further Dow, 2011). Starting instead from foundations which focus analysis on conditions where risk may be quantified, the prevailing mainstream analysis limits the scope for understanding why the quantitative models of market players, policymakers and economists broke down. A foundational belief in the stabilising capacity of markets also limits the scope for contemplating policy measures to restore stability and confidence in that stability. But alternative theories focus on the uncertainty of knowledge and the behavioural and institutional mechanisms developed to deal with that. This focus on uncertainty as a general feature of knowledge (not just something which arises in times of crisis) is relevant to market players and their handling of risk assessment as well as to policymakers and economists in their attempts to prevent a recurrence of such a serious crisis. In particular, the conventional judgments of markets are often the product of theoretical ideas, such that the reduction of large budgetary deficits may be seen as the top priority, based on mainstream supply-side analysis. But considering theory which sees the uncertainty of knowledge underpinning potential demand-side problems (however healthy the supply side), boosting aggregate demand in times of crisis is seen as the top priority (creating the conditions for attending to deficits in due course).

Different foundations produce different analyses and different policies. Engaging in debate about different approaches not only reveals possibilities for policy solutions but also hones our skills in judgement and the kind of lateral thinking required for making new connections. But the first step towards facilitating such debate is the recognition of the possibility of different foundations than one's own, and the willingness and ability to defend (and possibly amend) one's own foundations.

This requires some effort in understanding where economics stands now (which in turn requires some understanding of how we got here). Current economic problems are pressing and the problems of the future are as yet unforeseen. The focus of this volume has been to encourage the building of foundations on which new economic thinking can be developed in order to address them.

Bibliography

Agassi, J. (1965) 'The Nature of Scientific Problems and their Roots in Metaphysics, in M. Bunge (ed.), *The Critical Approach to Science and Philosophy* (New York: Collier-Macmillan).

—— (1979) 'The Legacy of Lakatos', *Philosophy of Social Sciences*, vol. 9, 316–26.

Aikman, D., P. Barrett, S. Kapadia, M. King, J. Proudman, T. Taylor, I. de Weymarn and T. Yates (2010) 'Uncertainty in macroeconomic policy making: art or science?' *Journal of Regulation and Risk North Asia*, 2 (summer/fall).

Akerlof, G. A. and W. T. Dickens (1982) 'The economic consequence of cognitive dissonance', *American Economic Review*, 72, 307–319.

Akerlof, G. A. and R. Shiller (2009) *Animal Spirits* (Princeton: Princeton University Press).

Allen, B. (2000) 'The Future of Microeconomic Theory', *Journal of Economic Perspectives*, 14, 143–50.

Amariglio, J. L. (1988) 'The Body, Economic Discourse and Power: An Economist's Introduction to Foucault', *History of Political Economy*, 20 (4), 583–613.

—— (1990) 'Economics as a Postmodern Discourse', in W. J. Samuels (ed.), *Economics as Discourse* (Boston: Kluwer).

—— and D. F. Ruccio (1995) 'Keynes, Postmodernism and Uncertainty', in S. C. Dow and J. Hillard (eds), *Keynes, Knowledge and Uncertainty* (Aldershot: Edward Elgar).

Anderlini, L. (1986) 'Competitive banking in a simple model', in J. Edwards et al. (eds), *Recent Developments in Corporate Finance* (Cambridge: Cambridge University Press).

Andrews, P. (1982) 'Manufacturing fixed investment and the Great Depression', Unpublished PhD dissertation, University of California, Berkeley

Andrews, P. W. S. (1949) *Manufacturing Business* (London: Macmillan).

Arndt, H. W. (1984) 'Political economy', *Economic Record*, 60, September, 266–73.

Arrow, K. J. and F. H. Hahn (1971) *General Competitive Analysis* (San Francisco: Holden-Day).

Bank of England (1999) *Economic Models at the Bank of England* (London: Bank of England).

Backhouse, R. E. (1988) 'The value of post Keynesian economics: a neoclassical response to Harcourt and Hamouda', *Bulletin of Economic Research*, 40, 35–41

—— (1991) 'The Neo-Walrasian Research Program in Macroeconomics', in N. de Marchi and M. Blaug (eds), *Appraising Economic Theories* (Aldershot: Edward Elgar).

—— (1992a) 'The Constructivist Critique of Economic Methodology', *Methodus*, 4 (1), 65–82.

—— (1992b) 'Should we Ignore Methodology?', *Royal Economic Society Newsletter*, July

—— (1992c) 'Rejoinder: Why Methodology Matters', *Methodus*, 4 (2), 58–62.

Backhouse, R. E. (1993) 'Lakatosian Perspectives on General Equilibrium Analysis', *Economics and Philosophy*, 9 (2), 271–82.
——, ed. (1994) *New Directions in Economic Methodology* (London: Routledge).
—— (1997) *Truth and Progress in Economic Knowledge* (Aldershot: Edward Elgar).
—— (1998a) 'If Mathematics is Informal, Then Perhaps We Should Accept that Economics Must Be Informal Too', *Economic Journal*, 108 (451), 1848–58.
—— (1998) 'The Transformation of U.S. Economics, 1920-1960', in M. S. Morgan and M. Rutherford (eds), *From Interwar Pluralism to Postwar Neoclassicism. History of Political Economy*. 30: Annual Supplement, pp. 85–108.
—— (2000) 'Progress in Heterodox Economics', *Journal of the History of Economic Thought*, 22,149–56.
—— (2005) 'Economists, Values and Ideology: A Neglected Agenda', *Revue de Philosophie Economique*, 11, 49–73.
—— (2010) *The Puzzle of Modern Economics - Science or Ideology?* (Cambridge: Cambridge University Press).
Bank of England (1999) *Economic Models at the Bank of England* (London: Bank of England).
Barro, R. J. (1984) 'Rational expectations and macroeconomics in 1984', *American Economic Review, Papers and Proceedings*, 74, May, 179–82.
Bateman, B. W. (1987) 'Keynes's changing conception of probability', *Economics and Philosophy*, 3, 97–119
—— and J. B. Davis, eds (1991) *Keynes and Philosophy: Essays on the Origin of Keynes's Thought* (Aldershot: Edward Elgar).
Baumol, W. J. (1991) 'Towards a Newer Economics: The Future Lies Ahead!', *Economic Journal*, 101 (404), 1–8.
Bausor, R. (1983) 'The Rational-Expectations Hypothesis and the Epistemics of Time', *Cambridge Journal of Economics*, 7, 1–10
Begg, D. K. H. (1982a) 'Rational Expectations, Wage Rigidity and Involuntary Unemployment', *Oxford Economic Papers*, 34, 23–47
—— (1982b) *The Rational Expectations Revolution in Macroeconomics: Theories and Evidence* (Oxford: Philip Allan).
Bell, D. and I. Kristol (1981) *The Crisis in Economic Theory* (New York: Basic Books).
Berger, L. A. (1989) 'Economics and Hermeneutics', *Economics and Philosophy*, 5 (2), 209–34.
Bertalanffy, L. von (1968) *General System Theory* (New York: George Braziller).
Bewley, T. F. (1995) 'A Depressed Labor Market as Explained by Participants', *American Economic Review, Papers and Proceedings*, 85, 250–54.
Binmore, K. (1987) 'Modelling Rational Players: Part I', *Economics And Philosophy*, 3 (2), 179–214.
Blanchard, O. (1997) *Macroeconomics*, third edition (NSR NJ: Prentice-Hall).
—— and S. Fischer (1989) *Lectures in Macroeconomics* (Cambridge, MA: MIT Press).
Blaug, M. (1976) 'Kuhn versus Lakatos on Paradigms versus Research Programmes in the History of Economics', in S. J. Latsis (ed.), *Method and Appraisal in Economics* (Cambridge: Cambridge University Press).
—— (1980) *The Methodology of Economics*, second edition 1992 (Cambridge: Cambridge University Press).
—— (1991) 'Afterward', in N. de Marchi and M. Blaug (eds), *Appraising Economic Theories* (Aldershot: Edward Elgar).

Blaug, M. (1999) 'The Formalist Revolution or What has Happened to Orthodox Economics after World War II', in R. E. Backhouse and J. Creedy (eds), *From Classical Economics to the Theory of the Firm: Essays in Honour of D. P. O'Brien* (Cheltenham: Edward Elgar).

Bleaney, M. (1991) 'An Overview of Emerging Theory', in D. Greenaway et al, (eds), *Companion to Contemporary Economic Thought* (London: Routledge).

Bohm, D. ([1957] 1984) *Causality and Chance in Modern Physics* (London: Routledge & Kegan Paul).

Boland L. A. (1981) 'On the Futility of Criticizing the Neoclassical Maximization Hypothesis', *American Economic Review*, 71, 1031–6.

—— (1982) *The Foundations of Economic Method* (London: George Allen and Unwin).

—— (1989) *The Methodology of Economic Model Building: Methodology after Samuelson* (London: Routledge).

—— (1991) 'The Theory and Practice of Economic Methodology', *Methodus*, 3 (2), 6–17.

Boulding, K. (1956) 'General System Theory, the Skeleton of a Science', *Management Science* 2 (3), 197–208, reprinted in *Modern Systems Research for the Behavioral Scientist*, W. Buckley, ed. (Chicago: Alaine).

Boumans, M. and J. B. Davis (2010) *Economic Methodology: Understanding Economics as a Science* (London: Palgrave Macmillan).

Brainard, W. (1967) 'Uncertainty and the effectiveness of policy', *American Economic Review Papers and Proceedings*, 57, 411–25.

Braithwaite, R. B. (1973) 'Editorial Forward' to J. M. Keynes (1921).

Bray, J. et al. (1995) 'The interfaces between policy-makers, markets and modellers', *Economic Journal*, 105 (431), 989–1000.

Brown, V. (1994) 'The Economy as Text', in R. E. Backhouse (ed.), *New Directions in Economic Methodology* (London: Routledge).

Brown-Collier, E. and R. Bowser (1988) 'The epistemological foundations of the General Theory', *Scottish Journal of Political Economy*, 35 (August), 227–41.

Buchanan, J. M. (1991) 'Economics in the Post-Socialist Society, *Economic Journal*, 101 (404), 15–21.

Caldwell, B. J. (1982) *Beyond Positivism: Economic Methodology in the Twentieth Century* (London: Allen & Unwin).

——, ed. (1984) *Appraisal and Criticism in Economics* (London: Allen and Unwin).

—— (1986) 'Towards a Broader Conception of Criticism', *History of Political Economy*, 18, 675–81

—— (1988) 'The Case for Pluralism', in N. de Marchi (ed.), *The Popperian Legacy in Economics* (Cambridge: Cambridge University Press).

—— (1989) 'Post-Keynesian Methodology: An Assessment', *Review of Political Economy*, 1 (1), 43–64.

—— (1990) 'Does Methodology Matter? How Should It Be Practiced?', *Finnish Economic Papers*, 3(1), 64–71.

—— (1991a) 'Clarifying Popper', *Journal of Economic Literature*, 29 (1), 1-33.

—— (1991b) 'Has Formalisation gone too Far in Economics: A Comment', *Methodus*, 3 (1), 27–9.

——, ed. (1993) *The Philosophy and Methodology of Economics*, vols I-III (Aldershot: Edward Elgar).

Caldwell, B. J. (1997) 'Varieties of Pluralism: A Comment on Dow and Samuels', in A. Salanti and E. Screpanti (eds), *Pluralism in Economics: Theory, History and Methodology* Cheltenham: Edward Elgar).

—— and S. Boehm, eds (1992) *Austrian Economics: Tensions and New Directions* (Boston: Kluwer).

—— and A. W. Coats (1984) 'The Rhetoric of Economists: A Comment on McCloskey', *Journal of Economic Literature*, 22 (2), 575–8.

Capra, F. (1975) *The Tao of Physics: an Exploration of the Parallels between Modern Physics and Eastern Mysticism* (London: Wildwood).

Carabelli, A. M. (1985) 'Keynes on cause, chance and possibility', in T. Lawson and H. Pesaran (eds), *Keynes' Economics: Methodological Issues* (London: Croom Helm).

—— (1988) *On Keynes's* Method (London: Macmillan).

—— (1991a) 'Organic interdependence and Keynes's choice of the units of quantity and of measure in *The General Theory*', in B. Gerrard and J. Hillard (eds), *Perspective on Keyne* (Aldershot: Edward Elgar).

—— (1991b) 'The Methodology of the Critique of the Classical Theory', in B. W. Bateman and J. B. Davis (eds), *Keynes and Philosophy: Essays on the Origin of Keynes's Thought* (Aldershot: Edward Elgar).

—— (1995) 'Uncertainty and Measurement in Keynes: Probability and Organicness', in S. C. Dow and J. V. Hillard (eds), *Keynes, Knowledge and Uncertainty* (Aldershot: Edward Elgar).

Caserta, M. (1993) 'Capacity Utilisation, Effective Demand and Unsteady Growth', Ph.D. Dissertation, University of London (UCL).

Casson, M. (1981) *Unemployment: a Disequilibrium Approach* (Oxford: Martin Robertson).

Cencini, A. (1995) *Monetary Theory: National and International* (London: Routledge).

Chick, V. (1977) *The Theory of Monetary Policy*, second edition (Oxford: Basil Blackwell).

—— (1983) *Macroeconomics After Keynes: A Reconsideration of the General Theory* (Oxford: Philip Allan).

—— (1983) *Macroeconomics after Keynes: A Reconsideration of The General Theory* (Oxford: Philip Allan and Cambridge, MA: MIT Press).

—— (1995) 'Order Out of Chaos in Economics', in S. C. Dow and J. Hillard (eds), *Keynes, Knowledge and Uncertainty* (Aldershot: Edward Elgar).

—— (1997) 'The Multiplier and Finance', in G. C. Harcourt and P. A. Riach (eds), *A 'Second Edition' of The General Theory* (London: Routledge).

—— (1998a) 'On Knowing One's Place', *Economic Journal*, 108 (451), 1859–69.

—— (1998b) 'A struggle to escape: equilibrium in *The General Theory*', in S. Sharma (ed.), *John Maynard Keynes: Keynesianism into the Twenty-First Century* (Cheltenham: Edward Elgar).

—— (2004) 'On open systems', *Brazilian Review of Political Economy*, 24 (1), 1–16.

—— and M. Caserta (1997) 'Provisional equilibrium and macroeconomic theory', in P. Arestis, G. Palma and M. C. Sawyer (eds), *Markets, Employment and Economic Policy: Essays in Honour of G. C. Harcourt*, vol. 2 (London: Routledge).

—— and S. C. Dow (2001) 'Formalism, Logic and Reality: A Keynesian Analysis', *Cambridge Journal of Economics*, 25(6), 705–22.

Chick, V. (2005) 'The Meaning of Open Systems', *Journal of Economic Methodology*, 12, 363–81.

—— (2001) 'Formalism, Logic and Reality: A Keynesian Analysis', *Cambridge Journal of Economics*, 25(6), 705–22.

Clements, M. P. and D. Hendry (1995) 'Macroeconomic forecasting and modelling', *Economic Journal*, 105 (431), 1001–31.

Coates, J. (1996) *The Claims of Common Sense: Moore, Wittgenstein, Keynes and the Social Sciences* (Cambridge: Cambridge University Press).

—— (1997) 'Keynes, Vague Concepts and Fuzzy Logic', in G. C. Harcourt and P. A. Riach (eds), *A 'Second Edition' of the General Theory*, vol. 2 (London: Routledge).

Coats, A. W. (2000) ' Opening Remarks for Roundtable on the Progress of Heterodox Economics', *Journal of the History of Economic Thought*, 22, 145–8.

Coddington, A. (1975) 'The Rationale of General Equilibrium Theory', *Economic Inquiry*, 13 (4), 539–58.

—— (1975) 'The rationale of general equilibrium theory', *Economic Inquiry*, 13, 539–58

—— (1976) 'Keynesian Economics: The Search for First Principles', *Journal of Economic Literature*, 14, 1258–73.

—— (1982) 'Deficient Foresight A Troublesome Theme in Keynesian Economics', *American Economic Review*, 72, 480–7

Colander, D. C. (2000a) 'The Death of Neoclassical Economics', *Journal of the History of Economic Thought*, 22, 127–43.

—— (2000b) 'New Millennium Economics: How Did It Get This Way, and What Way Is It?', *Journal of Economic Perspectives*, 14, 121–32

—— and R.S. Guthrie (1980-81) 'Great Expectation: What the Dickens do "Rational Expectations" Mean?', *Journal of Post Keynesian Economics*, 3 (2), 139–53.

—— and A. Klamer (1987) 'The making of an economist', *Journal of Economic Perspectives*, 1, 95–112

Crotty, J. R. (1980) 'Post Keynesian Economic Theory: An Overview and Evaluation', *American Economic Review*, 70 (2), 20–5.

Cuthbertson, K. (1979) *Macroeconomic Policy: The New Cambridge, Keynesian and Monetarist Policies* (London: Macmillan).

Darnell, A. C. and J. L. Evans (1990) *The Limits of Econometrics* (Aldershot: Edward Elgar).

Davidson, P. (1978) *Money and the Real World* 2nd edn (London: Macmillan).

—— (1982-83) 'Rational Expectations: A Fallacious Foundation for Studying Crucial Decision Making', *Journal of Post Keynesian Economics*, 5, 182-98

—— (1991) 'Comment on "Keynes on Probability, Expectations and Uncertainty"', in R. M. O'Donnell (ed.), *Keynes as Philosopher-Economist* (London: Macmillan).

Davie, G. (1961) *The Democratic Intellect: Scotland and her Universities in the Nineteenth Century* (Edinburgh, Edinburgh University Press).

Davis, J. B. (1994) *Keynes's Philosophical Development* (Cambridge: Cambridge University Press).

—— (1997) 'Comment' in A. Salanti and E. Screpanti (eds), *Pluralism in Economics* (Aldershot: Edward Elgar.).

—— (1999a) 'Postmodernism and Identity Conditions for Discourses' in R. F. Garnett Jr (ed.), *What Do Economists Know?: New Economics of Knowledge*, London: Routledge, pp. 155–68.

Davis, J. B. (1999b) 'Common Sense: A Middle Way between Formalism and Post-structuralism?', *Cambridge Journal of Economics*, 23 (4): 503–15.

—— (2003) *The Theory of the Individual in Economics: Identity and Value* (London: Routledge).

—— (2006a) 'The Turn in Economics: Neoclassical Dominance to Mainstream Pluralism?', *Journal of Institutional Economics*, 2, 1–20.

——, ed. (2006b) *Recent Developments in Economic Methodology*, 3 vols (Cheltenham: Edward Elgar).

——, D. W. Hands and U. Mäki, eds (1998) *The Handbook of Economic Methodology* (Cheltenham: Edward Elgar).

——, A. Marciano and J. Runde, eds (2004) *The Elgar Companion to Economics and Philosophy* (Cheltenham: Edward Elgar).

de Marchi, N., ed. (1988) *The Popperian Legacy in Economics* (Cambridge: Cambridge University Press).

—— (1991) 'Introduction', in N. de Marchi and M. Blaug (eds), *Appraising Economic Theories* (Aldershot: Edward Elgar).

——, ed. (1992) *Post Popperian Methodology of Economics: Recovering Practice*, (Boston: Kluwer).

—— and M. Blaug, eds (1991) *Appraising Economic Theories: Studies in the Methodology of Research Programs* (Aldershot: Edward Elgar).

Deane, P. (1983) 'The scope and method of economic science', *Economic Journal*, 93 (March), 1–12.

Debreu, G. (1959) *Theory of Value* (New York: John Wiley and Sons).

—— (1991) 'The Mathematization of Economic Theory', *American Economic Review*, 81, 1–7.

DellaVigna, S. (2009) 'Psychology and Economics: Evidence from the Field', *Journal of Economic Literature*, 158(2): 315–72.

Doherty, J., E. Graham and M. Malek, eds (1992) *Postmodernism and the Social Sciences* (London: Macmillan).

Dow, A. C. (1984) 'The hauteur of Adam Smith', *Scottish Journal of Political Economy*, 31 (November), 284–5.

—— and S. C. Dow (1985) 'Animal Spirits and Rationality', in T. Lawson and H. Pesaran (eds), *Keynes' Economics: Methodological Issues*. London: Croom Helm, 46–65.

—— and S. C. Dow (2011) 'Animal Spirits Revisited', *Capitalism and Society*, 6 (2), article 1, at http://www.bepress.com/cas/vol6/iss2/art1/

Dow, S. C. (1980) 'Methodological Morality in the Cambridge Controversies', *Journal of Post Keynesian Economics*, 2, 368–80.

—— (1985) *Macroeconomic Thought A Methodological Approach* (Oxford: Basil Blackwell), republished in revised form as *The Methodology of Macroeconomic Thought* (Aldershot: Edward Elgar, 1996).

—— (1987) 'The Scottish political economy tradition', *Scottish Journal of Political Economy*, 34, November 335–48.

—— (1988) 'What happened to Keynes's economics?', in O. Hamouda and J. Smithin (eds), *Keynes and Public Policy after Fifty Years*, vol. 1: *Economics and Policy* (Aldershot: Edward Elgar).

—— (1990a) 'Beyond Dualism', *Cambridge Journal of Economics*, 14(2), 143–58.

—— (1990b) 'Post Keynesianism as Political Economy: A Methodological Discussion', *Review of Political Economy*, 2 (3), 345–58.

—— (1991) 'Keynes's epistemology and economic methodology', in R. M. O'Donnell (ed.), *Keynes as Philosopher-Economist* (London: Macmillan).

Dow, S. C. (1992) 'Historical Reference: Hume and Critical Realism', *Cambridge Journal of Economics*, 26(6), 683–97.

—— (1997a) 'Methodological Pluralism and Pluralism of Method', in A. Salanti and E. Screpanti (eds), *Pluralism in Economics: Theory, History and Methodology* (Cheltenham: Edward Elgar).

—— (1997b) 'Endogenous Money', in G. C. Harcourt and P. A. Riach (eds), *A 'Second Edition' of the General Theory*, vol. 2 (London: Routledge).

—— (1998) 'Editorial Introduction to the Formalism in Economics Controversy', *Economic Journal*, 108 (451), 1826–8.

—— (1999a) 'Rationality and Rhetoric in Smith and Keynes', in R. Rossini, G. Sandri and R. Scazzieri (eds), *Incommensurability and Translation* (Aldershot: Edward Elgar).

—— (1999b) 'Post Keynesianism and Critical Realism: What is the Connection?', *Journal of Post Keynesian Economics*, 22(1),15–33.

—— (2001) 'Modernism and Postmodernism: A Dialectical Analysis', in S. Cullenberg, J. Amariglio and D. F. Ruccio (eds), *Postmodernism, Economics and Knowledge* (London: Routledge).

—— (2002) *Economic Methodology: An Inquiry* (Oxford: Oxford University Press).

—— (2003a) 'The Babylonian Mode of Thought', in J. King (ed.), *The Elgar Companion to Post Keynesian Economics* (Cheltenham: Edward Elgar). Second edition forthcoming.

—— (2003b) 'Probability, Uncertainty and Convention: Economists' Knowledge and the Knowledge of Economic Actors', in S. Mizuhara and J. Runde (eds), *Perspectives on the Philosophy of Keynes's Economics: Probability, Uncertainty and Convention* (London: Routledge).

—— (2004a) 'Structured pluralism', *Journal of Economic Methodology*, 11 (3), 275–90.

—— (2004b) 'Uncertainty and Monetary Policy', *Oxford Economic Papers*, 56, 39–61.

—— (2008) 'Plurality in orthodox and heterodox economics', *Journal of Philosophical Economics* 1(2), 73–96.

—— (2009) 'Smith's Philosophy and Economic Methodology', in J. T. Young (ed.), *Elgar Companion to Adam Smith* (Cheltenham: Edward Elgar).

—— (2010) 'Psychology of Financial Markets: Keynes, Minsky and Emotional Finance', in D. B. Papadimitriou and L. R. Wray (eds), *The Elgar Companion to Hyman Minsky* (Cheltenham: Edward Elgar).

—— (2011) 'Cognition, Market Sentiment and Financial Instability: Psychology in a Minsky Framework', *Cambridge Journal of Economics*, 35(2), 233–50.

—— (forthcoming, a) 'Keynes on Knowledge, Expectations and Rationality', in E. S. Phelps and R. Frydman (eds), *Microfoundations for Modern Macroeconomics*. Princeton NJ: Princeton University Press.

—— (forthcoming, b) 'Economics and Moral Sentiments: The Case of Moral Hazard', in V. Neves and J. C. Caldas (eds), *Facts, Values and Objectivity* (London: Routledge).

—— (forthcoming, c) 'Policy in the Wake of the Banking Crisis: Taking Pluralism Seriously', *International Journal of Applied Economics*

—— (forthcoming, d) 'What are Banks and Bank Regulation For? A Consideration of the Foundations for Reform', *Intervention*.

—— and P. E. Earl (1982) *Money Matters: A Keynesian Approach to Monetary Economics* (Oxford: Martin Robertson).

Dow, S. C. and D. Ghosh (2009) 'Fuzzy Logic and Keynes's Speculative Demand for Money', *Journal of Economic Methodology*, 16 (1), 57–69

—— and J. Hillard, eds (1995) *Keynes, Knowledge and Uncertainty* (Aldershot: Edward Elgar).

Downward, P. and A. Mearman (2008) 'Decision-making at the Bank of England: A Critical Appraisal', *Oxford Economic Papers* 60(3), 385–409.

Dubois, D. and H. Prade (1980) *Fuzzy Sets and Systems: Theory and Applications* (London: Academic Press).

Dutt, A. K. (1990) *Growth, Distribution and Uneven Development* (Cambridge: Cambridge University Press).

Earl, P. E. (1983a) 'A behavioural theory of economists' behaviour', in A. S. Eichner (ed.), *Why Economics is Not Yet a Science* (London: Macmillan).

—— (1983b) *The Economic Imagination: Towards a Behavioural Theory of Choice* (Brighton: Wheatsheaf).

—— (1984) *The Corporate Imagination: How Big Companies Make Mistakes* (Brighton: Wheatsheaf).

——, ed. (1989) *Behavioural Economics*, vols. 1 and 2 (Aldershot: Edward Elgar).

—— (1990) 'Economics and psychology: A survey', *Economic Journal*, 100, 718–55

—— (1991) 'The complementarity of economic applications of cognitive dissonance theory and personal construct theory', in S. E. G. Lea, P. Webley and B. M. Young, (eds) *New Directions in Economics Psychology* (Aldershot: Edward Elgar).

Eatwell, J. (1979) 'Theories of Value and Employment', *Thames Papers in Political Economy*, Summer

Eichner, A. S. (1985) 'The Lack of Progress in Economics', *Nature*, 313 (7), 427–8.

European Central Bank (2000) 'The Two Pillars of the ECB's Monetary Policy Strategy', *ECB Monthly Bulletin*, November, 37–48.

Evans, G. (1983) 'The Stability of Rational Expectations in Neoclassical and Keynesian Macroeconomic Models', in R. Frydman and E. S. Phelps (eds), *Individual Forecasting and Aggregate Outcomes: 'Rational Expectations' Examined* (Cambridge: Cambridge University Press).

Festinger, L. (1957) *A Theory of Cognitive Dissonance* (Evanston, IL: Row Peterson).

Feyerabend, P. (1970) 'Consolations for the specialist', in I. Lakatos and A. Musgrave (eds), *Criticism and the Growth of Knowledge* (Cambridge: Cambridge University Press).

—— (1978) *Science in a Free Society* (London: New Left Books).

Feynman, R. P. (1965) *The Character of Physical Law* (Cambridge, MA: MIT Press).

Fish, S. (1980) *Is There a Text in the Class? The Authority of Interpretive Communities* (Cambridge, MA: Harvard University Press).

Fishburn, P.C. (1991) 'Decision Theory: The Next 100 Years?' *Economic Journal*, 101 (404), 27–32.

Fitzgibbons, A. (1988) *Keynes's Vision: A New Political Economy* (Oxford: Clarendon).

Friedman, M. (1953) 'The Methodology of Positive Economics', in *Essays in Positive Economics* (Chicago: Chicago University Press).

Friedman, M. (1991) 'Old Wine in New Bottles', *Economic Journal*, 101 (404), 33–40.

—— and D. Meiselman (1963) 'The Relative Stability of Monetary Velocity and the Investment Multiplier in the United States, 1897-1958', in E. C. Brown et al. (eds), *Stabilization Policies* (Englewood Cliffs, N. J.: Prentice-Hall).

—— and A. Schwartz (1963) 'Money and Business Cycles', *Review of Economics and Statistics*, 45 (supplement), 32–64.

Frydman, R. and E. S. Phelps, eds (1970) *Microeconomic Foundations of Employment and Inflation Theory* (New York: Norton).

Fullbrook, E. (2003) 'Real Science is Pluralist', in E. Fullbrook (ed), *The Crisis in Economics* (London: Routledge).

Fuller, S. (2000) *Thomas Kuhn: A Philosophical History of Our Times* (Chicago: University of Chicago Press).

—— (2003) *Kuhn vs Popper* (Cambridge: Icon Books).

Fulton, G. (1984) 'Research Programmes in Economics', *History of Political Economy*, 16, (2), 187–205.

Gale, D. (1982) *Money: In Equilibrium* (Cambridge: Cambridge University Press).

—— (1983) *Money: In Disequilibrium* (Cambridge: Cambridge University Press).

Garner, C. (1982) 'Uncertainty, Human Judgement, and Economic Decisions', *Journal of Post Keynesian Economics*, 14, 413–24.

Garnett, R. (2006) 'Paradigms and Pluralism in Heterodox Economics', *Review of Political Economy*, 18 (4), 521–46.

Gerrard, B. (1989) *Theory of the Capitalist Economy: Toward a Post-Classical Synthesis* (Oxford: Basil Blackwell).

—— (1990) 'On Matters Methodological in Economics', *Journal of Economic Surveys*, 4 (2), 197–219.

—— (1991) 'Keynes's *General Theory*: Interpreting the Interpretations', *Economic Journal*, 101 (405), 276–87.

—— (1992) 'Human Logic in Keynes's Thought', in P. Arestis and V. Chick (eds), *Recent Developments in Post-Keynesian Economics* (Aldershot: Edward Elgar).

——, ed. (1993) *The Economics of Rationality* (London: Routledge).

—— (1995) ' The Scientific Basis of Economics: A Review of the Methodological Debates in Economics and Econometrics', *Scottish Journal of Political Economy*, 42 (2), 221–35.

—— and J. Hillard, eds (1992) *The Philosophy and Economics of J.M. Keynes* (Aldershot: Edward Elgar).

Gillies, D. and G. Ieto-Gillies (1991) 'Intersubjective Probability and Economics', *Review of Political Economy*, 3, 393–417.

Giocoli, N. (2003) *Modelling Rational Agents: From Interwar Economics to Early Modern Game Theory* (Cheltenham: Edward Elgar).

Glass, J.C. and W. Johnson (1989) *Economics: Progression, Stagnation or Degeneration?* (Brighton: Harvester Wheatsheaf).

Goldfeld, S. M. (1976) 'The Case of the Missing Money', *Brookings Papers on Economic Activity*, 3, 683–730.

Goodhart, C. A. E. (1999) 'Central bankers and uncertainty', *Bank of England Quarterly Bulletin*, February, 102–16.

Goodwin, C. D. (2000) 'Comment: It's the Homogeneity, Stupid!', *Journal of the History of Economic Thought*, 22 (2), 179–84.

Gordon, S. (1991) *The History and Philosophy of Social Science* (London: Routledge).

Grandmont, J. M. (1977) Temporary General Equilibrium Theory', *Econometrica*, 45, 535–72.

Graziani, A. (1990) 'The Theory of the Monetary Circuit', *Economies et Sociétés, Monnaie et Production*, no. 7, 7–36.

Greenspan, A. (2009) 'We need a better cushion against risk', *Financial Times*, 27 March.

Groenewegen, P. D. (1985) 'Professor Arndt on political economy: a comment', *Economic Record*, 61 (December), 744–51.

Haas, D. J. (1993) 'A Historical Narrative of Methodological Change in Principles of Economics Textbooks', *Journal of Economic Issues*, 27 (1), 217–30.

Hacking, I. (1981) 'Introduction', in I. Hacking (ed.), *Scientific Revolutions* (Oxford: Oxford University Press).

Hahn, F. H. (1952) 'Expectations and Equilibrium in Economics', *Economic Journal*, 72, 802–19.

—— (1973) *On the Notion of Equilibrium in Economics* (Cambridge: Cambridge University Press).

—— (1977) 'Keynesian economics and general equilibrium theory: Reflections on some current debates', in G. C. Harcourt (ed.), *The Microfoundations of Macroeconomics* (London: Macmillan).

—— (1981) 'General Equilibrium Theory', in D. Bell and I. Kristol (eds.), *The Crisis in Economic Theory* (New York: Basic Books).

—— (1983) *Money and Inflation* (Cambridge, MA: MIT Press).

—— (1984) *Equilibrium and Macroeconomics* (Oxford: Basil Blackwell).

—— (1986) 'Living with uncertainty in economics', *Times Literary Supplement*, August 1.

—— (1989) 'Robinson-Hahn love-hate relationship: An interview' in G. R. Feiwel, (ed.), *Joan Robinson and Modern Economic Theory* (Londo:, Macmillan).

—— (1991) 'The next hundred years', *Economic Journal*, 101, 47–50.

—— (1992) 'Reflections', *Royal Economic Society Newsletter*, April

—— and M. Hollis, eds (1979) *Philosophy and Economic Theory* (Oxford: Oxford University Press).

Hamouda, O. F. and J. Smithin (1988) 'Some remarks on "uncertainty and economic analysis"', *Economic Journal*, 98, 159–64.

Hands, D. W. (1990) 'Thirteen Theses on Progress in Economic Methodology', *Finnish Economic Papers*, 3 (1), 72–6.

—— (1991) 'The Problem of Excess Content: Economics, Novelty and a Long Popperian Tale', in de N. Marchi and M. Blaug (eds), *Appraising Economic Theories* (Aldershot: Edward Elgar).

——(2001) *Reflection Without Rules: Economic Methodology and Contemporary Science Theory* (Cambridge: Cambridge University Press).

Hargraves-Heap, S. (1989) *Rationality in Economics* (Oxford: Basil Blackwell).

Harcourt, G. C. (1972) *Some Cambridge Controversies in the Theory of Capital* (Cambridge: Cambridge University Press).

—— (1987) 'The legacy of Keynes: theoretical methods and unfinished business', in D. A. Reese (ed.), *The Legacy of Keynes, Nobel Conference XXII* (New York: Harper and Row).

Harris, L. (1979) 'Catastrophe Theory, Utility Theory and Animal Spirit Expectations', *Australian Economic Papers*, 18, 268–82.

Harrod, R. F. (1939) 'An Essay in Dynamic Theory', *Economic Journal*, 49, 14–33.

Harvey, M. (1999) 'How the Object of Knowledge Constrains Knowledge of the Object', *Cambridge Journal of Economics*, 23 (4), 485–501.

Hausman, D. (1984) *The Philosophy of Economics: An Anthology* (Cambridge: Cambridge University Press).

—— (1989) 'Economic Methodology in a Nutshell', *Journal of Economic Perspectives*, 3 (2), 115–27.

—— (1992) *The Inexact and Separate Science of Economics* (Cambridge: Cambridge University Press).

Hayek, F. A. (1931) *Prices and Production* (London: George Routledge).

—— (1945) 'The Use of Knowledge in Society', *American Economic Review*, 35, 519–30.

—— (1975) 'Full Employment at any Price', *Hobart Paper*, 45 (London: IEA).

—— (1978) 'Denationalisation of Money: The Argument Refined', *Hobart Special Paper* No. 70.

—— (1979) *The Counter-Revolution of Science*, second edition (Indianapolis: Liberty Press).

Henderson, W., T. Dudley-Evans and R. E. Backhouse, eds (1993) *Economics and Language* (London: Routledge).

Hendry, D. F. and J. Doornik (1994) 'Modelling Linear Dynamic Econometric Systems', *Scottish Journal of Political Economy*, 41 (1), 1–33.

Hey, J. (1993) 'Rationality Is as Rationality Does', in B. Gerrard (ed.), *The Economics of Rationality* (London: Routledge).

Heyting, A. (1971) *Intuitionism: an Introduction* (Amsterdam: North-Holland).

Hicks, J. R. (1939) *Value and Capital* (Oxford: Clarendon).

——. (1974) *The Crisis in Keynesian Economics* (Oxford: Basil Blackwell).

—— (1980-81) 'IS-LM: An Explanation', *Journal of Post Keynesian Economics*, 3, 139–54.

Hodgson, G. M. (1986) 'Behind methodological individualism', *Cambridge Journal of Economics*, 10, September 211–24.

Hodgson, G. M. (1988) *Economics and Institutions: A Manifesto for a Modem Institutional Economics* (Oxford: Polity).

—— (1997) 'Metaphor and Pluralism in Economics: Mechanics and Biology', in A. Salanti and E. Screpanti (eds), *Pluralism in Economics: Theory, History and Methodology* (Aldershot: Edward Elgar).

—— (1999) *Evolution and Institutions: On Evolutionary Economics and the Evolution of Institutions* (Cheltenham: Edward Elgar).

—— (2004) 'On the problem of formalism in economics', *Post-Autistic Economics Review*, 28 (October).

Hong, H. and J. C. Stein (2007) 'Disagreement and the Stock Market', *Journal of Economic Perspectives*, 21 (2), 109–28.

Hoover, K. D. (1994) 'Pragmatism, Pragmaticism and Economic Method', in R. E. Backhouse (ed.), *New Directions in Economic Methodology* (London: Routledge).

Hughes, P. (2010) 'Trust: Economic Notions and its Role in Money and Banking', unpublished PhD thesis, University of Stirling.

Hutchison, T. W. ([1938] 1965) *The Significance and Basic Postulates of Economic Theory* (New York: Augustus M. Kelley).

Hutchison, T. W. (1977) *Knowledge and Ignorance in Economics* (Oxford: Basil Blackwell).

—— (1988), 'The Case for Falsification', in N. de Marchi (ed.) *The Popperian Legacy in Economics* (Cambridge: Cambridge University Press).

Johnson, H. G. (1971) 'The Keynesian Revolution and the Monetarist Counter-Revolution', *American Economic Review, Papers and Proceedings*, 61, 82–93.

—— (1973) *The Theory of Income Distribution* (London: Gray-Mills).

Johnston, J. (1991) 'Econometrics: Retrospect and Prospect', *Economic Journal*, 101 (404), 51–5.

Kahneman, D. (2003) 'Maps of Bounded Rationality: Psychology for Behavioral Economics', *American Economic Review* 93(5), 1449–75.

—— and R. Sugden (2005) 'Experienced Utility as a Standard of Policy Evaluation', *Experimental and Resource Economics*, 32, 161–81.

Kaldor, N. (1985) *Economics Without Equilibrium* (Cardiff: University College Cardiff Press).

Kantor, B. (1979) 'Rational Expectations and Economic Thought', *Journal of Economic Literature*, 17, 1422–41.

Katouzian, H. (1980) *Ideology and Method in Economics* (London: Macmillan).

Kaul, N. (2008) *Imagining Economics Otherwise* (London: Routledge).

Kenyon, P. (1980) 'Discussion' of Tarshis (1980), *American Economic Review Proceedings*, 70, 25–6

Keynes, J. M. ([1921] 1973) *A Treatise on Probability, Collected Writings*, vol. VIII (London: Macmillan, for the Royal Economic Society).

—— ([1930] 1971) *A Treatise on Money. Part I: The Pure Theory of Money, Collected Writings*, vol. V (London: Macmillan for the Royal Economic Society).

—— ([1936] 1973) *The General Theory of Employment, Interest and Money, Collected Writings*, vol. VII (London: Macmillan, for the Royal Economic Society).

—— ([1937] 1973) 'The General Theory of Employment', *Quarterly Journal of Economics* 51, 209–23, reprinted in Keynes (1973b, pp. 109–23).

—— ([1938] 1979) Letter to Hugh Townshend, reprinted in Keynes (1979, pp. 293–4).

—— (1972a) 'Francis Ysidro Edgeworth, 1845-1926', in *Essays in Biography, Collected Writings*, vol. X (London: Macmillan for the Royal Economic Society).

—— (1972b) 'Newton, the man', in *Essays in Biography, Collected Writings*, vol. X (London: Macmillan for the Royal Economic Society).

—— (1972c) 'Bernard Shaw and Isaac Newton', in *Essays in Biography, Collected Writings*, vol. X (London: Macmillan for the Royal Economic Society).

—— (1973a) *The General Theory and After*, Part I: *Preparation, Collected Writings*, vol. XIII (London: Macmillan for the Royal Economic Society).

—— (1973b) *The General Theory and After*, Part II: *Defence and Development, Collected Writings*, vol. XIV (London: Macmillan for the Royal Economic Society).

—— (1979) *The General Theory and After: A Supplement, Collected Writings*, vol XXIX (London: Macmillan for the Royal Economic Society).

King, J. E. (2002) 'Three Arguments for Pluralism in Economics', *Journal of Australian Political Economy*, 50, 82–8, reprinted in *Post-autistic Economics Review*, 23:5, 2004.

—— (2009) 'Microfoundations', La Trobe University *mimeo*.

Kirman, A. P. (1989) 'The intrinsic limits of modem economic theory: The emperor has no clothes', *Economic Journal*, 99 (supplement), 126–39.

Kirman, A. P. (1992) 'Whom or What does the Representative Individual Represent?' *Journal of Economic Perspectives*, 6, 117–36.

Klamer, A. (1988) 'Economics as Discourse', in N. de Marchi (ed), *The Popperian Legacy in Economics* (Cambridge: Cambridge University Press).

——, D. N. McCloskey and R. M. Solow (eds+ (1988) *The Consequences of Economic Rhetoric* (Cambridge: Cambridge University Press).

Klant, J. J. (1990) 'Refutability', *Methodus*, 2 (2), 6–8.

—— (1994) *The Nature of Economic Thought: Essays in Economic Methodology* (Aldershot: Edward Elgar).

Kornai, J. (1974) *Anti-Equilibrium: On Economic Systems Theory and the Tasks of Research* (Amsterdam: North-Holland).

Kregel, J. A. (1976) 'Economic Methodology in the Face of Uncertainty', *Economic Journal*, 86, 209–25.

—— (1980) 'Economic Dynamics and the Theory of Steady-State Growth', *History of Political Economy*, 12 (1), 97–123.

—— (1985) 'Is the Invisible Hand a Fallacy of Composition?' *Cahiers d'Economie Politique*, 10–11, 33–49.

Krugman, P. (2011) 'Mr. Keynes and the Moderns', presented to the Cambridge conference commemorating the 75th anniversary of the publication of *The General Theory of Employment, Interest, and Money*, June.

Kuhn, T. S. ([1962] 1970) *The Structure of Scientific Revolutions* (Chicago: Chicago University Press).

—— (1970) 'Reflections on my critics', in I. Lakatos and A. Musgrave (eds), *Criticism and the Growth of Knowledge* (Cambridge: Cambridge University Press).

—— (1974) 'Second Thoughts on Paradigms', in. F. Suppe (ed.), *The Structure of Scientific Theories* (Urbana: University of Illinois Press).

—— (1977) *The Essential Tension* (Chicago: Chicago University Press).

—— (1990) 'Remarks on Incommensurability and Translation', in R. Favretti, G. Sandri and R. Scazzieri (eds), *Incommensurability and Translation* (Cheltenham: Edward Elgar).

Lachmann, L. M. (1973) *Macroeconomic Thinking and the Market Economy* (London: Institute of Economic Affairs).

Laidler, D. E. W. (1974) *Introduction to Microeconomics* (Oxford: Philip Allan).

—— (1981) 'Monetarism: An Interpretation and an Assessment', *Economic Journal*, 91, 1–28.

—— (1991) *The Golden Age of the Quantity Theory* (London: Harvester Wheatsheaf).

Lakatos, I. (1970) 'Falsification and the Methodology of Scientific Research Programs', in I. Lakatos and A. Musgrave (eds), *Criticism and the Growth of Knowledge*. (Cambridge: Cambridge University Press).

—— and A. Musgrave, eds (1970) *Criticism and the Growth of Knowledge* (Cambridge: Cambridge University Press).

Langlois, R. N. (1983) 'Internal Organization in a Dynamic Context', C. V. Starr Center for Applied Economics *Research Report*, 83–04.

Latsis, S. J., ed. (1976) *Method and Appraisal in Economics* (Cambridge: Cambridge University Press).

Lavoie, D., ed. (1990) *Economics and Hermeneutics* (London: Routledge).

Lawson, T. (1981) 'Keynesian Model Building and the Rational Expectations Critique', *Cambridge Journal of Economics*, 5, 311–26.

Lawson, T. (1985a) 'Keynes, predictions and econometrics', in T. Lawson and H. Pesaran (eds), *Keynes' Economics: Methodological Issues* (London: Croom Helm).

—— (1985b) 'Uncertainty and economic analysis', *Economic Journal*, 95, December, 909–27.

—— (1987) 'The relative/absolute nature of knowledge and economic analysis', *Economic Journal*, 97, 951–70.

—— (1988) 'Probability and uncertainty in economic analysis', *Journal of Post Keynesian Economics*, 11 (1), 38–65.

—— (1989a). 'Realism and instrumentalism in the development of econometrics', *Oxford Economic Papers*, 41, 236–58.

—— (1989b), 'Abstractions, Tendencies and Stylised Facts: A Realist Approach to Economic Analysis', *Cambridge Journal of Economics*, 13(1), 59–78.

—— (1992) 'Methodology: Non-optional and Consequential', letter to editor, *Royal Economic Society Newsletter*, October, 2-3.

—— (1994a) 'Why Are So Many Economists Opposed to Methodology?' *Journal of Economic Methodology*, 1 (1), 105–34.

—— (1994b) 'A Realist Theory for Economics', in R. E. Backhouse (ed.), *New Directions in Economic Methodology* (London: Routledge).

—— (1995a) 'A Realist Perspective on Contemporary Economic Theory', *Journal of Eocnomic Issues*, 29 (1), 1–32.

—— (1995b) 'Economics and Expectations', in S. C. Dow. and J. Hillard (eds), *Keynes, Knowledge and Uncertainty* (Aldershot: Edward Elgar).

—— (1997a) *Economics and Reality* (London: Routledge).

—— (1997b) 'Situated Rationality', *Journal of Economic Methodology*, 4 (1), 101–25.

—— (2003) *Reorienting Economics* (London: Routledge).

—— (2004) 'Reorienting economics: on heterodox economics, themata and the use of mathematics in economics', *Journal of Economic Methodology*, 11, 329–40.

—— (2009) 'The Current Economic Crisis: its nature and the course of academic economics', *Cambridge Journal of Economics*, 33 (4), 759–77.

—— and M. H. Pesaran, eds (1985) *Keynes's Economics: Methodological Issues* (London: Croom Helm).

Lecq, F. van der (1998) *Money, Coordination, and Prices* (Groningen: Rijksuniversiteit Groningen and Cheltenham: Edward Elgar).

Leijonhufvud, A. (1976) 'Schools, "Revolutions", and Research Programmes in Economic Theory', in S. Latsis (ed.), *Method and Appraisal in Economics* (Cambridge: Cambridge University Press).

—— (1981) *Information and Coordination: Essays in Macroeconomic Theory* (Oxford: Oxford University Press).

Lipsey, R. G. (1983) *An Introduction to Positive Economics* (6th edn) (London: Weidenfeld and Nicolson).

Loasby, B. J. (1976) *Choice, Complexity and Ignorance*, Cambridge University Press, Cambridge.

—— (1983) 'Economics of Dispersed and Incomplete Knowledge', in I. M. Kirzner (ed.), *Method, Process and Austrian Economics: Essays in Honor of Ludwig von Mises* (Lexington, MA: Lexington Books).

—— (1989) *The Mind and Method of the Economist* (Aldershot: Elgar).

—— (1991) *Equilibrium and Evolution* (Manchester: Manchester University Press).

Loasby, B. J. (1999), *Knowledge, Institutions and Evolution in Economics: the Graz Schumpeter Lectures* (London: Routledge).

—— (2003) 'Closed Models and Open Systems', *Journal of Economic Methodology*, 10, 285–306.

Lucas, R.E. Jr. (1976) 'Econometric Policy Evaluation: A Critique', in K. Brunner and A. H. Meltzer (eds), *The Phillips Curve and Labor Markets*, North-Holland, Amsterdam, and Carnegie-Rochester *Conference Series on Public Policy*, vol. 1, a supplementary series to the *Journal of Monetary Economics*.

—— (1980) 'Methods and Problems in Business Cycle Theory', *Journal of Money, Credit and Banking*, 12, 696–715.

—— and E. C. Prescott (1971) 'Investment under Uncertainty', *Econometrica*, 39, 659–81.

Maas, H. (1999) 'Mechanical Rationality: Jevons and the Making of Economic Man', *Studies in the History and Philosophy of Science*, 30 (4), 587–619.

Machlup, F. (1967) 'Theories of the Firm: Marginalist, Behavioural, Managerial', *American Economic,Review*, 57, 1–33.

Mair, D. and A. G. Miller, eds (1991) *A Modern Guide to Economic Thought: An Introduction to Comparative Schools of Thought in Economics* (Aldershot: Edward Elgar).

Mäki, U. (1988) 'How to Combine Rhetoric and Realism in the Methodology of Economics', *Economics and Philosophy*, 4 (1), 89–109.

—— (1990) 'Methodology of Economics: Complaints and Guidelines', *Finnish Economic Papers*, 3 (1), 77–84.

—— (1992) 'On the method of isolation in economics', *Poznan Studies in the Philosophy of the Sciences and the Humanities*, 26, 317–51.

—— (1997) 'The One World and the Many Theories', in A. Salanti and E. Screpanti (eds), *Pluralism in Economics: Theory, History and Methodology* (Cheltenham: Edward Elgar).

—— (1988) 'How to Combine Rhetoric and Realism in the Methodology of Economics' *Economics and Philosophy*, 4, 89–109.

—— (1999) 'Science as a Free Market: A Reflexivity Test in an Economics of Economics', *Perspectives on Science*, 7, 486–509.

Malinvaud, E. (1991) 'The Next Fifty Years', *Economic Journal*, 101 (404), 64–8.

Marshall, A. N. (1925) *Memorials of Alfred Marshall*, edited by A. C. Pigou (London: Macmillan).

Mayer, T. (1993) *Truth Versus Precision in Economics* (Aldershot: Edward Elgar).

McCloskey, D. N. (1983) 'The Rhetoric of Economics', *Journal of Economic Literature*, 21, 481–517.

—— (1986) *The Rhetoric of Economics* (Brighton: Wheatsheaf).

—— (1988) 'Two Replies and a Dialogue on the Rhetoric of Economics: Mäki, Rappoport, Rosenberg', *Economics and Philosophy*, 4 (1), 150–66.

—— (1994) *Knowledge and Persuasion in Economics* (Cambridge: Cambridge University Press).

Mearman, A. (2002) *A Contribution to the Methodology of Post Keynesian Economics*, Leeds University, unpublished Ph.D. thesis, University of Leeds.

—— (2005) 'Sheila Dow's concept of Dualism: Clarification, Criticism and Development', *Cambridge Journal of Economics*, 29, 1–16.

Meltzer, A. H. (1981) 'On Keynes's *General Theory*: A Different Perspective', *Journal of Economic Literature*, 19, 34–64.

Menger, C. (1963) *Problems of Economics and Sociology* (Urbana, IL: University of Illinois Press).

Milberg, W. (2001) 'Decentering the Market Metaphor in International Economics', in S. Cullenberg, J. Amariglio and D. F. Ruccio (eds), *Postmodernism, Economics and Knowledge* (London: Routledge).

Minsky, H. P. (1975) *John Maynard Keynes* (London: Macmillan).

—— (1986) *Stabilizing an Unstable Economy* (New Haven: Yale University Press).

Mirowski, P. (1987) 'Shall I Compare Thee to a Minkowski-Ricardo-Leontief-Metzler Matrix of the Mosak-Hicks Type? Or, Rhetoric, Mathematics, and the Nature of Neoclassical Economic Theory', *Economics and Philosophy*, 3 (1), 67–95.

—— (1989) *More Heat Than Light* (Cambridge: Cambridge University Press).

Morgan, M. S. (1988) 'Finding a Satisfactory Empirical Model', in N. de Marchi (ed.), *The Poppereian Legacy in Economics* (Cambridge: Cambridge University Press).

—— (1990) *The History of Econometric Ideas* (Cambridge: Cambridge University Press).

—— (2005) 'Experiments versus Models: New Phenomena, Inference and Surprise', *Journal of Economic Methodology*, 12, 317–29.

—— and M. Rutherford (1998) 'American Economics: The Character of the Transformation' in M. S. Morgan and M. Rutherford (eds), *From Interwar Pluralism to Postwar Neoclassicism. History of Political Economy*, 30: Annual Supplement, 1–26.

Morishima, M. (1991) 'General Equilibrium in the Twenty-First Century', *Economic Journal*, 101 (404), 69–74.

Morishima, M. (1992) *Capital and Credit: A New Formulation of General Equilibrium Theory* (Cambridge: Cambridge University Press).

Moss, S. J. (1981) *An Economic Theory of Business Strategy* (Oxford: Martin Robertson, 1981).

Muth, J. F. (1961) 'Rational Expectations and the Theory of Price Movement', *Econometrica*, 29, 315–35.

Myrdal, G. (1953) *The Political Element in the Development in Economic Theory* (London: Routledge & Kegan Paul).

Nash, S. J. (2004) 'On closure in economics', *Journal of Economic Methodology* 11 (1): 75-89.

Nelson, J. (1996) *Feminism, Objectivity and Economics* (London: Routledge).

O'Donnell, R. M. (1989) *Keynes's Philosophy, Economics and Politics: the Philosophical Foundations of Keynes's Thought and their Influence on his Economics and Politics* (London: Macmillan).

—— (1990) 'Keynes on mathematics: Philosophical foundations and economic applications', *Cambridge Journal of Economics*, 14, 29–47.

—— (1991) 'Keynes on Probability, Expectations and Uncertainty' in R. M. O'Donnell (ed.), *Keynes as Philosopher-Economist*: (London: Macmillan).

Pagan, A. (1987) 'Three Econometric Methodologies: A Critical Appraisal', *Journal of Economic Surveys*, 1 (1), 3–24.

Patinkin, D. (1965) *Money, Interest and Prices* (New York: Harper & Row).

—— (1982) *Anticipations of the General Theory* (Oxford: Basil Blackwell).

—— and J. C. Leith, eds. (1977) *Keynes, Cambridge and the General Theory* (London: Macmillan).

Pencavel, J. (1991) 'Prospects for economics', *Economic Journal*, 101 (404), 81–7.
Pesaran, M. H. (1982) 'A Critique of the Proposed Tests of the Natural Rate - Rational Expectations Hypothesis', *Economic Journal*, 92, 529–54.
Pheby, J. (1988) *Methodology and Economics: a Critical Introduction* (London: Macmillan).
Phelps, E. S. (1990) *Seven Schools of Macroeconomic Thought* (Oxford: Oxford University Press).
Pigou, A. C. (1936) 'Mr J. M. Keynes's *General Theory of Employment, Interest and Money*', *Economica*, 3 (10), 115–32.
Pocock, J. G. A. (1983) 'Cambridge paradigms and Scotch philosophers', in I. Horn and M. Ignatieff (eds), *Wealth and Virtue* (Cambridge: Cambridge University Press).
Polak, J. J. (1957) 'Monetary analysis of income formulation and payments problems', *IMF Staff Papers*, 6, 1–50.
Poole, W. (1970) 'Optimal choice of monetary policy instruments in a simple stochastic macro model', *Quarterly Journal of Economics*, 84 (May), 197–216.
Popper, K. R. (1957) *The Poverty of Historicism* (Boston: Beacon Press.).
—— (1959) *The Logic of Scientific Discovery* (London: Hutchinson).
—— (1963a) *The Open Society and Its Enemies* (Princeton: Princeton University Press).
—— (1963b) *Conjectures and Refutations*. London: Routledge.
—— (1970) 'Normal science and its dangers', in I. Lakatos and A. Musgrave (eds), *Criticism and the Growth of Knowledge* (Cambridge: Cambridge University Press).
—— (1982) The Open Universe: An Argument for Indeterminism (London: Routledge).
Potts, J. (2000) *The New Evolutionary Microeconomics: Complexity, Competence and Adaptive Behaviour* (Cheltenham: Edward Elgar).
Pratten, S. (1993) 'Structure, Agency and Marx's Analysis of the Labour Process', *Review of Political Economy*, 5 (4), 403–26.
Prigogine, I. and I. Stengers (1984) *Order out of Chaos: Man's New Dialogue with Nature* (London: Heinemann).
Ramsay, F. (1931) *Foundations of Mathematics* (R. Braithwaite, ed.) (London: Kegan Paul).
Rappaport, S. (1998) *Models and Reality in Economics* (Cheltenham: Edward Elgar).
Redman, D. A. (1989) *Economic Methodology: A Bibliography with References to Works in the Philosophy of Science (1860-1988)* (Westport, Conn.: Greenwood Press).
—— (1991) *Economics and the Philosophy of Science* (Oxford: Oxford University Press).
Richardson, G. B. (1953) 'Imperfect Knowledge and Economic Efficiency', *Oxford Economic Papers*, 5, 136–56
—— (1960) *Information and Investment* (Oxford: Oxford University Press).
Robinson, A. (1990) 'Letter', Royal Economic Society *Newsletter*, 69, 16–9.
Robinson, J. (1953-54) 'The Production Function and the Theory of Capital' *Review of Economic Studies*, 21, 81–106.
Robinson, J. (1973) *After Keynes* (Oxford: Basil Blackwell).
—— (1979) *Collected Economic Papers*, vol.V (Oxford: Basil Blackwell).

Rorty, R. (1979) *Philosophy and the Mirror of Nature* (Princeton: Princeton University Press, Oxford: Basil Blackwell, 1980).

Rosenberg, A. (1986) 'Lakatosian Consolations for Economics', *Economics and Philosophy*, 2 (1), 127–39.

—— (1987) 'Weintraub's Aims: A Brief Rejoinder', *Economics and Philosophy*, 3 (1), 143–4.

Roth, A. E. (1991) 'Game Theory as a Part of Empirical Economics', *Economic Journal*, 101 (404), 107–14.

Rothschild, K. W. (1989) 'Political economy or economics?' *European Journal of Political Economy*, 5, 1–12

Runde, J. (1990) 'Keynesian uncertainty and the weight of arguments', *Economics and Philosophy*, 6, 275–92.

—— (1991) 'Keynesian Uncertainty and the Instability of Beliefs', *Review of Political Economy*, 3 (2), 125–45.

—— (1998) 'Assessing Causal Economic Explanations', *Oxford Economic Papers*, 50 (2), 151–72.

—— (2002) 'Filling in the background', *Journal of Economic Methodology*, 9, 11–30.

—— and S. Mizuhara, eds (2003) *The Philosophy of Keynes's Economics: Probability, Uncertainty and Convention* (London: Routledge).

Russell, B. (1946) *History of Western Philosophy* (London: George Allen and Unwin).

Rutherford, M. (1994) *Institutions in Economics: the Old and the New Institutionalism* (Cambridge: Cambridge University Press).

Salanti, A. (1989) 'Internal criticism in economic theory: Are they really conclusive?', *Economic Notes*, 19, 1–14.

—— (1991) 'Roy Weintraub's Studies in Appraisal: Lakatosian Consolations or Something Else?', *Economics and Philosophy*, 7 (2), 221–34.

—— (1993a) 'A Reply to Professor Weintraub', *Economics and Philosophy*, 9 (1), 139–44.

—— (1993b) 'Lakatosian Perspectives on General Equilibrium Analysis: A Reply', *Economics and Philosophy*, 9 (2), 283–7.

—— (1997) 'Introduction' in A. Salanti and E. Screpanti (eds), *Pluralism in Economics: Theory, History and Methodology* (Aldershot: Edward Elgar).

Samuels, W. J., ed. (1990) *Economics as Discourse* (Boston: Kluwer).

—— (1993) 'In (Limited but Affirmative) Defence of Nihilism', *Review of Political Economy*, 5 (2), 236–44.

—— (1997), 'The Case for Methodological Pluralism', in A. Salanti and E. Screpanti (eds), *Pluralism in Economics: Theory, History and Methodology* (Aldershot: Edward Elgar).

—— (1998) 'Methodological Pluralism', in J. B. Davis, D. W. Hands and U. Mäki (eds), *The Handbook of Economic Methodology*, Cheltenham: Edward Elgar.

Samuelson, L. (2004) 'Modelling Knowledge in Economic Analysis', *Journal of Economic Literature*, 62, 367–403.

—— (2005) 'Economic Theory and Experimental Economics', *Journal of Economic Literature*, 43, 65–107.

—— and J. Swinkels (2006) 'Information, Evolution and Utility', *Theoretical Economics*, 1, 119–42.

Sargent, T. J. (1999) 'Comment', in J. Taylor (ed.), *Monetary Policy Rules* (Chicago: University of Chicago Press).

Schmalensee, R. (1991) 'Continuity and Change in Economic Inquiry', *Economic Journal*, 101 (404), 115–21.

Screpanti, E. (1997) 'Afterword: Can Methodological Pluralism be a Methodological Canon?', in A. Salanti and E. Screpanti (eds), *Pluralism in Economics: Theory, History and Methodology* (Aldershot: Edward Elgar).

Searle, J. R. (1995) *The Construction of Social Reality* (London: Free Press).

Sen, A. K. (1963) 'Neoclassical and Neo-Keynesian Theories of Distribution', *Economic Record*, 39, 54–64.

Sent, E.-M. (1998) *The Evolving Rationality of Rational Expectations* (Cambridge: Cambridge University Press).

—— (2004) 'Behavioural Economics: How Psychology Made Its (Limited) Way Back into Economics', *History of Political Economy*, 36(4), 735–60.

—— (2006) 'Pluralisms in Economics', in S. Kellert, H. Longino and K. Waters (eds), *Scientific Pluralism* (Minneapolis: Minnesota Studies in Philosophy of Science).

Shackle, G. L. S. (1955) *Uncertainty and Economics* (Cambridge: Cambridge University Press).

—— (1974) *Keynesian Kaleidics* (Edinburgh: Edinburgh University Press).

—— (1979) *Imagination and the Nature of Choice* (Edinburgh: Edinburgh University Press).

—— (1983-84) 'The romantic mountain and the classical lake: Alan Coddington's Keynesian economics', *Journal of Post Keynesian Economics*, 6, 241–57.

Simon, H. A. (1955) 'A Behavioural Theory of Rational Choice', *Quarterly Journal of Economics*, 69, 99–118.

—— (1976) 'From Substantive to Procedural Rationality', in S. J. Latsis (ed.), *Method and Appraisal in Economics* (Cambridge: Cambridge University Press).

Simpson, D. (1988) 'What economists need to know', *The Royal Bank of Scotland Review*, no. 160, 3–11.

Skidelsky, R. (1983) *John Maynard Keynes Vol. 1: Hopes Betrayed 1883-1920* (London: Macmillan).

—— (2011) 'The Relevance of Keynes', *Cambridge Journal of Economics*, 35 (1), 1–13.

Skinner, A. S. (1976) *A System of Social Science: Papers Relating to Adam Smith*, second edition (Oxford: Clarendon).

—— (1979) 'Adam Smith: an aspect of modern economics?', *Scottish Journal of PoliticalEconomy*, 26(June) 109–25.

Smith, A. ([1759] 1976) *The Theory of Moral Sentiments*, edited by D. D. Raphael and A. L. Macfie (Oxford: Clarendon).

—— ([1762-3] 1983) *Lectures on Rhetoric and Belles Lettres*, ed. by J. C. Bryce (Oxford: Oxford University Press).

—— ([1776] 1976) *An Inquiry into the Nature and Causes of the Wealth of Nations*, edited by R. H. Campbell and A. S. Skinner (Oxford: Clarendon).

—— ([1795]1980) 'History of astronomy', in W. P. D. Wightman (ed.), *Essays on Philosophical Subjects* (Glasgow edition) (Oxford: Clarendon).

Snowdon, B., H. Vane and P. Wynarczyk (1994) *A Modern Guide to Macroeconomics: An Introduction to Competing Schools of Thought* (Aldershot: Edward Elgar).

Solow, R. M. (1988) 'Comments from Inside Economics', in A. Klamer, D. McCloskey and R. M. Solow (eds), *The Consequences of Economic Rhetoric* (Cambridge: Cambridge University Press).

Soros, G. (2008) *The New Paradigm for Financial Markets: The Credit Crisis of 2008 and What it Means* (London: Perseus Books).

Stiglitz, J. E. (1991) 'Another Century of Economic Science', *Economic Journal*, 101 (404), 134–41.

—— (2010) 'The Non-existent Hand', *London Review of Books*, 32 (8), 17–8.

—— and A. Weiss (1986) 'Credit rationing and collateral', in J. Edwards *et al.* (eds), *Recent Developments in Corporate Finance*(Cambridge: Cambridge University Press).

Stohs, M. (1983) " 'Uncertainty" in Keynes' *General Theory*: A Rejoinder', *History of Political Economy*, 15 (spring), 87–91.

Sugden, R. (2005) 'Introduction to the Symposium on the Role of Experiments in Economics', *Journal of Economic Methodology*, 12, 177–84.

Vickers, D. (1995) *The Tyranny of the Market* (Ann Arbor: University of Michigan Press).

Tarshis, L. (1980) 'Post-Keynesian Economics: A Promise that Bounced?' *American Economic Review, Papers and Proceedings*, 70, 10–14.

Tennant, N. (1987) *Anti-Realism and Logic* (Oxford: Clarendon).

—— and C. R. Sunstein (2009) *Nudge: Improving Decisions About Health, Wealth, and Happiness* (New Haven NJ: Yale University Press).

Thomas, J. (2005) 'Fair Pay and a Wage-bill Argument for Low Real Wage Cyclicality and Excessive Employment Variability', *Economic Journal*, 115, 833–59.

Tobin, J. (1958) 'Liquidity Preference as Behaviour Towards Risk', *Review of Economic Studies*, 25, 65–96.

Togati, T. D. (1999) 'On the Generality of the *General Theory*', paper presented to the ESHET Conference, Valencia.

Torr, C. (1999) 'Equilibrium and Incommensurability', in S. C. Dow and P. E. Earl (eds), *Contingency, Complexity and the Theory of the Firm: Essays in Honour of Brian J. Loasby*, vol. 2 (Cheltenham: Edward Elgar).

Townshend, H. (1937) 'Liquidity Premium and the Theory of Value', *Economic Journal*, 47 (185), 157–69.

Tribe, K. (1999) 'Adam Smith: Critical Theorist?', *Journal of Economic Literature*, 37 (2), 609–32.

Tucket, D. (2011) *Minding the Markets: An Emotional Finance View of Financial Instability* (London: Palgrave Macmillan).

—— and R. Taffler (2008) 'Phantastic Objects and the Financial Market's Sense of Reality: A Psychoanalytic Contribution to the Understanding of Stock Market Instability', *International Journal of Psychoanalysis*, 89 (2), 389–412.

Turnovsky, S. J. (1991) 'The Next Hundred Years', *Economic Journal*, 101 (404), 142–8.

Tylecote, A. (1981) *The Causes of the Present Inflation* (London: Macmillan).

Vickers, D. (1995) *The Tyranny of the Market* (Ann Arbor, MI:P University of Michigan Press).

Wallich, H. and S. Weintraub (1971) 'A Tax-Based Incomes Policy', *Journal of Economic Issues*, 5, 1–19.

Walker, D. A. (1987) 'Walras's Theories of Tatonnement', *Journal of Political Economy*, 95, 758–74.

Walras, L. ([1926] 1954) *Elements of Pure Economics* (trans. W. Jaffé) (New York: George Allen & Unwin).

Weintraub, E. R. (1979) *Microfoundations* (Cambridge: Cambridge University Press).

—— (1985a) *General Equilibrium Analysis* (Cambridge: Cambridge University Press).

—— (1985b) 'Appraising General Equilibrium Analysis', *Economics and Philosophy*, 1 (1), 23–37.

—— (1985c) 'Review of S. C. Dow (1985)', *Economic Journal*, 95, 1116–8.

—— (1987) 'Rosenberg's "Lakatosian Consolations for Economists"': Comment', *Economics and Philosophy*, 3 (1), 139–42.

—— (1989) 'Methodology Doesn't Matter, but the History of Economic Thought Might', *Scandinavian Journal of Economics*, 91, 477–93.

—— (1992) 'Roger Backhouse's Straw Herring', *Methodus*, 4 (2), 53–7.

—— (1993) 'But Doctor Salanti, Bumblebees Really Do Fly', *Economics and Philosophy*, 9 (1), 135–8.

—— (1998) 'Axiomatisches Mißverständnis', *Economic Journal*, 108 (451), 1837–47.

—— (1999) 'How Should we Write the History of Twentieth-Century Economics?', *Oxford Review of Economic Policy*, 15(4), 139–52.

—— (2002) *How Economics Became a Mathematical Science* (Durham, NC: Duke University Press).

Weintraub, S. (1978-79) 'The Missing Theory of Money Wages', *Journal of Post Keynesian Economics*, 1, 60–2.

Whitehead, A. N. (1938) *Modes of Thought* (Cambridge: Cambridge University Press).

Whynes, D. K. (1984) *What is Political Economy? Eight Perspectives* (Oxford: Basil Blackwell).

Wiles, P. (1979-80) 'Ideology, Methodology and Neoclassical Economics', *Journal of Post Keynesian Economics*, 2 (winter), 155–80.

Wimsatt, W. C. (1981) 'Robustness, reliability and over-determination', in M. B. Brewer and B. E. Collins (eds) *Scientific Inquiry and the Social Sciences* (San Francisco: Jossey Bass).

Winch, D. N. (1997) 'Adam Smith's Problems and Ours', *Scottish Journal of Political Economy*, 44 (4), 384–402.

Winslow, T. (1986a) 'Keynes and Freud: psychoanalysis and Keynes's account of the "animal spirits" of capitalism', *Social Research*, 53 (Winter), 549–78.

—— (1986b) 'Human logic and Keynes's economics', *Eastern Economic Journal*, 12, October-December 413–30.

Woo, H. K. H. (1986) *What's Wrong with Formalism in Economics?: An Epistemological Critique* (Hong Kong: Victoria Press).

Wray, L. R. (1998) *Understanding Modern Money*. (Aldershot: Edward Elgar).

Wren-Lewis, S. (1992) 'Macroeconomic Theory and UK Macromodels: Another Failed Partnership?', *University of Strathclyde Discussion Paper*, no. 9.

Ziman, J. M. (1978) *Reliable Knowledge: an exploration of the grounds for belief in science* (Cambridge: Cambridge University Press).

Index

abstraction, 10, 11, 38, 59–60, 64, 67, 144–5, 153, 179, 186n5, 190, 192–3
accelerator principle, 40–1
adaptive expectations, 24, 27–32, 41, 45
aesthetics, 92
agency, 174, 217
aggregate behaviour, 20–2
aggregate demand, 19, 22, 33, 34, 39, 47
aggregation conditions, 189
analogy, 99
animal spirits, 14, 27, 33–51, 60, 75, 82, 98
anti-methodology position, 117
applied theory, 118, 119, 136
Arrow-Debreu model, 102
asset prices, 8
asset valuation, 4, 38–9
atomism, 53, 149–60, 187
axioms, 8, 48, 56, 58, 87, 100, 109, 118–22, 134, 141, 231

Babylonian thought, 53, 57–71
   consistency in, 59–60
   expectations in, 61–2
   political economy as, 66–9
   probability in, 61–2
   relativism in, 62–6
   uncertainty in, 60
Backhouse, R. E., 106, 213, 227
banking, socialisation of, 4
Bank of England, 159, 204, 208, 222
Bayesian theory, 109–10
behavioural economics, 8, 22, 213, 214, 215, 226, 227, 228
Blanchard, O., 214–15
Blaug, M., 107, 110, 111–12, 117
Boland, L. A., 110, 117, 136
boundaries, 189–91, 193–5
bounded rationality, 30, 44n10, 200

Caldwell, B. J., 108, 114–15, 137–8, 170, 212, 217
capital controversies, 164
capital theory, 26, 98
Cartesian/Euclidean thought, 53, 56–7, 59–62, 66, 69–71
catastrophe theory, 47
categories, 54–6, 65–6, 173–4, 177
central banks, 197–8, 208
certainty, 90, 91, 99, 126, 153, 205
Chick, V., 191, 216
classical logic, 53, 56, 69–70, 85, 91, 96, 100, 124, 126, 130–1, 144, 146, 148, 150, 152, 153, 160, 172, 204–5
closed systems, 11, 81, 87, 101–3, 130–1, 136–7, 142, 143, 149, 152, 160, 163, 171–4, 184–5, 195–6, 216–17
   conditions for, 182–3, 187–92
   definition of, 181–2
   event regularities and, 187–8
   knowledge and, 203
   models, 186
closure, 149–53, 156, 187–96, 203–4, 206
Coats, J., 214
Coddington, A., 102
cognitive dissonance, 92, 94
Colander, D. C., 217
communication, 166–7, 226
complex systems, 156–7, 161, 200–1
concepts, meaning of, 2
confidence, 34–40, 47
consistency, 59–60, 223
consumer preference, 43
consumption function, 159
contracts, 93
conventions, 8–14, 24, 75, 81, 90–4, 102, 205
coordination failure, 19–20
coordination success, 19
correspondence problem, 57

corridor theory, 47
creativity, 92
critical pluralism, 137, 138
critical rationalism, 109–10, 114–16, 126–8
critical realism, 125–8, 163, 173–4, 179, 187–92, 193–4
criticism, 166–7, 170, 228
cultural pluralism, 123

Davidson, P., 73
Davis, J. B., 149, 214, 216
decision-making, 48
    investment, 97–8
    by policy makers, 197–8
    rational, 49–50, 61–2
    under uncertainty, 34–40, 43–4, 50, 80, 120–2, 172–3, 197–8
    using conventions, 81, 90–4
deductivism, 10, 13, 100, 108–9, 117
de Marchi, N., 111–12
demi-regularities, 158–9, 188, 190
demonstrative logic, 85, 90, 100
deregulation, 4
Derrida, J., 123
descriptivism, 126
dialectics, 55
direct knowledge, 39, 89–91, 99–100, 104, 149, 156, 205
disciplinary matrix, 17
disequilibrium, 19–21
distortion, 189, 194, 195
Dow, S. C., 191, 204, 213
Dow conditions, 187–8
dualism, 7–8, 52–7, 71, 152, 190
Duhem-Quine problem, 54, 88, 91, 109, 111, 217

econometrics, 101–2, 118–19, 161, 192, 196
economic methodology, 1–12
    alternative, 125–7
    developments in, 107–17
    of mainstream economics, 86–9, 105–28
    pluralism in, 129–39, 210–30
    role of, 128
    schools of thought and, 52–71, 164–8, 227–8
    societal trends and, 122–5

economic policy, 67, 197–8
    mainstream, 13
    uncertainty and, 202–8
economic theory, 1–4
    see also specific theories
    changes in, 16–17
    divergence between practice and, 87–8
    empirical work and, 118–19
    falsification of, 49
    financial crisis and, 4–14
    history of, 3
    plurality in, 210–30
    rationality and, 97–8
    synthesis in, 16, 17
emotions, 7, 11
empirical testing, 18
empiricism, 108
employment, 22, 151
endogeneity, 48, 51, 101
endogenous variables, 25, 151
Enlightenment, 123
entrepreneurs, 27, 28n22
epistemic pluralism, 133–5, 138
epistemic uncertainty, 199–202
epistemology, 65, 66, 132, 169
    closed-system, 130–1, 136–7
    Keynes's, 84–6, 89–96, 99–104, 125–6, 135, 172–3
    open-system, 130–1, 135, 136
    of science, 124
    shifts in, 123
equilibrium, 20, 23–7, 155
European Central Bank, 208, 222
event regularities, 127, 141–2, 187–8, 191, 196
exogeneity, 48, 51, 101
exogenous variables, 25, 45, 49, 87, 151, 157
expectations, 20, 24, 151, 157
    adaptive, 27–32, 41, 45
    in Babylonian thought, 61–2
    formation of, 44
    Keynesian, 27–9, 33
    long-run, 33–4, 37, 41–3, 48–51, 91, 97–8, 152, 188
    rational, 30–1, 44–7, 49–50
    short-term, 28, 188
    under uncertainty, 205
expected return, 26

experiments, 142–3
extraordinary science, 65, 81, 103, 165–6, 174–6
extrinsic conditions, 189

fallibilism, 133
falsificationism, 109–11, 118, 119
fear, 9
Feyerabend, P., 63, 64, 123
financial crisis, 16n2, 234
financial instability, 5
financial markets, 4, 5
  uncertainty in, 8–9
fiscal policy, 4, 207
Fish, S., 113
fixprice markets, 21
flexprice markets, 21
formalism, *see* mathematical formalism
formal logic, 85, 89, 91, 101, 102, 104
formal models, 11
free markets, 4–5, 20, 229
Friedman, Milton, 16, 16n1, 18, 112–13, 144n7, 147
Fullbrook, E., 168
full employment, 19, 33
full knowledge assumption, 8
fuzzy logic, 124

game theory, 87, 215
Garnett, R., 167
general equilibrium theory, 6–7, 17, 25–7, 42, 56–7, 104, 173, 213
  certainty in, 91
  expectations in, 31–2, 45–6
  limitations of, 89
  methodology of, 87
  microfoundations, 18–20
Gerrard, B., 119
global financial crisis
  economics and, 4–14
  explanations of, 4–5
Goodwin, C. D., 214, 227
Gordon, S., 128
Great Depression, 47
greed, 9
growth, warranted rate of, 25–6
growth models, 25–6

Hahn, F. H., 87, 117, 143, 207

Harrod, R. F., 25–6
Hayek, F. A., 206–7
Hegel, G. W. F., 54, 55
hermeneutics, 65, 67, 70–1, 113–15, 134, 136, 137, 167, 226
Hicks, J. R., 103
historiography, 211
Hodgson, G. M., 70, 186, 226
holism, 62
humanism, 206–8
human logic, *see* ordinary logic
human nature, 147, 200, 227
Hume, David, 92, 165–6, 200, 203
Hutchison, T. W., 107, 110

ideology, 93, 165, 213, 227
ignorance, 76, 79, 80–2
imperfect competition, 103
imperfect information, 20
inconsistency, 59–60, 223
indirect knowledge, 89–91, 99–100, 104, 156
individual behaviour, 19, 20
individualism, 113
induction, 54, 126, 200
inference, 90
inflation, 159
information, 29–30, 31, 49
  imperfect, 20
institutionalist theory, 9
instrumentalism, 112–13, 144n7
internal consistency, 143
intersubjectivity, 75
intrinsic conditions, 189
investment, 35, 37, 39, 41, 47
  decision-making, 97–8
invisible hand, 93, 229
irrationality, 7, 9, 29, 39, 43, 61–2
isolation, 186n5, 190

Kaldor, N., 106
Kant, I., 54
Keynes, J. M., 8, 13–14, 25–6, 48–9, 157–8, 160, 184
  see also Keynesian economics
  Babylonian thought and, 58
  on basis of action, 204–5
  concept of weight and, 75–6, 99–100
  consumption function, 159

Keynes – *continued*
    on conventions, 90–4
    on econometrics, 161
    epistemology of, 84–6, 89–96,
        99–104, 125–6, 135, 172–3
    probability theory of, 61–2, 74,
        89–90
    on uncertainty, 60, 73–5, 78–81,
        84, 153, 201–2
Keynesian economics, 21–3, 33–51
    see also post-Keynesian economics
Keynesian expectations, 27–9, 33
Keynesian revolution, 18
Klant, J. J., 110
knowledge, 49, 60, 79–82, 89–92, 126,
        202–3
    see also epistemology
    acquisition of, 156
    construction of, 218
    direct, 39, 89–91, 99–100, 104, 149,
        156, 205
    indirect, 89–91, 99–100, 104, 156
    scientific, 123, 124, 148, 172–3,
        205, 221
    vs. theory, 109–10
    uncertainty and, 200–1, 207–8, 234
Kregel, J. A., 186
Kuhn, T. S., 16–17, 54–5, 62–6, 85,
        110–11, 123, 133, 165, 174–5, 177,
        205, 219–20, 1166–8

labour market, 19, 215
Laidler, D. E. W., 15–16
Lakatos, I., 6, 111
language, 10–11, 47n15, 58, 65, 95,
        173, 175, 177, 226
Lawson, T., 74, 117, 142, 143n5, 148,
        158–9, 173, 187–94, 196
liquidity preference, 27, 38, 74–5, 152,
        204
Loasby, B., 154–5, 202–3
logic, 54, 85, 90, 95, 100, 101
    classical, 53, 56, 69–70, 85, 91, 96,
        100, 124, 130–1, 144, 146, 148,
        150, 152, 153, 160, 172, 204–5
    demonstrative, 85, 90, 100
    formal, 85, 89, 91, 101, 102, 104
    fuzzy, 124
    meaning and, 146–9

non-demonstrative, 90, 100
    ordinary, or human, 126, 130, 148,
        149, 152–3, 155, 161, 205
logical empiricism, 108, 116–18, 128
logical positivism, 10, 18, 18n6, 19,
        22, 108, 111, 133
long-run equilibrium, 20, 24
long-run expectations, 33–4, 37,
        41–3, 48–51, 91, 97–8, 152, 188
Lucas, R. E., 206

macroeconomics, 19
mainstream economics, 6–17
    appeal of, 83–104
    equilibrium in, 23–4
    expectations in, 45–6
    methodology of, 86–9, 105–28
    microfoundations, 18–20
    ontological position of, 133
    theory in, 192–3
    uncertainty in, 72–3, 81
    variety in, 210–30
Mair, D., 213
Mäki, U., 190
market-clearing equilibrium, 23
market sentiment, 8, 9
Marshall, A. N., 154–5, 160
Marshallian theory, 22n14
Marxism, 113
mathematical formalism, 58, 86–98,
        100–4, 119–20, 140–61, 223–5,
        227, 228, 232–3
    limitations of, 153–4
    meaning and, 147–8
    method of, 141–6
    pluralism and, 212, 215, 223
mathematics, 10–11, 69
Mayer, T., 118, 136
McCloskey, D. N., 64, 66, 67, 88,
        93–4, 96, 97, 112–13, 114, 115,
        117, 128, 169, 220, 222, 224, 228
meaning, 146–9, 224
Menger, C., 202
methodological pluralism, 10–13,
        137–9, 162–4, 167–72, 176–7,
        210–32
methodology, *see* economic
    methodology
microeconomics, 18–23

microfoundations, 18–23
  mainstream theory, 18–20
  neo-Austrian economics, 20–1
  post-Keynesian economics, 21–3
Miller, A. G., 213
Minnesota Agnostics, 118, 119
Minsky, H. P., 5
models, 184–6, 195, 215–16
modernism, 124
modes of thought
  see also schools of thought
  Babylonian thought, 53, 57–71
  Cartesian/Euclidean thought, 53,
    56–62, 66, 69–71
  dualism, 52–7, 71
  economic methodology and, 52–71
modified pluralism, 132
monetarism, 159, 213
monetary policy, 9, 159, 197, 199,
    206–8
money, 147, 151, 152, 157
money supply, 19, 23–4, 42, 159
monism, 132, 168–9, 171, 204, 219
Moore, G. E., 39, 48
moral hazard, 4, 234
Morgan, M. S., 218–19

Nash, S. J., 190
negative analogy, 99
Nelson, J., 216
neo-Austrian economics, 5, 6, 12, 15,
    17, 147, 198
  equilibrium in, 25
  expectations, 31
  microfoundations, 20–1
  uncertainty in, 81
neoclassical economics, 7, 18–19, 19n9,
    87, 93–4, 145, 169, 207–8, 213
network theory, 5
New Classical economics, 87, 144n7,
    206, 207, 208
New Keynesian theory, 8
nihilism, 152
non-demonstrative logic, 90, 100
normal science, 174–5, 176

objective uncertainty, 201–2
O'Donnell, R. M., 95, 207
Ohlin, B., 36

ontological pluralism, 132–3
ontology, 132, 187
open systems, 11, 101–3, 124, 130–1,
    135–6, 151–2, 157, 160, 163,
    171–3, 178–96, 217
  conditions for, 182, 187–92
  conventions, 183
  definition of, 181–2
  event regularities and, 187–8
  real world as, 201–2
  theories as, 194
  uncertainty and, 201
ordinary logic, 101, 104, 126, 130,
    148, 149, 152–3, 155, 161, 205
organicism, 149–53, 158
orthodox economics, *see* mainstream
    economics

paradigms, 16–18, 62–7, 85, 110–11,
    133, 165–7, 174–7
paradigm shifts, 54–5, 64, 175,
    205–6, 219–20
Patinkin, D., 19, 36
Pencavel, J., 118, 211
persuasion, 96, 97, 112–13, 166
pessimism, 47
Phelps, E. S., 213, 220
Philips curve, 19, 20
philosophy of science, 54–5, 63, 64,
    108, 117, 165, 174–5, 219–20
physics, 156–7
Pigou, A. C., 157, 158
pluralism, 10, 11, 13, 70, 114–15, 123,
    129–39, 204
  critical, 137, 138
  in economics, 132
  epistemic, 133–5, 138
  formalism and, 212, 215, 223
  methodological, 135–7, 162–4,
    167–72, 176–7, 210–32
  modified, 132
  ontological, 132–3
  open and closed systems and,
    130–1
  structured, 162–77, 228
political economy, 66–9, 81
Popper, K. R., 63, 91, 97, 103, 109–10,
    123, 133, 135, 165, 175, 201, 217,
    228

portfolio choice, 26
positivism, 85, 108, 111, 117, 133, 217,
 220, 225
Post-Keynesian economics, 5, 6, 15,
 17, 32–3, 213
 equilibrium in, 24–5
 microfoundations, 21–3
postmodernism, 113–14, 118, 124,
 128, 132–6, 207, 220
prescriptive methodology, 65, 112–16,
 126–8, 136, 169, 220
present value, 39
prices
 asset, 8
 inflexible, 23
primary propositions, 89
private sector, 96
probability, 78–9
 and weight, 99
probability theory, 44, 51, 61–2, 74,
 89–90
progress, 144
propositions, 40, 89–90
psychological theory, 9
psychology, 92
public sector, 96

quantitative easing, 4
Quantity Theory of Money, 16n1
quantum mechanics, 54

randomness, 87, 199
rational expectations, 24, 30–1, 44–7,
 49–50
rationalisation, 86
rationality, 5–8, 33–4, 43, 49,
 61–2, 109
 bounded, 44n10, 200
 concept of, 2
 definition of, 43–4
 economic theory and, 97–8
 Keynes on, 39–40
 relativism and, 62–6, 70
 situated, 148
rationality axioms, 100, 119, 120–2,
 196, 225n5, 231
real business cycle theory, 24n17
reality, 13, 57, 64, 130–1, 133–4,
 144–5, 160–1, 173–4
 boundaries of, 189–91

distortion of, 189, 194
 nature of, 216–18
 theorising and, 192–6
reasoning, 18, 48, 97–8
reconstituted reductionism, 21
Redman, D. A., 107, 115
regularities, 127, 133, 135–6, 141–2,
 158, 187–8, 191, 196
relativism, 60, 62–6, 70, 232
relevance, 99–100
representative individual, 19
revolutions, 64, 166
 see also scientific revolutions
rhetoric, 65, 66, 88, 93–4, 113, 114,
 124, 134, 136, 137, 205
risk
 expected return and, 26
 pricing of, 4
 quantifiable, 198–9
 systemic, 5
 unquantifiable, 9, 198–9
risk assessment, 8, 9
Robinson, J., 43, 106, 125
Rorty, R., 65, 113, 134
Runde, J., 102, 190–1
Russell, B., 39
Rutherford, M., 218–19

Salanti, A., 98, 168
Samuels, W., 168, 170
Samuelson, L., 215
Sargent, T. J., 204
savings, 22
scarcity, 19
schools of thought, 15–32, 164–9,
 174, 176, 177, 227–8
 see also economic theory
scientific communities, 165, 205,
 220–1, 232
scientific knowledge, 123, 124, 148,
 172–3, 205, 221
scientific method, 18n7
scientific progress, 111, 115–16, 144,
 146, 219–20
scientific revolutions, 16, 166, 175
Scottish Enlightenment, 68
Searle, J. R., 227
segmentation, 152–60, 172–3, 176–7
self-interest, 92, 102, 147
Sen, A. K., 150, 151

shocks, 199
  exogenous, 87
  random, 24, 32
  technology, 24n17
short-term expectations, 28, 188
situated rationality, 148
Smith, A., 63, 67–9, 92, 93, 102, 147,
    165–6, 177, 184, 202–3
social conventions, *see* conventions
social sciences, 16, 174–5, 176
social structures, 189–90
social systems, 180–1, 194, 216–17
societal trends, 122–5
sociology of scientific knowledge, 221
speculation, 35
speculators, 27
stabilisation policies, 73
standards, 112
Stiglitz, J. E., 144
structured pluralism, 11, 162–77,
    228
subjective uncertainty, 201–2
subjectivism, 74–5
subsystems, 185–6
surprise, 47
systemic risk, 5
systems
    see also closed systems; open
        systems
    defined, 179–81
    economic thinking and, 184–5
    subsystems, 185–6
systems theory, 181n1

technology shocks, 24n17
theory, 56
    see also economic theory
    changes in, 145–6, 174
    falsification of, 110–11
    limits of abstract, 154
    models of, 195
    reality and, 192–6

systems and, 184–5
testing, 142–3
Thomas, J., 215
time, 26
Tobin, J., 26
Togati, T. D., 151, 157
trade cycle, 26
truth-value, 134

uncertainty, 8–13, 72–82, 126, 153,
    197–209, 215, 234
  in Babylonian thought, 60
  categorisation of, 74–6
  concept of, 72–3
  conventions and, 90–4
  decision-making under, 34–40,
      43–4, 50, 80, 120–2, 172–3,
      197–8
  definition of, 74–6
  of economic actors, 202–6
  of economics, 202–6
  epistemic, 199–200, 201, 202
  Keynes on, 34–40, 84, 89–90
  monetary policy and, 206–8
  nature and sources of, 198–202
  objective, 201–2
  parametric, 76
  structural, 76
  subjective, 201–2
  taxonomy of, 76–80
undemonstrative logic, 86

values, 227

wages, 19, 23, 152
Walras, L., 145, 157
warranted rate of growth, 25–6
weight, concept of, 75–6, 79, 99–100
Weintraub, E. R., 94, 97, 111, 134, 169,
    211, 213
Whitehead, A. N., 58, 59, 60
wonder, 92